CW01667386

EVERGREEN ASSETS

THE 'DO THE WORK ONCE, REAP THE REWARDS AGAIN AND AGAIN (AND AGAIN!)' CONTENT MARKETING ECOSYSTEM

JOHN LAMERTON

COPYRIGHT

Title: Evergreen Assets: The 'Do The Work Once, Reap The Rewards Again And Again (And Again)' Content Marketing Ecosystem'

First published in 2021

Address: Big Idea Books, PO Box 74, Plymouth, Devon, PL7 1ZN

The author specifically disclaims any liability, loss or risk which is incurred as a consequence, directly or indirectly, of the use and application of any contents of this work.

ISBN: 978-1-915222-00-8 (Paperback)
ISBN: 978-1-915222-01-5 (Ebook)

Copyright © 2021 John Lamerton

The right of John Lamerton identified as the author of this work, has been asserted in accordance with The Copyright Designs and Patents Act 1988.

All rights reserved. No part of this work may be reproduced in any material form (including photocopying or storing by any electronic means and whether or not transiently or incidentally to some other use of this publication) without written permission of the copyright holder except in accordance with the provisions of the copyright, Designs and Patents Act 1988.

Applications for the copyright holder's written permission to reproduce any part of this publication should be addressed to the publishers.

This guide is not endorsed by or affiliated with any other website or organisation mentioned in this book in any way.

Book Interior and E-book Design by AmitDey | amitdey2528@gmail.com

For Sarah. My greatest Evergreen Asset.

CONTENTS

1. INTRODUCTION

"Someone is sitting in the shade today because someone planted a tree a long time ago"

– *Warren E. Buffett*

NODDY HOLDER'S RETIREMENT FUND

In 1967, a young musician and songwriter by the name of Neville John Holder wrote a song called *Buy Me a Rocking Chair* for his band The 'N Betweens. It was based on the popular flower-power trend of the time (Sgt. Pepper, Bob Dylan etc.) with the chorus:

"Buy me a rocking chair to watch the world go by; Buy me a looking glass, I'll look you in the eye."

Unimpressed, Neville discarded the song along with the flower-power influences and instead found a passion for a new genre of music that would come to embrace the early 1970s – glam rock.

Neville John Holder became Noddy Holder and The 'N Betweens became Slade. By 1973, Slade were one of the most popular bands in Britain, having achieved two No1 singles in three months. In the boiling hot summer of that year, Slade's manager Chas Chandler suggested the band release a Christmas song. The lads were initially against the idea, until bassist Jim Lea remembered Noddy's discarded *Buy Me a Rocking Chair.*

After an evening's hard drinking with the band, Noddy worked through the night at his mother's house in Walsall, amending the lyrics and tweaking the melody.

"Buy me a rocking chair to watch the world go by" became, "So here it is Merry Christmas, everybody's having fun", while "Buy me a looking glass, I'll look you in the eye" was tweaked to, "Look to the future now, it's only just begun."

Merry Xmas Everybody was recorded in a boiling hot New York studio in August 1973 and became the official UK Christmas No1 that year, selling 500,000 copies in the first week and more than a million overall, remaining in the charts until February 1974.

It would turn out to be the last No1 single Slade would have.

But the story doesn't end there.

As I write this, 48 years have passed since Noddy Holder pulled a drunken all-nighter at his mum's house. Almost five decades since he first yelled: "It's Christmaaaaaas!" (when it very much wasn't). Nearly 50 years on from creating a three-minute, 26-second song most people wouldn't want to listen to for 90 per cent of the year.

Merry Xmas Everybody re-enters the top 40 every year. You'll hear it at any shopping centre from early October. It's often the "most streamed" song on Spotify each December. No self-respecting Christmas compilation album would be complete without it. It's been covered hundreds of times by artists such as Oasis, Girls Aloud and Robbie Williams (with Holder receiving the royalties). In 2009, PRS for Music announced that 42 per cent of the world's population has listened to the song.

Merry Xmas Everybody is Noddy Holder's pension fund, earning him an estimated £500,000 a year in royalties. Half a million a year every year for five decades based on one night's work writing a three and a half minute tune, and a day pretending it's December in a sweaty New York studio in the height of summer.

Noddy Holder did the work once and reaped the rewards again and again (and again).

He created an Evergreen Asset.

Look to the future now – it's only just begun.

2. WHAT ARE EVERGREEN ASSETS?

Evergreen Assets are an ecosystem of content-led resources that you can repeatedly deploy to create a content marketing machine, with dozens of individual assets interacting with each other and all contributing towards the machine that is your business.

There are six Evergreen Asset classes. They are:

- Lead Assets.
- Nurture Assets.
- Sales Assets.
- Fulfilment Assets.
- Admin Assets.
- Viral Assets.

Each of these six has its own section in the book, so you can learn about them in-depth and see how they fit into your machine. There are also examples of specific assets you can create.

To make things simple – and to ensure you maximise your return on investment – there is a detailed "One Asset To Rule Them All" in each asset class. As you may have guessed, this is the one you should prioritise above all others in that class.

If you do nothing more than build and integrate these six cogs into your machine, you're going to experience exponential growth far above the energy expended, thanks to the power of compounding.

The six Evergreen Assets asset classes build upon one another, holding your clients' hands through the entire customer journey – generating leads, nurturing the client relationship, making the sale, fulfilling the sale, ensuring everything runs like clockwork and, finally, turning one customer into more than one.

THEY ARE THE WORLD'S LARGEST MERRY-GO-ROUND

Deer Shelter Rock in rural Wisconsin is home to the world's largest merry-go-round. It features 269 animals (none of which are horses), 182 chandeliers, hundreds of mannequin angels hanging from the ceiling, and more than 20,000 lights.

It requires a lot of energy to get a machine like that moving – but considerably less to *keep* it moving.

Merry-go-rounds are built that way. With the rails greased and resistance minimised, the amazing feat of engineering kicks in so that once you have some forward momentum, it is harnessed to maximise and maintain forward progress using the least amount of external energy.

Without some external energy (an electric generator or a big bloke from Wisconsin giving it a shove), it will eventually grind to a halt. But not immediately. The more momentum built, the more rotations the merry-go-round will complete before slowing and stopping.

Your Evergreen Assets ecosystem is just like the world's largest merry-go-round, giving you that elusive missing ingredient from your marketing mix – momentum.

Sure, you'll need to work hard to get those Evergreen Assets moving, but once the ecosystem is up and running, with plenty of momentum behind it, you can take your hands off the ride and just give it a little push every now and then to get it back up to speed.

Evergreen Assets are *almost* "do it once and reap the rewards forever" pieces of the machine that is your business. Almost, but not quite. After all, if you give the world's largest merry-go-round a really big push, build up a lot of momentum, and let go – never applying any energy whatsoever to it again – then your merry-go-round will eventually crawl to a stop.

Creating your Evergreen Assets ecosystem is not a "one and done" job. Sure, most of the hard work is front-loaded. You'll do most of the heavy lifting in creating that ecosystem in the first place – building new assets and integrating them into your machine.

Then, once you've got some momentum, you can step back and do other things (like running your business rather than creating content to generate business). But you'll keep an eye on the merry-go-round to notice when it's starting to slow. And when it does, you'll apply some external energy – either in the form of two hands and a great big shove or in the form of a permanent power source.

Eventually, you'll relish every opportunity to grease the wheels, reduce friction and resistance, and replace old, worn parts with shiny new ones. You'll try new things with a curious mindset of "better or worse?".

There are only three ways to grow a business:

1. Get more clients.
2. Get each client to spend more.
3. Get each client to buy more often.

Getting more clients is the sledgehammer that always cracks the walnut, and it's why I've made marketing the number one activity in every one of my businesses for the last two decades.

But once you've got that forward momentum of regular clients coming in (and, of course, your Evergreen Assets will be the system that routinely ensures that happens), you can start to add some smaller cogs to the machine to tweak some of the finer points to your merry-go-round.

Because clients flow all the way through your machine, every cog and gear that you can optimise and improve will compound on all the other cogs in the machine.

For example, let's say you currently have 800 customers, who each buy a £100 product from you twice a year.

800 x £100 x 2 = £160,000.

Now let's see what happens when we improve all three cogs – the number of clients, the amount they spend, and how often they buy – by just 15 per cent.

We now have 920 customers, spending £115, 2.3 times per year (on average).

920 x £115 x 2.3 = £243,340.

We've improved the output of our machine by 52.1 per cent for a mere 15 per cent effort.

By now, you're probably thinking, "That sounds great John, but I don't have a clue how to get a one per cent improvement, let alone 15." Don't worry. While there are only three ways to grow your business (more clients, more spend, more frequency), there are hundreds of ways that you can impact each of these three cogs – and you will learn dozens of them throughout this book.

You'll see how I achieved a 48 per cent increase in clients by changing a few words on a webpage. You'll read how *removing* some ads increased my sales by 16 per cent. And you'll learn how reducing prices led to a 31 per cent increase in customer spend and a 58 per cent increase in the frequency of purchase.

And if those numbers seem scary and impossible right now, I'll show you how making just a single one per cent improvement every week can deliver a 68 per cent uplift to your machine.

THEY ARE PART OF A MACHINE – AND YOU'RE THE ENGINEER

Ray Dalio is one of the world's most successful investors with a current portfolio of more than £110billion ($154bn), more than 1,500 employees, and a well-established 30-year-plus track record of market-annihilating returns.

In his 2017 book *Principles*, Dalio lays bare how he's achieved those results, how he thinks, how he acts, why he does what he does, and exactly how to replicate his thought process.

Dalio has made *Principles* required reading for every person in his company, and you can understand why. He wants every one of the 1,500 members of his team to think the same way he would – to reach the same decisions using the same frameworks. It's the next best thing to cloning himself 1,500 times over.

One of the first principles that Dalio shares is that everything is a machine.

> *"The structure and evolution of galaxies, the formation of our own solar system, the makeup of Earth's geography and ecosystems, our economies and markets, and each of us – we individually are machines made up of different machines: our circulatory system, our nervous system that produces our thoughts, our dreams, our emotions...*
>
> *All of these different machines evolve together through time to produce the realities we encounter every day."*

Everything is a machine. You are a machine. Your business is a machine. Your Evergreen Assets ecosystem is a machine.

If everything is a machine, isn't it about time you treated the machine like a machine, stuck your head under the bonnet once in a while, figured out how the machine works, and how you can make the machine work better?

The Evergreen Assets ecosystem is a content marketing machine with dozens of individual assets interacting with each other and all contributing towards the machine that is your business.

If you're going to play around with a machine, you need to put on your engineer hat and visualise how it works – being able to see all the cogs, gears, and other moving parts in your head. This will allow you to understand how when one cog turns (making a sale), it causes others to move (onboarding, fulfilment, and billing).

Where you have problems in your business, it's usually caused by an inefficiency in the machine somewhere. Time to call the engineer (that's you, by the way.).

You will become head engineer – the expert in your business machine. Think of this book as the Haynes Manual for your business. You'll be able to confidently take the machine apart and replace all the worn-out parts with shiny, new titanium steel. You'll grease the wheels and get everything running faster, smoother, quieter, and more effectively, which will mean less stress for you and a better customer journey for your clients.

THEY ARE A DIRECT DEBIT INTO THE BANK OF GOODWILL

Evergreen Assets is not a numbers game. It's a relationships game. You're going to hear that a *lot* throughout this book.

We're all familiar with bank accounts. Your income gets paid into one and your bills come out. Hopefully, there's some money left at the end of the month (rather than some month left at the end of the money).

We know the pitfalls of going into the red – overdraft fees, £25 letters from the bank, and "transaction declined" at the checkout.

Your relationship with your prospects and clients also has a bank account – a Goodwill Bank account. Every time you give value, you make a deposit into the Goodwill Bank account. Every time you try and flog people something, you make a withdrawal.

Actively listen to someone = make a deposit.

Brag about your new car = withdrawal.

Send a handwritten card or a small gift = big deposit.

Send a nine-email sales campaign = big withdrawal.

With the Goodwill Bank account, you can only draw out what you've put in. There's no overdraft facility. No extended credit. No payday loan. If your Goodwill Bank balance is low and you send that nine-email sales campaign, you're not going to sell many (or indeed any). Send that same campaign when your Goodwill Bank balance is high and you can afford that withdrawal, not a problem.

Most businesses don't have a sales problem. They simply have a lack of available funds in their Goodwill Bank account. Evergreen Assets act like a reverse Direct Debit, automatically making deposits into your Goodwill Bank account, so that when you want to make a withdrawal, there's plenty of funds available to you.

Evergreen Assets do the hard work, which makes the selling easy. You can take that to the bank.

THEY ARE THE MINIMUM EFFECTIVE DOSE

To boil water, you need to heat it to 100°C. Heating it further doesn't make it more boiled. Boiled is boiled. Heating water to 150°C just wastes energy, achieving the same result.

In pharmacology, the minimum effective dose is the amount of a drug that produces a biological response. Any less than the minimum effective dose and it won't be, erm, effective. But as you increase the dosage above the MED, you achieve ever-diminishing returns on your investment.

Twice the MED is not twice as effective.

You'll design your Evergreen Assets to hit the minimum effective dose to deliver a great return on investment (ROI) and to maximise your investment of time, money, energy, and resources. For some assets, you'll keep building well beyond the MED. But as you do so, you'll be aware of the ever-diminishing ROI that you'll see as you keep building and growing that asset, eventually choosing to achieve a better ROI by diverting your attention towards bringing a different asset up to the MED standard.

From not boiled to boiled. From off to on. From not effective to effective.

First and foremost, we want to design a diverse ecosystem containing a wide range of effective assets, all working together and compounding on one another to deliver a fantastic ROI. Bringing each asset up to the minimum effective dose standard is more effective than boiling water to 300°C.

KEEPING IT SIMPLE

If you're worried that all this talk of ecosystems, cogs, machines, engineering, and physics sounds scary, then please don't panic. Your guide and teacher for this topic is me – a normal bloke from Plymouth. I've got a GCSE in physics, but I haven't studied it since 1994. I know nothing about machines, engineering, or anything technical. The toolkit in my garage consists of a hammer, some duct tape, and a can of WD-40.

I like to keep things simple. That way, I can understand them too!

There are six Evergreen Asset classes, which form the structure of the rest of this book. All six asset classes have the same theme running throughout them, and each Evergreen Asset you create will serve one of these three objectives:

1. Find out what they want.
2. Give them what they want.
3. Make damn sure they've got what they want.

That's it. Easy, eh?

Easy to say, much harder to do. After all, if it were that easy, everyone would be doing it and there'd be no need for me to be writing this book or you to be reading it, would there?

Where most business owners go wrong with their content marketing is that it tends to be missing the mark on one of these three simple objectives.

FIND OUT WHAT *THEY* WANT.

It's not what you want to create. Not what some Silicon Valley algorithm wants or what some "guru" told you is what's working right now. It's what your customers want. As Walmart tycoon Sam Walton said: "There is only one boss – the customer. And he can fire everybody in the company, from the chairman on down, simply by spending his money elsewhere."

GIVE THEM WHAT *THEY* WANT.

I've gone wrong here myself, many times. I've created a product that I love, of which I'm really proud, and that my heart and soul has been poured into. But it wasn't what my customers wanted, so only one man and his dog bought it – and the dog was nonplussed. Likewise, if you ordered a pepperoni pizza and received a ham and pineapple one, you'd be none too happy. Yet that's the experience many business owners give their customers – delivering amazing ham and pineapple pizzas to people who would rather have pepperoni.

MAKE DAMN SURE THEY'VE GOT WHAT *THEY* WANT.

Let's stay in the pizza restaurant for a moment. You've taken the customer's order (find out what they want). You've asked the chef to cook it and the front of house staff to deliver it (give them what they want). So, with hundreds of orders flying in and out of the kitchen throughout a busy lunchtime service, what does the front of house team need to go and ask the customer?

> *"Is everything OK with your meal? Do you have everything you need? Can I get you anything else?"*

In other words, make damn sure they've got what they want. Make sure no one is sitting there moaning quietly in that oh-so-British way about how they don't like pineapple, but they'd rather pick the segments off than complain.

> *"It's OK, we won't cause a scene by letting the waiter know our order got mixed up. We'll simply leave them a negative review on TripAdvisor, tell all our friends how bad it was and vow never to come here again."*

This is why it's so important to make damn sure they're getting what they want.

Because happy and fulfilled customers don't leave, don't cancel, and don't ask for a refund. They just keep throwing money your way, leaving you positive reviews, and sending you referrals of more people just like them.

Find out what they want. Give them what they want. Make damn sure they've *got* what they want. Each Evergreen Asset you create will tick at least one of those three boxes.

I'LL TELL YOU WHAT THEY'RE NOT

Picture the scene. It's 8am on a grey, damp Sunday morning, and you're in the function room of a Holiday Inn Express somewhere on the M25 near Heathrow Airport.

You're about to watch some "guru" or "expert" (please note my incredibly heavy use of quotation marks there) perform a magic trick that convinces you that they have the answer to your greatest problem. However, in reality, neither your problem nor their solution exists.

Like any magician, they make great use of smoke and mirrors. In their mind, they are "selling from the stage". But they tell you they're just delivering a free training course, a courtesy seminar, a gratis workshop, all from the kindness of their heart, to help you.

The topic of this "free" session is "what's working right now".

It doesn't matter if you're there to learn about property investing, LinkedIn ads, Forex trading, email marketing or weight loss. The magic trick follows the same formula.

Now, I'm not a member of the personal development Magic Circle, so I'm free to tell you how this works. First of all, you need your audience to believe that you're just like them – or at least you *were* before you stumbled on this amazing secret that you're going to share with them today.

Next, you need to justify their fears. It's likely they're going to be sceptical and think to themselves: "I've tried something like this before and it didn't work."

How do you do that? You tell them that it's not their fault. They may have been using an outdated framework. Something that may have worked for some people in the past, but it's not "what's working right now". The reason they're failing is because they haven't heard about this new thing.

At this point, you should talk about what "successful people" do and what sets them apart from the failures. You should spend at least a few minutes talking about how painful it is to fail – to be overweight, to be poor, to be a bad parent, etc. Tug on those heartstrings now; it'll loosen the purse strings later.

By now, your audience should be sufficiently distracted by the smoke and mirrors of all the pain they're in (pain they were largely unaware of and unconcerned by a mere 20 minutes ago), and it's time for you to pull the rabbit out of the hat. And so you unveil "what's working right now".

You now start "teaching" the "new thing". I wish there were a separate set of quotation marks for such heavy sarcasm, but there aren't, so let me make this abundantly clear: There is no new thing and you're not actually going to teach anything.

All you're going to do is give a very brief overview of the model or framework you use.

> *"Our students log into the portal, and the software tells them with a few clicks whether to buy or sell," says one Forex trader selling from the stage.*
>
> *"Our workshops use these brand new ten-point techniques to turn anyone into a world-class public speaker," promises the public speaking coach.*

After this teaching session (which may contain as much as ten minutes of useful information in a 90-minute presentation), you roll out some (unbelievably vague) case studies as social proof.

> *"John from Plymouth was sitting where you are this time last year. He attended my course, learnt the new thing that's working right now, and now he's a gazillionaire."*

Your case studies should reveal nothing at all about *how* to do "what's working right now" but merely reinforce the idea that your audience *must* do what's working right now if they want to succeed.

What's the reason they're failing? Because they're not doing what's working right now.

That's the magic trick, in a nutshell.

However, now it's time for the magic wand – your £5,997 course.

But the first 50 people who run to the back of the room right now and pay in full can get it for just £1,997(+VAT).

Get a few stooges to start the stampede immediately and – abracadabra – you're up and running. Or rather your audience is.

Take your applause, and count your money.

It makes me vomit in my mouth a little every time I see one of these pitches.

EVERGREEN ASSETS ARE *NOT* "WHAT'S WORKING RIGHT NOW"

If your marketing strategy relies on "what's working right now", then you end up in a vicious circle of constantly chasing shiny new objects, having to learn all the new platforms, hacks, and models.

And when someone offers to show you "what's working right now" in exchange for spending your Sunday morning at a Holiday Inn Express, drinking shit coffee, and watching Reading's answer to Tony Robbins stumble through his thinly-veiled sales pitch, you find yourself hunting for shiny objects to chase.

Evergreen Assets are about creating an ecosystem of content-led resources you can deploy again and again. Sure, you may need to update some of the pieces as the world evolves, but as head engineer of your merry-go-round, you'll know that each time you update an asset, you'll be leveraging all the other assets too, and compounding every gain you make. The rising tide lifts all ships.

I recently picked up a copy of *Getting Everything You Can Out Of All You've Got* by Jay Abraham. My copy is well-thumbed, covered in notes and scribbles, with massive sections highlighted and entire chapters copied and sent to my team to implement in my Evergreen Assets ecosystem.

But then I came to the chapter about the internet. Not a single highlight. No scribbles. Nothing to ask the team to implement.

I've been running businesses on the net for more than two decades now. So I found it puzzling to read a book that said the internet is "still finding its legs" and that "50 per cent of online businesses fail".

It all seemed a little outdated and certainly wasn't "what's working right now".

At one point, Jay listed the top eight search engines:

- Lycos.
- AltaVista.
- HotBot.
- Northern Light.
- Excite.
- InfoSeek.

- WebCrawler.
- Yahoo!.

Now, I've only heard of half of these brands, most of them aren't even around anymore (looks like Jay's "50 per cent of online businesses fail" prediction wasn't far off), and, of course, where's the 800lb gorilla in the room? Why no mention of Google, which owns 92 per cent of the search market?

I found my answer in the copyright notice at the start of the book: "Getting Everything You Can Out Of All You've Got. Copyright © 2000 by Jay Abraham."

2000? The year of the Millennium Dome and Y2K bug fears? The year Wembley Stadium lost its twin towers, Big Brother started, and Madonna married Guy Ritchie? Back then, Britney Spears hadn't yet shaved her head, Oasis were still together, and not a single Harry Potter movie had been made.

And nobody had heard of Google.

Until I reached page 287, I didn't have any idea that I was reading a book that was more than 20 years old.

Now, that's an Evergreen Asset.

Never mind "what's working right now", Evergreen Assets are "what's *still* going to be working two decades from now".

So, what *is* going to be working two decades from now?

I would ask Jeeves, but I can't seem to find him.

3. LEAD ASSETS

You could build the best machine in the world, but if you don't have any leads coming into it, that machine's just going to sit there looking pretty. You're dead in the water, with nothing but a very expensive paperweight to show for it.

Gary Keller, author of *The ONE Thing*, says that every business's "one thing" should be to bring in leads, no matter what your industry or sector and regardless of your individual skills. You might be the world's best at what you do, but without leads, the world will never know.

I recognised this early on in my business journey and soon embraced lead generation as my bread and butter. I didn't capture a single lead in my first nine months of being in operation (part-time alongside the full-time day job from hell). I was busy "getting the word out there" by doing a lot of shouting and waving, working far harder than I needed (or wanted) to.

Then someone suggested I put an email sign-up box on my website. So I did and started sending weekly emails to anyone who wanted to hear more from me. Three months later, I was emailing 700 people a week and had enough business to be able to reduce my day job from hell to part-time hours. I'd found my minimum effective dose.

After another three months, I was sending my weekly emails to 3,000 people and could quit the day job from hell completely.

I established the routine of sending my weekly newsletter out every Thursday. One week, I was popping round to visit my parents after I'd sent my weekly email.

"I'll be with you in about an hour, Dad," I said. "I've got to send my weekly email first."

"Oh, OK son. How many people do you send that to?"

"Just over 3,000 now."

"3,000? Blimey! That must cost you a fortune in stamps!"

To this day, I still like to imagine that my dad thinks you need to stick a stamp on an email. But fast forward 20 years and I now send emails to somewhere in the region of a million people a month – all 100 per cent opted-in, fully GDPR compliant, and to people who want to hear from me.

Lead Assets are the most important cog in your machine.

ONE LEAD ASSET TO RULE THEM ALL - THE RIGHT BAIT

As a potential customer, why should I give you my email address? Or hand over my phone number? Or my business card? Or my home address?

If you're going to go fishing for leads, you need The Right Bait. Lead bait (sometimes also referred to as a lead magnet) offers a fair exchange of value, giving Joe Public something in return for giving up their personal information. I've used lots of different bait in the past – free horse racing tips, fridge magnets, magazines, and sample chapters of my books.

You might have entered my world to get "a new Big Idea from me every Wednesday lunchtime" or my "top 100 books for business owners" reading list.

Without The Right Bait, you offer no reason whatsoever for people to offer up their details. Twenty years ago, I could put a "subscribe to our newsletter" box on my website and get hundreds of people popping their email addresses in. If I had the same box on my website now, I'd be able to count the number of sign-ups after a year on my fingers and toes – and I probably wouldn't need to take my socks off.

That's because my newsletter is no longer The Right Bait. In the early 2000s, it was. There was still a novelty around email then. People signed up for just about anything so they could get that dopamine hit from the "You've got mail" notification. Meanwhile, your letterbox was rammed full of junk. How times have changed.

My newsletter was a lead magnet. It was an exchange of value. Back in the day, it was valued much more. Visitors to my website wanted to hear from me regularly, with a weekly digest of what was going on in my world. It was The Right Bait – at the time.

But as more and more companies came online, they almost all offered the chance for *their* customers to "get our newsletter", "join our mailing list", and "subscribe to updates". And before you knew it, your inbox was full of crap you didn't want – and that's before we talk about offers of little blue pills or estranged Nigerian princes looking to launder millions of dollars.

All of a sudden, my newsletter didn't hold the same value it once did. My newsletter is still lead bait, but it's no longer The Right Bait.

So, what is The Right Bait? It's something that's sufficiently juicy and tempting. Assuming you're fishing in the right place, when you cast your net into the water, The Right Bait will attract the right sort of fish and entice them to have a tiny nibble, a taste of what's to come. You're not giving them an entire meal and you're not using the cheapest possible bait. Instead, you're hitting the sweet spot of the minimum effective dose – the most attractive, most cost-effective worms and maggots that your fish can't wait to bite on.

The Right Bait.

The £125,000 fridge magnet

In 2007, I sold a website for £125,000. I got £125,000 because it had an active, engaged email list of more than 100,000 people. And the reason I had an active, engaged list of 100,000-plus people was thanks to a fridge magnet.

Two years before the sale, I bought a load of promotional fridge magnets featuring the website's logo. I gave them away for free, but only to people who joined my website.

Little did I know it, but I'd literally created a lead magnet. A little gift. Something of value in fair exchange for an email address.

Within two years of advertising that free fridge magnet, I'd grown the list to six figures and attracted a buyer for the site.

I probably gave away no more than 1,000 magnets at a cost of 27p each. Not everyone wanted the magnet, and because you had to send a stamped addressed envelope (Dad was right, there were stamps involved) to claim it, not many people did.

So my (literal) lead magnet cost me £270 and earned me the lion's share of £125,000.

Not a bad ROI, and from then on, I was hooked on lead magnets. There's barely a business that I've been involved in that hasn't offered a lead magnet of some description:

- Free fluffy bug.
- Free magazine.
- Free scratchcard.
- Free game of bingo.
- Free horse racing tips.
- Free chapter of my books.

- Free pin badge.
- Free trial of the full service.

What could be your £125,000 fridge magnet?

Remember it's bait – not the whole meal

The Right Bait for my sports betting business is a 32-page magazine dedicated to a particular sporting event. We started producing it for our paying members in 2013 and it got such great reviews that we decided to replicate it every year. We not only send a physical printed magazine to our members, but also produce a digital version to use as lead bait.

That's when we discovered this magazine was The Right Bait. Our standard bait for this business is to receive free daily horse racing tips from a professional tipster. This works pretty well most of the time, with a conversion rate of around 30 per cent for new traffic. Adding a free 32-page guide to the Cheltenham Festival, for example, enabled us to fish where the fish are – to find new audiences of horse racing fans. This bait doubled our conversion rates and brought in thousands of new leads in a few short weeks.

On the face of it, this was a win-win situation. We were already making the magazine for our paying members, so the costs (content, design, printing, and postage) were all fixed. Sending out a digital version as lead bait costs no more and, by bringing in thousands of leads, greatly increases the value of the asset to the business.

Or at least that was the plan.

One year, we decided to replicate the Cheltenham Festival lead bait for Royal Ascot, which is the highlight of the flat racing calendar and takes place each June, attended by the Queen.

We decided to make the bait *amazing* – the best it could possibly be. We expanded the magazine from 32 to 36 pages. We involved the entire team in the creation of the magazine, ensuring that everyone had a say. It was written, re-written, proof-read, and edited to within an inch of its life.

We opted for the heaviest possible paper, the glossiest cover, and the most luxurious envelopes, and sent the lot first class.

The feedback from our members and new leads was amazing. One of the many testimonials we received said: "This is top-notch! I don't know how you can afford to do this for free."

And they had a point. Because while the end result was very impressive, we didn't actually catch any more fish. In fact, because we spent so much time creating the bait, we forgot to cast our nets in the right places, so we caught fewer fish.

Also, because the entire team was dragged away from their day-to-day responsibilities, other areas of the business suffered, and we had a committee of seven people – on a combined salary of something like £250 an hour – doing proofreading.

We usually spend around £1,000 to create The Right Bait, which we know will bring in 10-15,000 leads – an investment of between 10p and 15p per lead.

On this occasion, we spent more than £3,000 creating the bait and only brought in 2,500 leads. We 10x'd our costs but not our returns. We went way past the minimum effective dose and saw ever-diminishing returns on our investment.

We kept heating our water well past boiling point.

LEAD ASSETS: EMAIL

You have got an email list, haven't you?

In 2012, Google kicked me in the balls. I'd spent several years building up a portfolio of online website businesses, all built on one single marketing pillar – SEO.

With one tweak of their algorithm, Google knocked that pillar out from underneath every one of my online businesses. And with that solitary pillar crumbling and no foundations in place, every one of those businesses saw their revenues tumble too.

Well, all except one. My sports betting business. What set that business apart was an email list of 14,000 people who wanted to hear from us daily. Our Google traffic may have dried up overnight, but the revenues for this business stayed consistent.

Google could take away my rankings. It could take away my traffic. But it'll never take my email list.

My email list is my greatest Evergreen Asset. It's mine. I own it. I control it. It still amazes me that I speak to business owners who either don't have an email list or, more frequently, have one that they never send an email to.

I spoke to a restaurant owner a few years ago and asked him if he had an email list. He replied: "Yeah, we've got 3,700 email addresses of people who've eaten here." My eyes lit up – that was 3,700 previous buyers with whom we could nurture a relationship and encourage to visit the restaurant more often. Happy days!

"How often do you email them?" I asked.

"Oh, I've never emailed them."

Oh. Let's just leave that money on the table then, shall we? How about that table over there? Or this table here? This restaurant is full of empty tables, every night. If only we had a way of tempting people who'd eaten here before to come back again.

If only.

Step one in creating your Email Lead Assets is to have an email list. Once you have that, step two is to actually email them – and regularly.

It's not a numbers game

But what if people don't like it? What if they unsubscribe or complain? Common questions but the answers are simple. If they want to leave, you let them and just keep talking to the people who do want to hear from you. You will get unsubscribers every time you send an email. Get OK with that from day one.

If people don't want to read your emails, they're unlikely to turn into a customer so let them go.

Evergreen Assets is not a numbers game. It's a relationships game. We're not looking to build the biggest list possible; we're looking to build the best relationship possible with that list, regardless of the size. The smaller the list you start with, the better, in my opinion, because you'll treat it as a two-way conversation with a friend rather than a broadcast to thousands. You'll build much stronger relationships that way.

You are sending weekly emails, aren't you?

In my book *Routine Machine*, I shared the email framework that's served me well for more than 20 years – weekly emails. I showed how others used that exact framework to win £30,000 tenders without pitching, land massive clients they had no idea were on their radar, and £350,000 orders from an inbound phone call.

I've appeared on almost 100 podcasts since writing that book. When asked what routine small business owners should put in place to give them the greatest ROI, without hesitation my answer is always the same – start sending weekly emails that don't sell anything (don't worry, I'll show you how to do this in the Nurture Assets section).

I host three group coaching calls for my One Percent Club members every month. On at least two of these calls, I'll either advise someone to start sending weekly emails or praise someone for the fantastic results they're getting from sending them.

Yet, most small business owners still aren't doing it. If you're not building an email list and nurturing that relationship on a weekly basis, then I implore you to start now.

Email is one of, if not *the* biggest cogs in the machine. Nearly every customer who will ever flow through the machine will pass through the email cog dozens, and possibly hundreds, of times.

Why don't more people send weekly emails? Perhaps they're scared. Scared of getting started, scared that they don't know how to manage an email list, scared that people won't read the emails or that they don't have the time to do it.

Maybe they don't know what to say? Perhaps they've sat staring at a blinking cursor for ten minutes before giving up. They might have scribbled a few sentences down, only to judge it as "not good enough" and thrown it out.

What if people unsubscribe? Or complain? Or send nasty replies? What about GDPR?

That's a lot of reasons (dare I say excuses!) not to send weekly emails. But let me make it simple for you.

Getting started is scary. Keeping going is not. So let's put on our grown-up pants, bite the bullet, and get started in the easiest way possible. Use an email marketing provider such as AWeber, Mailchimp or Active Campaign (I'll link to all of these in the resources section and help you find the right one for you) because they have user-friendly interfaces that make everything much easier.

They'll give you code to paste into your website, meaning people can sign up to your mailing list. Copy and paste. That's all you need to do at this point and you're on a par with me setting up my first email list.

At this point, you could add in The Right Bait to give people a reason to jump on your email list. But, to keep it simple, let's start by adding the people you already know to your list. No, not your friends and family, but your existing customers and prospects. Most email marketing providers let you import email addresses in bulk, as long as you have an existing relationship with them and permission to contact them.

Don't be a dickhead

This is where some people get the GDPR jitters. If you're not aware of GDPR (and you should be, seeing as it's been in law since May 2018), it's a strict set of rules that places limits on how organisations/businesses can use, process, and store the personal information of others.

Now, I'm no data protection expert, so I rely on the Information Commissioner's Office (the UK's independent authority that upholds information rights in the public interest) to tell me that's it's OK to keep chatting to my existing customers and prospects, without me being dragged through the courts:

> *"You can rely on legitimate interests for marketing activities if you can show that how you use people's data is proportionate, has a minimal privacy impact, and people would not be surprised or likely to object."*

When you read this, it's quite obvious stuff. Make sure you're only adding people to your mailing list who would expect to hear from you (I'm giving anyone who scrapes my email address off LinkedIn and adds me to their mailing lists without my permission the death stare right now).

If someone asks to be removed from the list, remove them. Don't spam people twice a day. Don't buy cold data. Don't make your email marketing strategy "throw enough shit at the wall and hope that some of it sticks".

You could sum up the entire GDPR legislation in four words: Don't be a dickhead.

There's no reason to be afraid of GDPR, unless you're planning on being a dickhead. You don't plan to be a dickhead, do you?

TL/DR:

After some of the longer or more complex assets, I'll briefly recap the main points and give you a nice, simple plan to follow with my TL/DR (which, for those unfamiliar with the term, stands for "too long, didn't read").

Here's your first TL/DR for Email Lead Assets:

Start an email list. Add people you already know (customers and prospects, not friends and family). Create The Right Bait. Offer The Right Bait to the right people by fishing in the right places.

Oh, and don't be a dickhead.

LEAD ASSETS: WEBSITE

Internet Marketing for Dummies

Two decades ago, I was a civil servant. A government employee. A pen-pusher. I knew *nothing* about marketing, how to run a business, or how to build a website. Hell, I didn't even own a computer! But this was the height of the dotcom bubble, and the Press was full of 20-somethings like me making millions of pounds on the internet, just for having *ideas*. Well, I have ideas!

But how to turn those ideas into reality? I didn't have a Scooby Doo. So I took a trip to WH Smith (remember when you used to leave the house to buy stuff?) and picked up a copy of *Internet Marketing for Dummies*. If ever there was a book title made for me, this was it!

I read the book and I followed the instructions. Sixteen months later, after many, many late nights, weekends, taking annual leave and the occasional sick day to work on my fledgling business, and with much blood, sweat and tears, I finally left the day job from hell to work full time on my new internet marketing business.

Now it's what I'm known for. I'm the guy who's been building businesses on the net for more than two decades. I still don't know more than the most basic HTML code, but I do know how to build a squeeze page, leverage SEO and get thousands of pounds worth of free traffic every month. I know how to design webpages and write copy so that they convert better, and I know how to turn my website into an Evergreen Asset – a 24/7 salesman who always delivers the perfect pitch.

Why am I telling you this? It's certainly not to show off my amazing web design skills (The average 15-year-old can probably build a better website than me), but rather to demonstrate my journey from knowing absolutely nothing about websites to earning a very good living for the rest of my days from them.

If the thought of working on a website scares you, then I want you to know that I understand. I was scared, too. But *Internet Marketing for Dummies* closed the knowledge gap for me. Evergreen Assets will do the same for you.

But I don't need a website!

Often when I'm coaching small business owners and I start talking about websites, I get a dismissive wave of the hand: "Oh, I don't need a website. I've got a Facebook group/Yell listing/Instagram account."

Oh really? So no one ever searches on Google for your product or service? If they do (and let me assure you, they *do*), would you rather be in control of what they see or are you happy for them to see your competitors, your Companies House listing, and that solitary one-star review that a disgruntled customer left on a review site years ago?

As Bill Gates famously said: "If your business is not on the internet, then your business will be out of business."

Others will say: "My Facebook page gets me all the business I need." Great. Well done. Good for you. I used to have a Facebook page, too, with 127,000 followers. I spent a six-figure sum with Facebook to build that up over a couple of years. That page gave *me* all the business I needed.

Until, one day, Facebook closed it down. From 127,000 followers to zero, overnight. From all the business I needed to none whatsoever. Facebook can (and will) do whatever it likes because it owns the platform. It's their football. If you're building your business on Facebook (or any third party platform), then you're building your business on someone else's land, and you're always going to be one tweak of the algorithm or breach of the terms and conditions away from your business crumbling to the ground.

A website is an Evergreen Asset that *you* own and *you* control. It's a massive cog in the machine, opening up several other assets – including SEO, Google Ads, squeeze pages, memberships, and customer fulfilment.

By all means continue with your Facebook group, directory listing or Instagram account. But remember, these are all someone else's football. That puts them in charge of the game and they can move the goalposts, change the rules, or take the football away from you if they want. They can't take your website away from you, though. *You* own that. *You* control that.

That's *your* asset, not theirs.

No, I can't build *you* a website!

"Nice to meet you. What do you do?"

"I run an internet marketing company."

"Oh cool, could you build me a website?"

Shudder. For years, I had this exact conversation every time I went to a networking event. For some reason, people thought that because I ran an online business, I must be a world-class web designer. They also thought I must know how to fix computers because I use one.

Using a laptop doesn't make you any more of a computer technician than using a toothbrush makes you a dentist. Yes, our company builds websites. No, we won't build yours.

Over the years, my web design "skills" went through the following evolution: In the early years, I did everything myself. I found a WYSIWYG (what you see is what you get) program that allowed me to make very (and I mean very) basic websites using drag and drop. A box here, some text there, an image at the top, and a link at the bottom.

I can't emphasise enough just how awful those websites I designed myself in those early years were. I used to receive frequent feedback from other business owners that my sites were "basic", "outdated", and "horrible to look at".

So I hired a team of designers and coders to build much more attractive websites. Those sites took a lot longer to go live (months rather than days) and cost a lot more (five people on salary rather than me on commission-only). And guess what? They didn't perform as well as my "ugly" sites.

Still, at least they looked pretty.

That seems to be most people's criteria for their website – it must look pretty. My criteria isn't to look pretty. It's to *convert*. It's to be effective. It's to turn cold traffic into warm leads, warm leads into paying customers, and paying customers into lifelong fans.

What do you want *your* website to do? Make the phone ring? Sell something? Capture leads? Signpost people to your offline store or office? To showcase you?

The primary purpose of your website should be to instigate the action you want the majority of visitors to take (and/or the action *they* want to take) – book an appointment, find out technical information, read reviews, get a quote, etc. – aka convert.

The vomit brochure

However, most web designers don't even think about this. Instead, they have a template for "business websites" and they all look pretty much the same: Nice big logo at the top, huge slider section filled with stock images and the entire site devoted to who we are and what we do.

It's an online version of a glossy brochure. It's designed to tell people how great we are, how we're the experts, and showcase all the things they could buy from us.

Oh, it's going to look pretty. But it won't convert (which is the primary purpose of your website, remember?). It won't help your prospects and customers to do what *they* want to do, and it won't result in those prospects and customers doing what *you* want them to do either.

What's the answer? Stop treating your website as a brochure. And stop vomiting all over it.

When most business owners plan what needs to go on their website, they think to themselves: "Well, people need to know who we are. They need to know the history of the company. They need to know all about our experience. They need to know that we sell blue widgets, red widgets, and green widgets. But we don't just sell widgets. We also sell thingies, too, in a variety of shapes and sizes. Oh, and whatchamacallits. We make those too. And we need to make sure we include a link to our

Facebook page and Twitter feed. And... And... Make sure we include *everything*!"

It's like you've force-fed your web designer your company brochure and they've vomited it all over your website. And just like a pool of vomit, it's a mess, it's all over the place, and it stinks.

We're not helping

Every time a user lands on a webpage, they start having a conversation in their head with that site:

> *"Am I in the right place? What shall I look at first? Where's the thing I'm looking for? Is this the same company I've been speaking to? Can these people help me? Where the hell is what I'm looking for? How do I find out the price? How do I contact them? Why does this look like someone's vomited their company brochure all over it? I can't find what I was looking for. Oh, I give up."*

That whole conversation took place in your website visitor's head. It took them less than 20 seconds, a few clicks to try to find what they wanted and they're now back at Google, checking out your competitor's website instead.

Go to your website now. Forget everything you know about yourself and put yourself in the shoes of a potential customer. Imagine you've just searched Google for the answer to a problem you have or a product you're interested in knowing more about.

What questions pop into your head? Forget for a moment that you know where to click to find stuff and consider if a complete stranger who's never heard of you and never seen your website will know where to go and what to do. Will they know they're even on the right website and that you can help them?

I'll tell you one thing: we're not helping matters. If you look at most businesses websites, you'll notice that they "we" a lot:

> "We are the number one choice for blue widgets."
>
> "We were established in 1974."
>
> "We do this."
>
> "We do that."
>
> "We're great."
>
> "Want to hear more about us? Sure, we've got a whole 'About Us' page dedicated to us (but really every page on this website is about us!)."
>
> "Anyway, enough about us. What do you think about us?"

Your website should talk to your ideal target market in *their* language, about *their* problems, *their* hopes and dreams – what *they* want. "Oh, and by the way, we're someone who can help you with that."

Most websites could massively increase their conversions if they simply took their current ratio of "we" versus "you" and flipped it on its head. Less about us, more about you.

Once you attract the right person to your site (which you will do if you're using The Right Bait and fishing in the right place), they should have the following reaction in their head: "Oh, I'm definitely in the right place. It's like they're talking *just to me*!"

What's the "big idea"?

How do you tell an anonymous website visitor that they're in the right place in fewer than three seconds?

Nope, not with a massive version of your logo. It's not a slider full of glossy stock images either. And it is most certainly not by you welcoming them to your website. For some reason, the opening gambit on most small business websites all around the world is some variation of: "Welcome to our website."

Would you take out a billboard ad on the busiest road in town and on that prime bit of advertising real estate lead with the words: "Welcome to my billboard"? No, of course you wouldn't, so don't do it on the prime real estate that is your website.

What's the biggest problem you solve for the majority of your customers? Before they come to you, what's keeping them up at night? What are they worried about? What concerns, false beliefs or objections do they have to overcome in order to become a client? What's in it for them? What's The Right Bait for them?

What's the one thing that, if you convince them of this one fact, all the other barriers come tumbling down?

That's your "big idea" and by shouting it from the rooftops, web visitors know without a shadow of a doubt in 0.4 seconds flat: "I'm in the right place. This is just what I've been looking for!"

In 2003, I was setting up a limited company to make my fledgling internet marketing business all official and grown-up. My accountant asked me what name I wanted to choose and I didn't have a clue.

Later, I jumped in the car with my springer spaniel Max to go for a walk at our local National Trust beauty spot. As I pulled up in the car park, I heard an advert on the radio with the headline: "What's the big idea, then?"

Hmm, I was *full* of big ideas. And so, Big Idea Media Ltd (Registered in England and Wales, No. 4758844) was born.

Nowadays, I refer to the "big idea" as our guiding light – the North Star that keeps us on track. The one concept that everyone can buy into.

My overarching, big idea is to create an ambitious lifestyle business. The One Percent Club's big idea is that it's not about growing your business; it's about improving your business – and that stacking up one per cent improvements each week is the key to steady, sustainable, stress-free growth.

My sports betting business's big idea is that using professional tipsters and data science helps everyday punters make better betting decisions.

For my book *Big Ideas... for Small Businesses*, the big idea was that lifestyle businesses are real businesses too, and can compete (and beat) the big boys at their own game.

For *Routine Machine*, it was that consistency is a superpower, and by outsourcing your actions to a collection of carefully designed daily habits and routines, you can make success inevitable.

This book's big idea is that working hard to create an Evergreen Asset once enables you to reap the rewards again and again (and again).

It doesn't matter whether you're writing a headline for your website, sending an email to 35,000 people, chatting to a small group on a Facebook thread, or talking one-to-one with a single prospect, your big idea will guide you. By finding out *what they want* – which "big idea" they buy into the most – you can naturally (and with a clear conscience) recommend the right product and service for them.

That's the big idea.

It's a bit of a squeeze

One of the best ways to grow your email list is with a dedicated lead-generation landing page, sometimes called a squeeze page.

Just like squeezing juice from an orange, landing/squeeze pages are there to *squeeze* leads out of web traffic that lands on the page. While they can be hosted on your website, they're more often than not stand-alone pages, with all the navigation menus and possible options removed.

There are only two things visitors can do on a squeeze page:

1. They can enter their details and sign up.
2. They can close the tab and get on with their day.

That's it. Sign up or go away. Shit or get off the pot.

Squeeze pages are much more effective than a simple sign-up box on your website, with conversion rates up to ten times higher.

The main focus of your squeeze page will be The Right Bait. All you need to do now is offer The Right Bait to the right people. Fish where the fish are, using the bait they love. When you've got a squeeze page that works, you just need to point the right people there, which can be done with paid traffic, SEO, social networking, podcasts, direct mail, or any of the other assets in this book.

Remember, we're creating an ecosystem here – a machine full of interacting cogs and gears. The squeeze page cog connects to the email cog, but it also has multiple smaller cogs feeding into it, ensuring a steady flow of potential leads coming into the machine at all times. If you remember, Gary Keller told us that lead generation should be every business's "ONE thing".

It's certainly mine. Let's make it yours.

Turn your homepage into a hug page

A squeeze page only gives users two choices – sign up or bugger off. But what if you want your homepage to not only capture leads, but also serve existing customers, signpost to customer service touchpoints, and provide self-serve or product research information?

Well, why not turn your homepage into a hug page? A hug page is like a squeeze page, only quite a bit softer.

Sure, the main objective on your homepage is going to be capturing a lead. Therefore the ideal set-up is:

"Big idea" headline > The Right Bait > sign-up form.

If I land on your website, I'm going to read the big idea headline, be enticed by The Right Bait, and pop my details in your sign-up form. But, unlike a squeeze page, that's not my only option. I can still navigate around the rest of the website as I wish as the standard menus are all in place. And if I scroll down past the call to action area, I might see other sections that are more relevant to me – "get a quote", existing members' login, a list of FAQs, etc.

I'm not being squeezed onto your email list; I'm being gently hugged into it. Your call to action (CTA) area should be above the fold (visible on all screen sizes, without scrolling), but not the only option.

TL/DR:

Don't be scared of websites. Everyone should have one.

Design for conversions, not awards. Every visitor is having a conversation in their head with your website. Stop vomiting and "we-ing" all over it. Share the "big idea" and The Right Bait. Make the most of squeeze pages and hug pages.

Oh, and no, I can't fix your computer.

LEAD ASSETS: SEARCH ENGINE OPTIMISATION

What has SEO ever done for me?

OK, so, apart from sending me tens of millions of pounds worth of highly-targeted traffic with users at every point on the buying journey (from the coldest of cold leads to those yelling "shut up and take my money"), and enabling me to employ dozens of full-time team members, raise my profile, and ultimately save me from the day job from hell, what has SEO ever done for me?

Email is the largest cog in my Evergreen Assets machine. The email cog is filled with leads from my website and my website gets most of its traffic from SEO.

Sure, I could still run my businesses without SEO, but then I'd have left a heck of a lot of money on the table every year.

When I first got my crayons out and started knocking up horrible looking websites, SEO was easy. All you needed to do was repeat the keywords you wanted to rank for (and every possible combination of them) on the webpage as many times as possible.

That's obviously going to look horrible for users, so I would make this text the same colour as the background. That way, users couldn't see it, but search engines could.

An important note: please do not attempt that hidden text, keyword stuffing tactic today. While it was "what's working right now" for me 20 years ago, it'll get you blacklisted by Google if you try it now.

At the time, I thought I was being clever but was actually cheating the system. The search engine algorithms soon realised and got a bit smarter and SEO got a bit harder.

Google was the first to take into account the number of links that each page had pointing to it, figuring that the more people link to a particular page or website, the better it must be. But website owners soon cottoned on again and an entire link building (and link buying) industry popped up off the back of it. So Google moved the goalposts again and made its algorithm even more complicated. So, SEO got even harder.

A game of cat and mouse then ensued with Matt Cutts, head of webspam at Google, changing the rules almost daily to stop people gaming the system, only for SEO-savvy webmasters to reverse engineer the current algorithm and game it anyway.

Eventually, something had to give. In 2012, Google rolled out two of the largest overhauls to its algorithm. Never mind moving the goalposts, Google's Panda and Penguin updates removed them completely and put them in a different city.

The algorithm got infinitely more complicated and SEO got infinitely harder.

That's when I gave up "doing" SEO. All of a sudden, SEO was hard and I no longer knew how it worked. So I focused instead on growing my email list, optimising my website for users (not Google), and sending paid traffic to my squeeze pages and hug pages. I stopped looking at the search results, stopped tracking every single rise and fall in search rankings, and just looked after my existing site visitors – including the trickle I was now getting from Google.

A few years later, I noticed I was getting a lot of organic traffic from Google again – and for many of the keywords I used to rank for. I dug deeper and, sure enough, my rankings for just about every keyword that I used to dominate when I was playing cat and mouse with Matt Cutts were at their pre-Panda/Penguin levels.

I was winning at SEO again without even trying.

SEO is simple again

What does Google actually want? It wants to deliver the best results for its users. The most relevant, most insightful, most helpful content that reliably, comprehensively solves the problems and queries that its users have.

That's all you need to know about SEO.

"Doing" SEO these days is simple (but not easy). Just make sure your website or webpage is "the internet's best answer to that question" or "the number one source of $$$ on the internet", or the most comprehensive, or the most user-friendly, or the most downloaded, the most bookmarked, the most…you get the idea.

Google doesn't care about you or your business and it has no obligation to send you any traffic whatsoever.

But if you care about Google's users, look after them when they're on your website, and give them what they want, Google is more likely to reward you with hundreds (or thousands, or tens of thousands) of highly targeted, ready-to-buy customers, who are looking for *exactly* what it is that you do – and that reward is free.

Google would charge you a few quid for every one of those clicks via Google Ads, but if you scratch its back (by giving Google's users what *they* want), it'll scratch yours. I've had millions of pounds worth of free traffic from Google.

Remember the three objectives of Evergreen Assets:

1. Find out what they want: Google wants the best possible results for its users.
2. Give them what they want: Make sure you're creating the internet's best answer to their question.
3. Make damn sure they've got what they want: Use analytics to spot where you're missing the mark and fix it, so that you are giving them what they want.

The internet's best answer to that question

It doesn't matter whether you're searching for "how long should I cook a 3kg turkey?", "who's the best accountant in my town?" or "what would a chair look like if your knees bent the other way?" (Yes, people do search Google for that!). What you want and what Google wants to give you is the internet's best answer to that question.

Swimming pool salesman Marcus Sheridan has created a bestselling book, public speaking career and training business out of this simple (but not easy) tactic of giving Google searchers what they're looking for.

He noticed lots of people were landing on his website for search terms such as "how much is a swimming pool?" or "what's the best swimming pool for a small garden?". In a lightbulb moment that seems painfully obvious in hindsight, Sheridan realised he *wasn't* giving them what they wanted.

How much is a swimming pool? Well, it depends on several factors. A small, standard-size, above-ground fibreglass pool will cost a lot less than a custom-made Olympic-sized pool in the shape of your favourite Teletubby. Most swimming pool companies answered the "how much is it?" question with a short: "It depends. Give us a call."

Every one of them. Not one company answered the question.

So Marcus did. He created a blog post that listed all the different factors that could affect the price of a swimming pool and gave ballpark prices for each type of pool. And then something scary happened. His phone started ringing less. Because he was giving the prices out publicly, people no longer needed to call to get what they were looking for.

Damn.

Or maybe not.

Because Marcus's conversion rate went through the roof.

The calls that stopped were from the tyre kickers – the "I wonder if I can afford a pool?" brigade who had a budget of $7,000 and would disappear when told they'd need at least $20,000.

And those that remained were warm prospects who already had a ballpark figure for the cost of a pool and were ringing Marcus to ask for a more precise quote for their exact requirements.

The time wasters de-selected themselves and the only people that Marcus spoke with were highly-qualified leads.

So, he continued to write blog posts that answered the most common questions his potential customers had (he knew what these questions were because they were the ones he answered every time he did a sales call or presented to a warm prospect):

> How much is a __________?
>
> What are the common problems with a __________?
>
> Should I choose a __________ or a __________?
>
> What are the __________ reviews like?
>
> What's the best __________ to buy?

Your potential customers are asking these questions right now. Start typing these questions into Google and you'll see the auto-suggest kick in, which means lots of other Google users search for that term. Google also helpfully includes a "people also ask" section, as well as displaying related searches, so you can find the questions that actual prospects are typing into Google right now. Finding out *what they want* is a piece of cake.

And all you need to do now is give them what they want. And what they want is their question answered fully, honestly, and without marketing spin.

That's what Marcus Sheridan did, turning his humble three-man company River Pool and Spas into one of the largest manufacturers and installers in the United States, as well as the most visited pool website in the world, attracting more than 750,000 visitors a month – mostly free of charge, courtesy of SEO.

Are we on the same page?

If your website truly is the internet's best answer to that question (or the internet's best resource for that search), then Google wants to reward you with a #1 ranking. And if someone delivers a better experience, it will promote that person over you. Remember, Google owes you nothing and simply wants to make damn sure its users have got what they want.

These days, I would estimate that off-page factors such as the links pointing at your website account for less than ten per cent of the algorithm determining your rankings and is far outweighed by on-page factors, such as basic optimisation and user experience.

Basic optimisation means tweaking a few settings within your website code to tell search engines what each page is about. If you're a business coach who works primarily with coffee shops in Cambridge, you want to let Google know that.

Google considers thousands of on-page factors, but let's look at the crucial two that carry almost all of the basic optimisation weight.

Meta Title

Meta Title is the page name that appears as the clickable link on the search results and should serve two purposes. First, to include your target keywords and, second, to encourage people to click from the search results (clickthrough rate is also a ranking factor). The most common mistake people make is not changing this at all. Hundreds of thousands of websites have an identical Meta Title, all saying simply "Homepage".

The second most common mistake is to use your company name as the Meta Title. Ranking for your own name should not be hard (or celebrated). By all means include your name, but not as the main focus.

So not "Homepage" and not "Dark Roast Coaching". But something like "Coffee Shop Business Coach Cambridge – Free Coffee Shop Business Plan".

There are a few keywords I'm targeting there:

- Coffee Shop Business.
- Business Coach.
- Business Coach Cambridge.
- Coffee Shop Business Cambridge.
- Coffee Shop Business Plan.
- Coffee Shop Business Coach.
- Coffee Shop Coach.

Note that I've also used The Right Bait ("Free Coffee Shop Business Plan") to hook people in and teased this in the search results to increase click-throughs. I've also capitalised every word (which I'm sure will have my editor pulling his hair out working through this section), but in my experience, this grammatical faux-pas actually leads to around a ten per cent bump in clicks.

Meta Description

You also need a Meta Description, which is a sentence or two that Google displays underneath your Meta Title in the search results.

If you don't choose one yourself, Google will scrape what it thinks is most relevant from your webpage and display that. Don't let it do that. Again, we're talking about prime real estate and an opportunity for you to tell Google and its users what your page is about and why they should choose you over the other 130trillion pages indexed by Google – including your competitors.

You don't have a lot of space to work with (up to 158 characters at the time of writing), so keep it short and punchy with your target keywords in there.

For example: "Get your free coffee shop business plan today from Cambridge's #1 coffee shop coach Dark Roast Coaching."

That's 103 characters. All variations of your target keywords are covered. The Right Bait is teased. It's about them, not you. It's a little bit clickbaity. And you've even included your business name. Box ticked!

You're probably thinking: "Bloody hell, John. That sounds complex. I'm no coder or web geek. I'm just Cambridge's #1 business coach for coffee shop owners."

Well, worry ye not. Get the coffee brewing (I'll have a double-caramel macchiato please), and I'll show you an easy way to tick all the on-page SEO boxes.

If you're using WordPress (as 35.2 per cent of the entire internet does), then all you need to do is download a free plugin called Yoast, which makes updating your on-page SEO as easy as filling in the blanks. Simply tell Yoast which keywords you'd like to target and you'll see a traffic lights system for each page, telling you how well optimised the page is for those keywords.

The plugin will even give you feedback and ideas to improve your scores. Most of the functionality is free but there is a paid version that is even more powerful and highly recommended for those serious about adding SEO as an Evergreen Asset.

Google also helps you to see exactly where the goalposts are by giving you free resources in your search console to see how your website is performing against its expectations. It expects your site to be mobile-friendly and fast loading with a set of "core web vitals" that it uses to monitor and rank websites. (Imagine your blood pressure, heart rate, and temperature being checked during a visit to the doctors).

Google says these vital signs "should be measured by all site owners and will be surfaced across all Google tools. Each of the Core Web Vitals represents a distinct facet of the user experience, is measurable in the field, and reflects the real-world experience of a critical user-centric outcome."

In other words, it's all about the user.

TL/DR:

Give Google what *it* wants (the internet's best answer/resource for the user's search) and Google will give you what *you* want (large numbers of highly-targeted leads from your exact target market).

Choose your keywords wisely, get the on-page basics ticked off using the free tools available (I'll include links to all the SEO tools, together with a two-part masterclass training video in the resources at the end of the book), and then focus entirely on the user experience.

Oh, and don't try to trick Google. It is way smarter than you or I.

LEAD ASSETS: GOOGLE ADS

The game-changer

Google Ads launched in the UK on February 23rd, 2002. I signed up on that first day and was able to buy clicks for half of one pence that were worth 15p a click to me. I was literally 30x'ing my money overnight (for a few weeks at least).

I spent £300 the first month and turned it into £9,000. The second month I spent £1,000, and turned that into £15,000. Eventually, the ROI dropped as more and more competition appeared on the terms

I was bidding on, but I was still doubling my money every month – £10,000 in, £20,000 out.

Google Ads was a proper game-changer for many people and some used it to grow huge businesses. My network is full of people who now run very successful businesses, are multimillionaires, and who have built up significant wealth over the last two decades. But I knew them before February 23rd, 2002, when they still worked in a biscuit factory or drove HGV lorries for a living and, like me, didn't have a pot to piss in.

Jamie worked full-time and ran a small wedding list website on the side – until that day in February. He started playing with Google Ads, saw similar returns to me and snowballed the lot. He turned a few hundred into a few thousand, a few thousand into ten thousand, and then went to his bank manager and took out a £20,000 personal loan.

Two months later, Jamie paid the loan off in full and deposited his commission cheques for five times that amount. The bank manager's eyes lit up and he offered Jamie an umbrella now that there was no chance of rain: "Would you like a coffee, Jamie? Is there anything we can do for you? How much would you like to borrow next?"

Jamie kept on building his snowball, compounding those amazing ROIs for a couple of years. In 2008, I picked up the Sunday papers, only to find his face staring out at me. He was featured in the Sunday Times Rich List "30 under 30" section with a net worth of £28million.

The same guy I chatted with online at 3am, munching on Marmite on toast while coding our own (horrible looking) websites, was worth £28million. And all thanks to Google Ads.

I know a shortcut

Google Ads is a shortcut to SEO. It puts you in control, enabling you to turn the taps on (or off) as your pipeline dictates. It's "pay to play", so you can immediately leapfrog the hundreds of competitors all vying for the top SEO spots by simply putting your hand in your pocket and paying for the privilege.

In the early days, it was a very simple auction. If I was willing to pay 14p a click and you bid 15p, then your ad would be shown above mine. If a third person offered 16p a click, they'd leapfrog us both.

This led to a lot of revenue for Google and its top advertisers, but it wasn't a great experience for Google's users. Remember, what Google wants is the best resource/answer/webpage for that search term – and that includes paid traffic as well as organic.

Maybe more so, because paid listings are given the prime real estate at the top of the results where most people will click.

So, while ad position is still loosely based on an auction system, it's a lot more advanced than the simple "highest bidder wins" model that they used back in the day. It's now more a case of the "best bidder wins" with Google taking into account dozens of factors, such as landing page relevance, user experience, clickthrough rate, bounce rate, and overall account quality, in addition to how much you're willing to spend.

The best place to bury a dead body

According to a study by IgniteVisibility.com, the first Google result will receive approximately 43 per cent of the clicks. This drops to 37 per cent for the second result, 30 per cent for the third result, all the way down to just three per cent for the tenth result. It's clear to see why lots of people want to pay to be top.

But do you need to be top? Sure, you'll get more clicks than any other position but you'll pay exponentially more for the privilege. The sweet spot could be somewhere in the top four. Fourth position, for example, averages a 19.38 per cent clickthrough rate – less than half that of top spot, but potentially costing less than half as much per click.

As you've read above, deep pockets alone won't suffice anymore because Google might charge you three times as much as me for the same ad spot. So why can I get the same ad much cheaper than you? Because I've taken the time to give Google what it wants. And what does Google want? It wants the best search experience for its users.

If a user clicks on your ad, visits your site, hits the back button, and clicks on someone else's ad, then not only have you lost the sale or failed to generate a lead, but you've also paid for that click, *and* sent a negative signal to Google Ads about the experience for their user. So, Google will charge you *more* for the next click, relegate you further down the results page or even bump you off the first page completely.

There's an old SEO joke: "Where's the best place to hide a dead body? Page two of the Google results."

Fewer than one in 20 users will make it as far as page two, and if you drop one place in the rankings from 10th (bottom of page one) to 11th (top of page two), you can expect your traffic to drop by around 140 per cent. Great if you're trying to hide a dead body. Not so good if you're trying to generate leads.

So how do we give Google what it wants? Relevancy is key. Your ad (as well as your landing page and user experience navigating your website) should be the most relevant to the user's search. Google Ads are not about showing billboards to loosely-targeted segments; they're about delivering exactly what the user is searching for.

Google isn't a big fan of squeeze pages, because one of their key user experience metrics is whether users interact with the website as a whole – ideally navigating around several pages, clicking on a couple of links, scrolling, reading, and ultimately taking some form of action on the site, ending that search session.

It's also against Google's advertising policies to send a user to a standalone landing page that isn't part of your website. So this would be a good place to deploy a softer hug page – still using a big idea-focused headline with The Right Bait and a prominent call to action above the fold. But also include your navigation menu and maybe some more content below the fold that can signpost other relevant pages on your site, particularly if it's relevant to the user's search or can help them decide whether to take the bait, which is your primary objective as a Lead Asset.

Make sure you track conversions, too. If you're using Google Ads to generate leads, you want to know what keywords and what ad copy results in leads so that you can divert more of your budget there. Strip out keywords that don't convert (or find out *why* they don't convert), and maybe redesign a poorly converting webpage or send them to a more relevant page.

Play "Winner Stays On" by split-testing different headlines, body copy, etc, in your ads. See if version A or version B works best. Then pit the winner against version C.

Conversion tracking is also important for Google's algorithm to learn how users convert for you, so that it can show your ads to the users most likely to result in a conversion. Feeding conversion data back into your Google Ads account teaches the algorithm to work in your favour.

Because you pay for every single click, you only want the highest quality potential leads – those with the greatest potential to provide a return on your investment. Therefore, make sure you're only targeting the most relevant of keywords. Indeed, you should be building a massive list of "negative keywords", the search terms for which you specifically don't want your ads to be shown. Your negative keyword list should be at least ten times the size of the keywords you're actively targeting.

Let's go back to our business coach in Cambridge. If you only serve your local area, you don't want to advertise to people looking for a business coach in Carlisle or to those looking to hire a 32-seater coach to travel to Cambridge.

So you would add words like Carlisle, seat, seater, and travel to your negative keywords list, and Google won't waste your money showing ads to people who are highly unlikely to buy.

At least once a month, look at the search terms that have resulted in clicks. These are actual clicks from real users that have cost you real money. You'll soon spot the searches that were never going to convert – those out of your area, those in different sectors, and those looking for free, cheap or second hand.

John Wanamaker, an American businessman in the 1800s known as a pioneer of marketing, famously said: "Half the money I spend on advertising is wasted…the trouble is, I don't know which half."

Well, if you're tracking conversions, you'll not only know which half is wasted, but you can turn that half off and double your ad spend on the other half – those search terms most likely to result in a conversion.

TL/DR:

Google Ads is a shortcut to SEO.

Remember, Google wants the best results for its users and you want to avoid wasting your money on ads that don't convert. You don't have to be #1, but you could hide a dead body on page two (at #11 and beyond). Be the most relevant advertiser – the best bidder wins, not the highest bidder. Track conversions. Play Winner Stays On by split-testing. Use hug pages. Build a massive negative keyword list.

Oh, and figure out which half of your ad spend is wasted and spend it on the other half instead.

LEAD ASSETS: FACEBOOK ADS.

I've tried to make this book as evergreen in its examples as possible. You wouldn't want to pick up a book today that tells you how to rank on Alta Vista, gain traction on Friends Reunited or build a better MySpace profile.

Facebook Ads have been an asset that's served me very well over the last decade, but I'm no fortune teller.

In the years that follow writing this, Facebook may still be a major player in the social networking landscape or it may implode and disappear up its own newsfeed. Everything you're about to read in this chapter (and in the subsequent Facebook Ads chapters) apply to *any* social networking platform where you can deploy pattern interrupt ads to clearly defined, interest-based demographics.

The Interrupting Cow

> Knock.
>
> Who's there?
>
> The Interrupting Cow.
>
> The Interrupt…
>
> Mooooo!

That's my daughter's favourite joke. I make no apologies for it.

Facebook Ads are a different beast to Google Ads. Advertising on Google is very much about "giving them what they want". In contrast, Facebook Ads are more about guessing what they might want and interrupting their newsfeed-scrolling session with something that grabs their attention.

You will need to nurture Facebook leads a bit more (give these guys some more Nurture Assets), as it's more "interruption marketing". For clarity, people might actively search for your product or service on Google, but you're hunting for them on Facebook.

When it comes to interrupting people, you need something… interesting…exciting…sexy. The Right Bait for the right people. Facebook users are not looking for your product or service. They're looking for photos of their friends or to argue with Karen from Stockport about the latest news topic du jour.

Their current pattern is scroll, scroll, scroll, hit like, scroll, scroll, scroll, angry emoji, scroll, scroll, enter debate about politics or religion, scroll, scroll, scroll.

We're looking to interrupt this pattern and create a new one: Scroll, scroll, scroll. STOP! What's this? This looks interesting...

Some of the best pattern interrupt campaigns I've seen include the use of a funny or interesting image combined with an intriguing headline. In our sports betting business, we've used photos of a smiling horse, a footballer missing an open goal, and a very ugly man with a nose shaped like a penis (hey, I never claimed to be high-brow!), and all have achieved that first objective – to interrupt the user's pattern.

I'm currently being targeted by a dog trainer with ads full of stuffed toy squirrels in funny positions (think Elf on the Shelf, but with squirrels), to promote their "Are you sexier than a squirrel?" dog training challenge.

The pattern interrupt in those ads (interesting/funny images plus an intriguing headline – who wouldn't want to be sexier than a squirrel?) means that I not only stopped scrolling, but I also read the ad in full. I also watched the accompanying video. And I clicked through to their squeeze page. And I joined their mailing list.

From idly scrolling Facebook to signing up for more information about a dog training course in which I previously had no interest and zero inclination to search for in about two minutes flat. That's a well-targeted pattern interrupt Facebook Ad at its best.

Our Survey Said

Imagine a survey that more than three billion people worldwide have spent more than a decade responding to – divulging all their innermost thoughts and secrets including the brands they buy, the places they visit, their political leanings, the media sources they listen to, the TV shows they watch, the music they listen to, and every single opinion they agree (or disagree) with. Everything they like and everything they hate.

How valuable would that be? Well, Facebook has that information at its fingertips and, at current estimates, its value is roughly £520billion.

If Justin Bieber wants to spend his hardly-earned money flogging his latest pile of noise, he can leverage Facebook's demographic data, diverting his ad spend towards people who have already indicated that they enjoy his "music" – which, as you may have guessed from this sentence, would not include myself.

But this is great for Justin and me. He doesn't waste any of his ad spend on me and I don't see ads for musicians whose songs I find less appealing than listening to cats fighting. The money that JB saves by not making my ears bleed can be spent elsewhere – maybe growing his email list (so he's not reliant on Facebook's football) by offering The Right Bait to the right people or getting powerful with his targeting.

Let's say Bieber is planning a UK tour next year with dates in Birmingham, London, Manchester and Glasgow. (As long as he stays at least 200 miles away from Plymouth, I'm happy).

He can laser-focus his targeting. He could include people who like his Facebook page. That's 76,462,560 people at the time of writing, which is way too broad. Just like Google Ads, Facebook rewards advertisers who target users with relevant ads. So the more JB can narrow his audience, the better.

He could target those fans who both like his page and live in the UK. But there's still lower hanging fruit to be had.

Why not start by targeting JB's Facebook fans + the social demographics of his typical gig-goer + people who live within a 25-mile radius of the stadium (or those who have checked into the venue before)?

Not only would we be left with a much smaller target audience than the 76million we started out with, but it will also be whittled down to the fans most likely (and most able) to buy a ticket.

Now, that is music to my ears.

It's like they're stalking me

We've all had that uneasy feeling. You have a conversation with a friend over a cuppa or chat to a mate on Messenger, maybe discussing whether your next car will be a BMW X1 or an Audi Q3.

Twenty minutes later, you're scrolling Facebook and a picture of an Audi Q3 appears in an ad in your newsfeed. What are the chances? They must be stalking you, surely?

Well, I'll leave the conspiracy theories to those who know more about personal information security than me. After all, the greatest lie ever told is: "I have read and understand the terms and conditions."

But make no mistake about it, you have been targeted for that ad. Probably not by Alexa spying on you and having a quick word with Audi's marketing department, but more likely by a combination of your demographics and browsing history.

How do "they" know that you're trying to decide between the X1 and Q3? Well, you've probably done a few Google searches for both cars (maybe starting with a larger field of potential candidates. You might have bookmarked a few websites and returned to certain ones more often than others. You might have searched for images of particular colour options (a stronger buyer intent signal) or visited the specs page of the dealer website.

You might have also looked at some reviews, watched a YouTube video or ten, and downloaded a brochure. You might have visited a number of websites to compare prices or find second-hand car dealers. You may well have found out how much it would cost to insure your new motor.

And unless you've done all this on a totally-secure, untraceable computer with your tin-foil hat on, you've given all those buying signals to the likes of Google and Facebook. These guys know more about you than you do, because they've studied the buying patterns of billions of people all over the planet. If you really want to know whether you're going to choose the X1 or the Q3, perhaps you should ask the online giants instead as they probably know before you do.

So, yes, the ad targeting available is scarily good. And for that reason, you need to straddle the fine line between "It's like they're talking to me" and "Oh my god, they are talking to me".

"It's like they're talking to me" is "Justin Bieber is returning to Manchester next year! Buy your tickets today", whereas "Justin Bieber (who you love) is playing just 8 miles from your house next year! Buy your tickets today" sounds a little bit too "I know where you live" for most user's liking. And Facebook won't allow you to use anything that indicates someone has been personally targeted in the ad copy for that exact reason.

Count me out

Rather than blasting ads to anyone who *could* buy, let's use a sniper approach and target those *most likely* to buy. As with Google Ads, the key to keeping your Facebook Ads costs down is to exclude people.

Treat your targeting as a deselection process. Aim to have as small (and as highly targeted) a demographic as possible. Digital marketer Brian Swichkow took this a little too far by creating an incredibly highly-targeted demographic, consisting of just one person – his flatmate – whom he bombarded with incredibly personal-ads:

"Does it seem ironic that swallowing swords is easy and then small pills make you gag?" (His flatmate was indeed a professional sword-swallower, who gagged on paracetamol).

"If you're the kind of coffee-drinking guy who has a black bandana in his pocket, watch this!" (Referencing a private conversation they'd had earlier that day).

And finally, the big reveal: *"Ever feel like your flatmate is creating Facebook Ads targeted to a niche of just you?"*

Thankfully, Facebook has made this level of targeting/stalking impossible now, but you should still be aiming to remove as many irrelevant users as possible.

You should also remove poorly performing ads and campaigns and double down on the ones that work. Play Winner Stays On, track conversions, and split test your ads, removing the worst performers and diverting budget towards the best.

TL/DR:

Facebook Ads are the interrupting cow and your ads need to be sexier than a squirrel.

The real power lies in the targeting – aiming to advertise to as small (but as relevant) an audience as possible. Maybe not just your flatmate, though! Facebook really does know its users better than they know themselves and if you can also define your target market well, it should be a match made in heaven.

Oh, and Zuckerberg? I'd better not start seeing Justin Bieber ads after writing this chapter.

LEAD ASSETS: SOCIAL NETWORKS

A quick caveat before we dive into this section. Once again, I've tried to avoid referring to specific social networking sites where possible, as it's quite likely that they will have been acquired, imploded, or have disappeared up their own arse in the time between me writing these words and you reading them.

So, if I do refer to a now-defunct network, please forgive me. However, the ideas contained within this section are designed to be evergreen and not platform-specific.

With that in mind, let's get sociable.

Antisocial Media

I've met more than my fair share of "experts" over the years and you can guess from the return of the heavily sarcastic quotation marks that they were anything but experts. Every sector and every industry has them. But one industry seems to attract more of them than any other.

Anyone with an Instagram account can suddenly call themselves a social media marketing expert – and they often do, despite possessing little marketing nous or business acumen.

I don't do social media. I do social networks. I joined Facebook and Twitter not long after they launched in the UK, using these social networking sites as I believe they were intended – to network with people, socially.

I'd keep in touch with old friends, chat with work buddies, and strike up conversations with relevant people in my industry.

Somewhere between then and now, the definition has changed. The social network is no more. It's all about social media these days. Now, I don't want you to confuse the two, so let's make this very clear. Media is one-way broadcasting. Chris Evans talks into a microphone, Tess Daley speaks to a TV camera and they are seen and heard by millions.

Networks, on the other hand, can have infinite connections. They can be one-to-one, one-to-five, ten-to-1,000, anything – but it's communication that goes both ways.

You talk to me and I listen. I respond and you listen. For those new to the concept, this is called having a conversation. It doesn't involve clicking "like" buttons, posting "describe your business using only emojis" BS, or copying and pasting "thanks for posting" comments on a hundred posts a day.

Social media is about vanity metrics, filters, and fame. It's about throwing enough shit at the wall and hoping some of it will stick.

Social networking is about sanity metrics, relationships, and real-life connections. It's about building an Evergreen Asset of relationships with real people that will serve you (and them) for years to come. Sanity over vanity.

My children are aged nine and 11. Both have a YouTube Channel. As do all their friends. They all want to be "famous YouTubers" when they grow up. As the adults in this relationship, we know it's not possible for them *all* to be famous. Yet many sensible, grown-up business owners have also fallen into the same trap. We've been fed the line that we can all be successful social media broadcasters and we should be (nay, *need* to be) on all platforms, constantly churning out new content every day.

I have a YouTube Channel. I've just checked and I have 201 subscribers. I've no idea who they are. I don't even know where my logins are.

I'm on Facebook, but post on my own timeline approximately ten times a year and have installed a news feed blocker so I don't see anyone else's posts either. I have a number of Facebook groups, for my One Percent Club members and ALB podcast listeners, and I spend a few minutes in those groups every day having actual conversations with real people.

Of course, it's Facebook's football, so I don't rely on these groups as my only way of speaking to these people and that's much easier to do when you actually know their names and are on speaking terms with them.

Engagement is vanity. Relationships are sanity

They say that what gets measured gets managed. Therefore, measuring social media metrics makes sense, surely? Well, it depends on what you're measuring. As Albert Einstein said, you wouldn't measure a fish's intelligence by its ability to climb a tree.

Yet when it comes to social media, that's exactly what most people do. They're obsessed with "engagement" – arbitrary, meaningless likes and comments – usually from other "influencers" who are trying to trick the social media platform's algorithm into showing *their* content to more people, so that they can get more "engagement" on *their* posts. Piling shit on top of shit and then flinging it at the wall, day after day.

And then they herald their strategy as a great success: "It must be working, because I'm getting tons of "engagement!". Great, but you can't pay for bread and milk with engagement. I checked, and Tesco,

Sainsbury's, and Waitrose all still want cold hard cash in return for you taking their goods.

That means you need to convert "engagement" into customers. The best way to do that is to build relationships and you don't build relationships by using the latest hacks or tricks to get engagement: "Wow! Have you seen what happens when you double-click here?"

Yes, double-clicking on an image automatically "likes" your post, giving you a ton of "engagement" and taking your post "viral". But did the user really like your post? Did you actually offer them any value? Do they know anything about you, what you offer, and how you can help them? Have you done anything to nurture a relationship with another human being and help them solve their greatest problems?

No. You simply tricked them into doing something that makes your vanity metrics look good.

You've got 178 likes, 34 comments (including around a third of people getting angry because you've tricked them), zero deposits in the relationships bank, and no true fans.

Dale Carnegie's 1,000 true fans

So how can we turn social media networks into an Evergreen Asset? By ignoring the word "media" and instead building true networks with real people by having actual conversations with other humans – what social networks were intended for before marketers came along and ruined everything. Forget about social media, and focus on social networks instead.

Don't obsess over fans or followers. Build friendships instead. My entire social networking lead generation strategy could be written on the back of a napkin: connect with the right people, then talk to them. That's it!

Born into poverty on a farm in Missouri in 1888, Dale Carnegie found success as a young man selling bacon and soap. He was so successful at sales that his territory of South Omaha, Nebraska, was the company's best performing area by some margin.

Naturally, people wanted to know how he was getting better results than anyone else. So Carnegie started telling people the secret to his success. Those who listened also reaped the rewards. So Carnegie started telling even more people, creating a new career as a public speaker. Again, those who listened reaped the rewards and Carnegie knew he was onto something. He wanted to help even more people.

In 1936, he released the book *How to Win Friends and Influence People*. By the time of Carnegie's death in 1955, the book had been translated into 31 languages and sold more than five million copies worldwide. At the time of writing, it's now estimated more than 30million copies have been sold and it's constantly among the most recommended business books in the world of sales.

So what's the big secret to winning friends and influencing people? It's listening. It's building real connections and empathy with a fellow human. It's thinking about them as a person, not a vanity metric. It's talking *with* them (not *to* them) – about them.

I think of my own social networking policy as Dale Carnegie meets 1,000 true fans.

In his essay "1,000 true fans", Kevin Kelly firmly dispels the myth of vanity metrics and engagement bait. He says:

> *"To be a successful creator, you don't need millions. You don't need millions of dollars or millions of customers, millions of clients or millions of fans. To make a living as a craftsperson, photographer, musician, designer, author, animator, app maker, entrepreneur, or inventor you need only thousands of true fans.*

> *A true fan is defined as a fan that will buy anything you produce. These diehard fans will drive 200 miles to see you sing; they will buy the hardback and paperback and audible versions of your book; they will purchase your next figurine sight unseen; they will pay for the 'best-of' DVD version of your free YouTube channel; they will come to your chef's table once a month. If you have roughly a thousand true fans like this (also known as super fans), you can make a living – if you are content to make a living but not a fortune."*

Stop trying to get 10,000 followers, 100,000 views or a million vanity likes. Focus instead on working towards 1,000 true fans.

Imagine you had a social network with 1,000 connections and I mean *real* connections, true fans. You know what makes them tick, their likes and dislikes, what's going on with their family, what's keeping them awake at night, and their hopes and dreams.

If you had that network of 1,000 true fans, do you think you'd ever be short of leads?

Of course not.

But how do you get 1,000 true fans? One at a time. Embrace your inner Dale Carnegie and start making friends and maybe worry less about "influencing people" – there's enough "influencers" out there already.

An Evergreen Social Network Lead is a true, real connection with another human. A true fan Carnegie himself would be proud of.

I see we have some mutual connections...

Every time I log into LinkedIn, I find my inbox full of messages and connection requests. I used to think: "Great, these people must have read my books and want to chat with me further about the ideas in them."

How naive could I be? Nope, they wanted to sell me something.

> *"Hi John, great to connect! Are you looking for a new mortgage?"*
>
> *"Hey John, thanks for connecting. Could you do with more leads in your business?"*
>
> *"Good afternoon, John. Would you like to be number 1 on Google?"*

Over the last year, I've spent more time on LinkedIn, building up my 1,000 true relationships. My "connect and pitch" radar is now finely tuned.

Every time I receive a connection request accompanied by phrases such as "looking to grow my network", "I see we have some mutual connections", and "thought we should connect", a massive red flashing warning light appears in my mind.

Because you know as well as I do that Mr Looking-to-expand-his-network is actually Mr Looking-to-cold-pitch-you-the-minute-you-accept-his-request.

"Looking to connect with like-minded individuals" = connect and pitch.

"See we have some mutual friends and thought it would be good to connect" = connect and pitch.

"Are you looking to save money on your gas and electricity?" = wow, you're not even waiting to *connect* before pitching.

When I receive a connection request from someone I don't know, I ask myself: Will this person's content improve my newsfeed and brighten my day or make me want to punch their face in because they're going to try and pitch to me the minute I accept?

Take a look at your profile right now. Do you look like the sort of person I'd *want* to see on my newsfeed? Do you look like the sort of person I'd *want* to speak to at a party or that I'd actually want to spend some time getting to know?

Does your profile scream, "Oh, they look interesting!" or does it make you look like the sort of person you'd dive behind the sofa to hide from if you saw them walking up your garden path?

We'll look at how to nurture those relationships in the Nurture Assets section coming up, but for now the aim is to grow a network of people you would want to nurture a relationship with.

TL/DR:

Build social networks rather than broadcast on social media.

You can't pay for bread and milk with online engagement. Embrace your inner Dale Carnegie, and build 1,000 true relationships.

Oh, and please don't connect and pitch.

LEAD ASSETS: SUMMARY

Every business's "ONE thing" should be to bring in leads.

Be sure to use The Right Bait (such as a £125,000 fridge magnet). My email list is my greatest Evergreen Asset. It's mine. I own it. I control it.

If your business is not on the internet, then your business will be out of business. Stop vomiting your brochure all over your website. Share your "big idea", combined with The Right Bait using squeeze pages and hug pages. Give Google what it wants and Google will give you what you want (millions of pounds worth of free SEO traffic).

Google Ads are a shortcut to SEO but it's pay to play. Figure out which half of your ad spend is wasted and spend it on what's working instead. Facebook (or other social media) ads are an interrupting cow. Laser-target the right people with something that's sexier than a squirrel.

You can't pay for bread and milk with engagement. So stop broadcasting on social media, and start building 1,000 true relationships with your network instead.

You might be the world's best at what you do, but without leads coming into your Evergreen Assets ecosystem, the world will never know.

4. NURTURE ASSETS

"I just want to help people. I know I can offer amazing value to my members, but no one's buying. I just can't seem to convince anyone to actually give me a go."

This was a conversation I had with a sports coach recently and it's a scenario that plays out time and time again in a lot of small businesses and especially so for coaches. You've spent years developing your techniques and honing your craft. You're *really* good at what you do. If only people would give you a chance and just try it out then they'd see.

You know you can help them. But still, no one's biting.

Why? Because they don't yet know, like and trust you.

In 1958, advertising agency McGraw-Hill created an ad featuring a grumpy-looking executive, sat facing the camera with his arms folded, accompanied by the following text:

I don't know who you are.

I don't know your company.

I don't know your company's product.

I don't know what your company stands for.

I don't know your company's customers.

I don't know your company's record.

I don't know your company's reputation.

Now – what was it you wanted to sell me?

More than 40 years later, it was voted the best b2b advert of the 20th century – and its message is as valid today as it was in 1958.

If people don't know who you are...

If they don't know your company...

If they don't know your products...

If they don't know what you stand for...

If they don't know who your current/ideal customers are...

If they don't know your track record or history...

If they don't know how good you are...

Then how the hell are you going to sell *anything* to them?

Before people buy anything, they have to know, like and trust you. All three and in that order.

You wouldn't buy something from someone you don't trust. You don't trust someone you don't like. And it's impossible to like someone you don't know.

Know > Like > Trust.

The "connect-and-pitch" brigade don't bother with this asset class at all. Any success they get is purely down to the numbers game – throwing enough shit at the wall that some of it must stick.

Evergreen Assets isn't a numbers game. It's a relationships game.

Building Nurture Assets is how you win that game.

Joe Bloody Wicks MBE

Let's compare two personal trainers. One you've probably heard of – Joe Wicks – and one you definitely haven't (because he's fictional), Joe Nobody.

Both Joes started their journey as personal trainers. Both have a similar product offering (an exercise and diet plan.) But one has a multi-million-pound business and one can't make rent. What's the difference?

As Joe Nobody would say to anyone who'll listen: "What's Joe bloody Wicks got that I haven't?" Well, Mr Nobody, what Joe Wicks has got that you haven't is an awful lot of people who know, like and trust him.

People know Joe Wicks. They like Joe Wicks. They trust Joe Wicks.

Why do they know, like and trust him? Because he's spent years building an ecosystem of Evergreen Assets, starting with nurturing true fan relationships with existing clients, creating valuable content for his social network, writing blog posts and books, doing personal appearances at schools and workplaces, leveraging PR opportunities, doing joint ventures with the likes of Jamie Oliver and Sir Mo Farah, creating YouTube videos, appearing on podcasts, email coaching content, and developing his own app.

During the Covid-19 national lockdown in 2020, Joe created a free daily live workout video every weekday for nearly four months (even after breaking his hand a few days in) which were viewed more than 70million times, broke the world record for the largest streamed workout on YouTube, and raised more than half a million pounds for NHS Charities Together.

None of which involved any selling whatsoever. The only benefit to Joe Wicks was that more people would know him, more people would like him, and more people would trust him.

Which probably explains how during 2020 "Joe bloody Wicks" picked up an extra million YouTube subscribers, sold a couple of hundred thousand books, landed thousands of new paid clients, a brand new £1million book deal, and even bagged himself an MBE.

Not bad for a year's work, focusing almost entirely on Nurture Assets.

Meanwhile, what did Joe Nobody do during this same period? Well, he moaned about "Joe bloody Wicks" getting all the attention, complained that no one was buying his stuff, and lamented that if only they'd give him a shot, he knows he could help them. He doesn't see the point in building Nurture Assets, insisting: "I'm better off spending my time speaking to actual paying customers rather than freebie hunters and tyre-kickers."

So, where *are* those paying customers? They're handing their money over to someone they know, like and trust.

Now you may be reading this and thinking: "Aha! I've found a flaw in your argument John. You see, I don't like Joe Wicks!" For every person who loves Joe Wicks, there's more than likely an equal (or maybe even greater) number who turn the TV over, switch the radio off, refuse to buy his books, or even hate him with a passion.

But Nurture Assets are not about getting *everyone* to know, like and trust you. They're about getting your true fans to know, like and trust you. If you ask ten people to agree on an ice cream flavour, you're going to end up with vanilla.

Don't be vanilla. Joe Wicks certainly isn't vanilla. He's probably some kind of weird Heston Blumenthal-style broccoli and Lycra flavoured sorbet.

Choose your flavour wisely. Leave bland, boring vanilla to the middle-of-the-road masses. Instead, be yourself – be locally made raspberry ripple gelato (with real raspberries), served in an M&Ms crusted waffle cone, topped with the finest Devon clotted cream. Not everyone's going to like it, but your true fans are going to *love* it.

ONE NURTURE ASSET TO RULE THEM ALL: WEEKLY EMAILS

Remember what happened when I first started sending emails? I put The Right Bait (a free fridge magnet) in front of the right people (those searching the internet for freebies) and started building my list. But I didn't just build a list and let it gather dust. I emailed that list every week. On the same day, at the same time, every week. Thursday morning at 11am. Without fail.

When I was earning enough money from my weekly emails that I could drop a couple of days at the day job from hell, one of the days I dropped to focus entirely on my business was a Thursday. Because Thursdays were "Net Free Stuff Newsletter" day.

Sometimes I sold things in my weekly email. More often than not, I didn't. My main aim each week was to highlight the cool new stuff that I'd added to the website in the previous seven days and showcase some of the most popular items that my members were interested in, even if those items didn't earn me a penny.

My weekly email served one purpose – to give as much value as possible to every reader.

Fast forward 20-plus years and that one tactic of sending weekly emails that don't necessarily sell anything but give the most value possible and build the best relationships possible remains the foundation of every business that I'm involved in.

I send a new "big idea" – a sort of a "mini-chapter" from me – every Wednesday lunchtime. If you'd like to receive it, I'll include it in the resources at the end of the book. You'll get one every week, forever. It's a Never-Ending Nurture Sequence. As long as you continue to get value from it, I'll keep writing one every week. And, true to the ethos of the weekly email, you'll notice I hardly ever try to sell you anything.

I want my weekly emails to demonstrate my expertise and experience. To nurture a relationship with you, my reader (that's "reader" singular, not "readers" plural because my weekly emails are designed to communicate *with* you, not broadcast *to* you).

I do the same for my sports betting business, regularly sending valuable "how-to" content that doesn't sell anything. Giving value, demonstrating expertise, and nurturing relationships, one person at a time.

Although I keep using the term weekly emails, when it comes to using this Nurture Asset for you and your business, it doesn't have to be email and it doesn't have to be weekly.

However, it does need to be regular and it does need to be a two-way communication rather than a one-way broadcast. For most business owners, the easiest way to do that is via a weekly email.

I won't go into the specifics of how to craft the perfect weekly email (my book *Routine Machine* has a chapter dedicated to this, including case studies, examples, and some tactics you can use to come up with ideas for content).

But what I will say is that despite writing that chapter on weekly emails, telling every podcast host and book club that sending weekly emails is the one routine that every business owner could do to impact their business most positively, and nagging my own One Percent Club coaching clients on a regular basis, most people I speak to still don't send weekly emails. So please, I implore you. This really is the one Nurture Asset to rule them all.

NURTURE ASSETS: EMAIL

It's not big, but it is clever

A common mistake many business owners make with email is focusing on building a big list. They start earning a little money from the first 100 people, get their calculator out, and start dreaming about what they'd be earning if only they had 10,000 or 100,000 people on their list.

You can do that, of course. But it's like trying to fill a leaking bucket just by adding more water.

A better way to do it would be to try to fix the holes in your bucket. Don't try to build a big list. Instead, focus on building an *engaged* list. Just like Facebook or Google have an algorithm to decide which content makes it to your newsfeed or which one of the 50 gazillion web pages to show first, email providers also use data to decide if your email will get through.

Their algorithms instantly decide whether you're a friend sending a cake recipe or a Nigerian prince asking for help smuggling $200million out of the country.

If you're anything like me, when you get home from a fortnight's holiday and sort through your post, you'll create three piles for all the mail that's arrived while you've been off sunning yourself – one for all the junk that's headed straight for the bin, one for boring bank statements and brown envelopes, and one for the exciting-looking stuff (which gets opened first).

Every time you email your list, your subscribers' email providers do the same. They put you into one of three "piles" – spammer, semi-spammer, or friend. If they label you a spammer, your emails will go straight into the online equivalent of the shredder – the junk folder – never to be seen, let alone read. Earn a semi-spammer tag and they might let some of your emails through, depending on how spammy each one is.

If they're absolutely sure you're a friend, you'll be ushered straight through to the inbox every time as long as you don't start acting like a spammer in future. The key to avoiding being labelled a spammer is to avoid doing spammy things!

People who fixate on building huge email lists do spammy things. They scrape emails from LinkedIn, adding people without their permission. They buy cold lists from brokers. They refuse to let people unsubscribe. And they would never, *never* dream of removing a subscriber willingly, just because their emails weren't getting opened, let alone read.

If you're doing stuff like this, you'd just as well have a big warning sign on every email you send that reads: "I am a spammer. I want to spam this person."

Email providers decide your deliverability based on how their users treat your emails. Do they open them? Do they open them multiple times? When they do open them, do they read everything? Do they scroll down? Do they click on any of the links? Do they reply to your emails or forward them to friends?

Email is not a numbers game, it's a relationships game. Have conversations with your readers rather than "blast your list". Ask questions. Give real value in every email and treat your subscribers with the same respect you would if you were emailing your grandmother.

The only people who should be on your list are those who want to hear from you. If people stop opening your emails (and that will happen), remove them from the list long before they finally get around to unsubscribing. I use an automated tool to purge my list every month (I'll include a link to it in the resources), which not only keeps my list costs down, but also keeps my open rates, engagement rates, and crucially my deliverability rates at some of the highest they've ever been.

I may have a smaller list, but as they say: "It's not how big it is, but what you do with it that matters."

Can I ask a rude question?

You need to find out what your subscribers want. The best way to do that is to ask them a rather direct question:

> "What part of x do you struggle with the most?"
>
> "What's your greatest challenge with x?"
>
> "What tips can I give you about x?"
>
> "What do you find hardest about x?"
>
> "Do you struggle with x, y, or z the most?"

Or to paraphrase all of these questions: "What do you want? What's keeping you awake at night? What problem are you hoping I can solve for you? What brought you here? What the hell do you want?"

You can't come out and say it quite like that, of course, because that's rude, so let's soften the blow somewhat.

If you sign up for my weekly emails, one of the very first ones you'll receive has the headline, "What made you think THIS was a good idea?" in which I talk about my own hopes and dreams for my business, how I arrived at my ideal job description (to do *what* I want, *when* I want, *how* I want, *where* I want, *if* I want), and then ask the direct question: "What lifestyle do *you* want?"

I end the email with a P.S: "Hit reply and let me know – what's *your* ideal job description?"

Now, that's a direct request to email me back and most people do. This ticks a number of boxes. Readers have opened, read, scrolled, and replied to my email. That's a big tick to show the email providers that I'm a friend, not a spammer.

I also find out critical information about my newest friends in discovering *what they want*. Most importantly, we've kicked off some personal communication. We can now chat person-to-person, outside of automated algorithms.

We can now truly get to know, like and trust each other.

This week, I 'ave been mostly...

What the hell are we going to write about? The examples I gave in *Routine Machine* included a human resources company having a weekly rant about bad HR practice, a marine engineering business sending "engineer porn" about the boats and engines they'd had in the workshop that week, and a web design agency writing about the worst websites they'd seen in the last seven days.

In '90s TV sketch show The Fast Show, a dishevelled character called Jesse would emerge from his tool shed and announce to the viewers, in a strong West Country accent, his latest diet, fashion choices or experiments, starting with the phrase: "This week, I 'ave been mostly..."

> *"This week, I 'ave been mostly eatin'... bourbon biscuits."*
>
> *"This week, I 'ave been mostly wearin' Dolce & Gabbana."*
>
> *"This week, I 'ave been mostly having a coil fitted."*

If you find yourself staring at a blinking cursor, simply embrace your inner Jesse and fill in the blank on the following sentence:

"This week, I 'ave been mostly... ______________"

I use this technique every week on my social networking posts to identify something that resonates with my audience:

> *This week, I have been mostly... vomiting 13,118 words all over a Google Doc.*

This week, I have been mostly... planning my work and working my plan.

This week I have been mostly... muting myself on Zoom until the dog stops barking at EVERY SINGLE PERSON WALKING PAST THE HOUSE!!!

What have you mostly been doing this week? Tell me more about that. How does that apply to me? Expand on that single line and you've got the basis of a great weekly email.

This week, I have been mostly telling people it's not as simple as calories in vs calories out.

This week, I have been mostly redesigning some frankly horrific looking websites.

This week, I have been mostly feeling chuffed to bits with the results my amazing clients are getting.

Sell by not selling

And what are we going to promote each week? Nothing. We're not going to sell *anything.*

Mic drop!

The real power of the weekly email is that it builds the relationship one week and one email at a time. The more weekly touchpoints you have *without* selling, the more that relationship will blossom and people will want to buy from you. Yells of "Shut up and take my money" will be ringing in your ears.

You will make more sales by not selling because there will be a "subtle sell" in every email. You'll add a P.S. signature that goes on the very bottom of every email, telling readers exactly how they can do business with you:

P.S. Here are three ways I can help you achieve your desired result(s):

1. Book a 1-2-1 call with me.
2. Join my next training course.
3. Become a member of my monthly membership club.

The main body of the email is used to make friends with people, build relationships, and demonstrate your knowledge and expertise. The selling is left to the "soft sell" in the P.S.

By appearing in your prospects' inboxes every seven days, you'll be top of mind, and therefore tip of tongue when they are reminded of the problems that you can help them fix.

It's your job to remind customers you exist, not their job to remember. When my local Italian restaurant sends me an email, I book a table. Without that email, the restaurant wouldn't have my money in their till and I wouldn't have their tiramisu in my belly.

They don't even need to sell anything in that email – just a sneak peek of the new summer menu or some information on how to make carpaccio at home is enough to remind me to book a table for my birthday next month, my wedding anniversary or a Friday cheat day.

Have I got your attention?

The email is written, you've got your topic of the week and soft sell P.S. but now you need a catchy subject line to lure them in.

There's nothing wrong with a bit of clickbait here. After all, a good curiosity-led headline is the right bait to get your emails opened.

A good headline is:

1. Intriguing.
2. Compelling.

3. Creative.
4. Relevant to your target market.

You don't have to tick off all four but the more boxes you tick, the higher your open rate will be.

You don't want a subject line that's a descriptive label, informing the recipient what's inside. That means that "Brand Name Newsletter" is out of the question, as is "Weekly Email #34".

Don't obsess over the perfect subject line, though. In my experience, the subject line is the second-greatest factor in getting your email opened. Far more important is what's in the "From" field – in other words, your name.

Optimising the "From" field takes a lot of work, a lot of time, and you can do untold amounts of damage, undoing all your hard work with just one email. You see, the "From" field isn't based on the words contained within your name. It's based entirely on the reader's relationship with you.

It's not a numbers game, it's a relationships game.

Think back to the last time you opened your email inbox and were greeted with a large number of new messages. Like most people, you probably filtered them in some way before working through them one at a time. My filtering process looks something like this:

1. Scan the "From" fields to find those emails I'm not going to read. Select. Delete all.
2. Scan the "From" fields again, this time looking for those senders whose emails I enjoy reading or whose message I've been expecting. I open these emails first.
3. From the remaining emails, I now scan the subject lines to see what looks intriguing, compelling, creative, and/or relevant to me.

What reaction do readers have when they see your name in their inbox? Do they immediately delete it, immediately open it, or decide whether to open it based on your subject line?

The answers to these questions lie in the relationship readers have with you and the quality of your email content. If you've got stunning, compelling subject lines but don't deliver on your promises, you're going to hurt the relationship. If you're constantly selling, you're going to hurt the relationship. If you treat email as a one-way broadcast medium, guess what? You're going to hurt the relationship. And that relationship is far more important than any subject line you could use.

Nurture on autopilot

Not everyone will reply to your "what do you want?" email. Even for those that do, you shouldn't make the mistake of thinking they're all warmed up after an email or two. A little chit-chat, and it's time to close the deal? Nope. We're going to spend more time wining and dining them first. A lot more time, asking questions, telling stories (and our best jokes), demonstrating that we're worthy of a second date before we ask for their hand in marriage.

The way we do this is with an automated nurture sequence. That's a nurture sequence, not a sales sequence. Stop trying to sell in every email. Instead, demonstrate expertise, build rapport, and showcase your personality. Find out what they want, and, once you know that, demonstrate you're the best person to give them what they want.

Send them the content *they* want to see. Use the language *they* use. Start conversations, and then use what you learn in those conversations to create your evergreen content.

"OMG, it's like they're talking to me!"

You're damn right we are. And we're going to keep on talking (without selling) every single week. This is a Never-Ending Nurture Sequence.

Give 'em what they want!

Once we've found out what they want and given them what they want, what's next? Make damn sure they've *got what they want*. Encourage them to "hit reply and let me know what you think". Ask the reader a specific question. When they reply, keep the conversation going, and find out what they like or don't like about your emails so far.

TL/DR:

Remember, I don't know who you are, what you stand for or how you can help me.

It's not how big your list is that matters, it's what you do with it. Create a Never-Ending Nurture Sequence and don't be afraid to ask direct questions to *find out what they want*, and to start two-way conversations. Then, send weekly emails that *sell without selling.*

Oh, and don't be a spammer. Just tell them what you 'ave been doing this week.

NURTURE ASSETS: WEBSITES

Do your own research

If there's one thing I've learned from home-schooling my children over the last few years, it's that you can ask the internet anything and get the answer in seconds:

> *"OK Google, when was the battle of Hastings?"*
>
> *"Alexa, why is the sky blue?"*
>
> *"Hey Siri, why do men have nipples?"*

Your prospects can do the same. In the past, if you wanted to buy a fridge freezer then you'd talk to a salesperson at a local electrical retailer, letting them know your budget, what size you need, and trusting them to recommend the best one.

You had to put all your trust in someone who (as you'll remember from that grumpy executive ad) you don't know anything about. You don't know them, their motives, whether they truly have your best interests at heart or whether they need to sell three more "lemons" this week in order to hit their sales target.

Today, you can simply ask Google: "What's the best A-rated, 200cm, free-standing fridge freezer with automatic defrost?" Big G will then show you the internet's best answer to that question and take you to a website where you could buy said appliance.

If you're still doing research and aren't quite ready to whip your credit card out, you can find reviews that allow you to easily compare dozens of different models. You'll discover whether you get what you pay for or if the cheaper model may also be the best. You can also find out common problems previous owners have reported and consider whether they are an issue for you.

Once you've concluded your "which fridge freezer is best?" research, you can now enter the final stage of your fact-finding mission – where to buy it for the least amount of money? You may head back to Google and search for the exact model number of your chosen appliance, adding terms like: "price comparison", "cheapest" or "prices".

This is why traditional, salesperson-led retailers have all but disappeared from the high street. But what's bad news for high street stores is good news for anyone with a website. Armed with the knowledge that most people do their own research before making a buying decision, it's crucial to ensure your website is a key part of that research.

My eyes! My eyes!

What's the first line of that McGraw-Hill ad with the grumpy exec?

> *"I don't know who you are."*

So if your website is to take visitors on a journey through the enchanted lands of Know, Like, and Trust, it needs to first tell them who you are.

Not in an "our company was founded in 1985 and we deliver outstanding customer service and great prices" way, where somebody could sneakily swap your company logo with that of your competitor and it would still make just as much sense.

I mean literally tell people who *you* are. What makes you, you. The person behind the business. Put your face front and centre. They have to know you, before they stand a chance of liking or trusting you!

Ling Valentine has taken the idea of putting your face on your website to another level. Her website *lingscars.com* is, well, ugly. Very ugly. In fact, I'd go as far as to say it's downright horrible. Psychedelic patterned backgrounds that wouldn't look out of place on 1970s wallpaper, animated gifs, strobing effects, 17 different colour schemes, eight different fonts, and a million things all flashing and shouting at you.

But once your eyes have recovered from the shock and awe treatment, two things appear on the page more than anything else. Ling's name and Ling's photo. The website screams at you:

> *"Hello! I am Ling! I'm the UK's hardest working car leasing provider, and I run LINGsCARS, the UK's favourite car leasing website.*
>
> *Don't be deceived... I may be a scruffy Chinese girl, but I have more happy new-car customers and supply more new cars*

than many of the anonymous (and some big-name!) leasing companies out there, combined."

I counted no fewer than 22 photos of Ling on her homepage alone and not a single one of them a professional headshot. Instead, you'll see her standing in front of a rocket launcher, mocked up as Kate Winslet from Titanic, in cartoon form as Superman, and immortalised by Viz magazine.

I stopped counting the number of times she uses her name after about 120. Spend 0.3 seconds on Ling's website and you'll know who she is and what she does. She tells you that she's scruffy, but hard working. She tells you that she's currently chatting to 191 clients on live chat, and responds in an average of eight minutes and 17 seconds.

She says that she treats customers like adults, not idiots. She tells you that she's from Chengdu in the People's Republic, and married a Yorkshireman (who talks rubbish) in Finland, taking over his business: "He was very successful, so I learnt the business and took over the reins. I must say I'm better at it than him!"

She compares her business to Ryanair, saying bluntly: "My cars are the UK's cheapest and my service is simply the best." She caps this off in her trademark low-key style with a cartoon Ryanair-style airplane with "LINGsCARS.com" emblazoned on it.

The more you read, the harder it is not to like Ling. She displays a great sense of humour, poking fun at her husband, her competitors, famous people and, more than anything, at herself.

Good luck swapping her logo (complete with animated traffic lights that change colour and a Rolling Stones inspired Union Jack-covered tongue that gently rocks from side to side) with A.N.Other Car Leasing Limited. There's no way you could possibly confuse Ling with anyone else!

Enough about me, what do you think about me?

Business owners know their way intuitively around every last corner of their website. As a result, they can't imagine what it's like to stumble across the site for the first time and not know where anything is or what they're supposed to do next.

Your business exists to solve problems for your customers. So why does your website say "we do x", "we're the leading manufacturer of y" or "we've been selling z since..."?

Your website is not about you. It's about how you can help the person that's just landed on your site who is hoping and praying you're the one to finally fix their most pressing problem.

When writing copy for your website, do so as if you were having a conversation with that person in front of you, face to face. Ask if they're experiencing those problems. List some of the most common issues they may be having and how they might be affecting their lives.

Discuss how much better their lives would be if they could get the results they're looking for and then (only then) demonstrate that you know a thing or two about getting those results.

First, show that you *know what they want*. Then, demonstrate that you're the most capable person to *give them what they want*.

Every time someone interacts with a web page, they have a conversation in their head with the site:

> *"Am I on the right website?"*
>
> *"Where's the thing I'm looking for?"*
>
> *"Am I on the right page?"*
>
> *"Hmm, I'm not sure I believe that."*
>
> *"How do I find out whether this will work for me?"*

"Where are the prices?"

"What should I do now?"

Ensure your website copy refers to "you" and "your" (the prospect) far more than "we" and "our" (the business). When your copy is centred on the reader rather than the writer, your website joins in the conversation:

Website: "Do you suffer with ______________?"

Website Visitor: "Yes, I do. Good, it seems like I'm in the right place."

Website: "Does ___________ affect your ability to ______________?"

"Website Visitor: "Yes, yes it does."

Website: "Does that make you feel __________________?"

Website Visitor: "It most certainly does. What the hell can you do about it though?"

Website: "Would you be interested in hearing how we've fixed this problem for hundreds of people like you?"

Website Visitor: "People like me? If they really are like me, then that would be amazing. What should I do next?"

Website: "Click here to see our case studies."

*Website Visitor: *click*.*

Now, I'll let you in on a little trade secret here that can supercharge these virtual conversations and massively increase your conversions. It involves leveraging another part of the Evergreen Assets ecosystem.

Remember the rude question from the email section where we found out what they want by directly asking what they struggled with, what their greatest challenge was, what help they wanted, and what they found hardest? When they replied to that email, we kept the conversation going – "tell me more about that?", "does that stop you from ________?" and "how does that make you feel?"

By recording these answers in a spreadsheet, you'll start to notice patterns. You'll see what people's greatest challenges are, how that affects them, what they've tried in the past, and how that makes them feel.

Pay close attention to the language they use and then mirror those exact words and phrases in your Nurture Assets, including on your website.

If you're a personal trainer whose prospects and customers are 40-year-old mums and dads telling you they want to "not be embarrassed at the beach", "be able to keep up with the kids", and "fit back into that dress I love", then why the hell would you fill your website with stock photos of 20-year-olds sporting six-pack abs, bulging biceps, and copy about "shredding body fat" and "getting into the shape of your life"?

Ideally, at some point during the conversation, your website visitors should be saying to themselves: "I don't believe it, it's like they're talking to *me*!" You should know your prospects so well that you could (and should) build a website for them, about them, telling them how you can solve their problems and what that means for them. In their words.

It's all about them. Find out what they want, tell them you know what they want, and demonstrate you're the person to give them what they want.

Yeah, so?

Marketing 101 dictates you should list benefits, not features. You're itching to tell prospects about all the cool stuff they'll get when they become a customer. But that doesn't help them work out what the cool stuff means for them – what difference it will make to their lives, and how much happier, wealthier, and wiser they'll be.

Again, let's imagine the two-way conversation between your website and the visitor:

Website: "You'll get this cool feature."

Website Visitor: "Yeah? So what?"

Website: "Erm, well, that means that you'll be able to _____________."

Website Visitor: "Right… so?"

Website: "So, that will free you up to _____________, give you an extra ______________ and make you feel _____________."

Website Visitor: "Ah, I see. What else do I get?"

The important words here are those spoken by the website visitor. If he or she is asking, "So what?" then you've either listed a benefit they don't care about or a feature.

If you're struggling to turn features into benefits, try adding "which means that" explainers to the copy:

"You'll get this cool feature."

"You'll get this cool feature, which means that…"

"You'll get this cool feature, which means that you'll be free to __________, you'll have an extra ___________ and you'll feel ___________."

And what goes in the blanks? The benefits that your prospects already told you, in their words, from the rude question. Like a mirror, you're reflecting back at them. I know what you want, and this is the product or service to deliver it.

Hey, that guy looks like me...

People buy from people like them. If you can demonstrate you've got the results your website visitors are looking for, and that you've delivered those results to other people (especially other people like them), then they're more likely to buy from you.

We like people like us. We listen to people like us. We trust people like us. We do business with people like us.

If you visit my website (www.bigidea.co.uk), the first thing you'll notice is a massive picture of me, smiling at you, together with my business partner Jason. The second thing you'll notice is a short video of me talking directly to you, sharing my "big idea", as well as telling you who I am and what I stand for. It's interspersed with "b-roll" footage of my backstory, some of the clients I work with, and the results I've been able to achieve for myself and others.

Within two minutes and 18 seconds, you know who I am. You know who Jason is. You know our company. You know our products. You know what we stand for. You know our customers. You know our record and you know our reputation. We're well on our way to building a lifelong friendship and it doesn't stop there.

The "John and Jason brand" is all about having fun and not taking ourselves too seriously. So you'll see me climbing through a massive hula hoop, Jason with his hands around my throat, me being punched in the face by a boxing glove, and Jason and I having a rather *heated* discussion.

There are photos of Jase and me with Santa hats on, my infamous "fat John" picture (when I weighed 70lbs more than I do today), and a great moment where the photographer caught Jason and me collapsing in fits of laughter while he was trying to take serious, professional headshots.

I've also used pictures of me with my family, talking on stage, and delivering coaching to One Percenters. There are snaps of me sitting in the BBC radio studio, standing next to Chewbacca from Star Wars, and pulling what can only be described as a gurning face. What you won't find are any boring, cookie-cutter stock images.

I use photos to demonstrate that I'm just like you. I'm a normal bloke from Plymouth. I've got kids and want to design my business around a lifestyle that serves me, which means family holidays and plenty of free time. I demonstrate my knowledge and expertise by showing you that I'm a regular guest on the BBC, I've written several books, and coach lots of people just like you.

There's barely a page on my site that doesn't contain a testimonial or case study featuring real people like you talking about how much they enjoyed reading *Routine Machine*, how the One Percent Club has helped them achieve the lifestyle they truly want, and how much fun they've had working with Jason and me.

Client testimonials and case studies should be a core element of your website's content. You should curate real-life testimony for every page on your site. Having a "testimonials" page is better than nothing, but if you've done the hard part of asking for a testimonial, why on earth would you then bury that prime piece of content on a "testimonials" page or add it as an afterthought to the bottom of a page?

Testimonials have maximum impact when they're most relevant. Within content about my books, I'll sprinkle a few book reviews. On my podcast page, I'll list some of the five-star reviews from existing listeners. And on my sales page for the One Percent Club, I'll hand over a large proportion of the available real estate with a "Meet the One Percenters" section where I present case studies from my existing clients for them to tell you (in their words) how it's helped them.

I include their full name, company name, and a photo of them. And if you were still left in any doubt that they were a real person, I've also included a link to a 45+ minute podcast interview with them, where you can hear them chat about their experience.

When you present an abundance of evidence in this way, objections, doubt, and uncertainty melt away. You demonstrate to those potential new clients that the risk that "this won't work out" is tiny because it's clearly working well for other people. And even more so if it's clearly working well for other people *like me*. People like me buy things like this.

Never trust anyone who says trust me?

You could say that Ling Valentine won't be winning any awards for her website. Well, you'd be wrong, because she has won an award – "the world's worst website", an award which she proudly displays on her homepage.

Ling's website doesn't exist to look pretty and win design awards. It's there to win customers. And it's doing a fantastic job of that with Ling leasing more than £85million of cars per year, mostly through her "awful" website.

Prospects want to know who they can trust. Ling tells them in her trademark, subtle-as-a-brick style with an animated image of her face and the words, "I AM LING YOU CAN TRUST ME" – all caps, no punctuation, and in an almost tasteful pink and white font, on a blue background, just above the yellow, pink, and green menu.

In 2011, I bought a live streaming football business. The website was awful. Unlike Ling's, mine was just ugly, and didn't convert very well. It didn't convert because I gave people no reason whatsoever to know, like or trust me. If you landed on that site and handed over your credit card details, you were a braver person than most.

The first thing I did was tidy up the design. I got a new professional logo and installed a WordPress theme so the site looked half decent, as opposed to something the cat killed, threw up and then dragged in.

Then I added a photo to the homepage of me wearing my Plymouth Argyle football shirt. I explained how I was a real fan just like you. And I told the story of how my love of football led to me buying the business (hat tip to Victor Kiam of Remington razors for the original "I liked the product so much that I bought the company" angle). But it wasn't really about me. It was about what I could do for my clients.

I submitted the service for awards and listed where we had been nominated, shortlisted, and (occasionally) won. I went on a PR blitz, sending press releases to many newspapers, magazines, bloggers, and websites. Then, I added an "as seen on" logo for every piece published.

I signed up with services like Buy With Confidence to demonstrate that Trading Standards knew about us for the right reasons. I showcased the large companies we worked with to demonstrate that the big boys trusted us. And I flooded the website with testimonials from real users – real football fans *just like you*, who had a great experience.

The results were astounding. The conversion rate increased seven-fold, from 0.3 per cent to 2.2 per cent, which opened up new Evergreen Assets like Google Ads as viable marketing platforms, compounding my gains even further. When I bought the business in 2011, it was earning £500 a month. Over the next three years, it earned a total of £500,000 before legislation around live streaming changed and we shut the service down.

From £500 to £500,000 and the only difference was making sure people knew, liked, and trusted us. In many ways, trust is the hardest of the three hurdles to overcome. But if you can do so, the rewards can be well worth the effort.

TL/DR:

Your website is not about you. It's about the problems you can solve for people like us.

Put your face all over it and your clients' faces too. Provide an abundance of evidence that you can be trusted and clearly demonstrate that *people like us, buy things like this.*

Oh, and the world's worst website is still better than yours.

NURTURE ASSETS: AWARDS

I hate awards. I've tried hard to win an award many times. I wrote letters and sent pictures to BBC Television Centre at least a dozen times, yet never got a Blue Peter badge. Even when I play Monopoly, second place in a beauty contest is my best hope.

I once entered a "best use of technology" industry award, putting together a formidable entry, demonstrating how we'd bootstrapped a software platform, solving a problem that had blighted the industry for more than a decade and done so with zero VC money. We lost to a VC-backed newbie who hadn't launched their product (but had sponsored another award).

I entered again the following year; this time losing out to the company that sponsored the free bar. One of the judges approached me after the ceremony, shrugged his shoulders and blew through his teeth. That told me all I needed to know about their criteria for picking the "best".

I once came second with a pitch so good that the awards organiser dedicated a 25-minute case study on it to the audience. It wasn't good enough to *win* the award, of course. I was destined to be forever the bridesmaid.

Or was I? One day, I was approached by an industry magazine, letting me know that my mobile phone insurance business had been shortlisted in the "best insurance provider" category in their upcoming annual awards. They wanted to know if I would be interested in taking out some ads in the mag to help sway voters.

"That's nice. No thanks," I said.

A few weeks later, they got in touch again, letting me know that I'd made the top five and asking if I would be interested in sponsoring an award.

"That's great news. No thanks," I said.

A month before the gala event, they reached out again to ask how many tables I'd like to buy.

"None, thanks," I said.

"Erm, well, this is awkward." They replied. "You see, you've kind of, well, you've won."

"Oh, that's amazing news! Here's my address to send the award."

So you see, I *have* won an award. One I never entered, did not sponsor, and didn't even turn up to collect the trophy. What I did do, though, was add the "Best Mobile Phone Insurance Provider 2016" image on our website – and increased conversions by 17 per cent as a result.

You see, it doesn't matter if you're bitter, like me, and believe awards are given to the popular kids, the biggest advertisers or the ones paying for the free bar. What matters is that "award-winning" is a shortcut to trust. If you can win an award, you should.

NURTURE ASSETS: ENDORSEMENTS

Ahead of Portugal's Euro 2020 match against Hungary, captain and football icon Cristiano Ronaldo took his seat for the press conference and smiled at the assembled journalists.

The smile vanished, though, when Ronaldo spotted two bottles of Coca-Cola placed in front of him on the table. As one of the tournament's main sponsors, Coke was keen to be associated with the world's best athletes.

That desire wasn't reciprocated. Ronaldo disdainfully glared at the two bottles of fizzy syrup and slid them to the other end of the table out of shot of all the cameras. Then he picked up an unbranded bottle of water from the table, held it aloft and proclaimed: "Agua!"

CR7's refusal to be associated with Coca-Cola coincided with a $4billion drop in the drinks giant's market value. Four. Billion. Dollars. Endorsements are a big deal. Like winning awards, they're a shortcut that can significantly accelerate the nurture process. If you know, like and trust Cristiano Ronaldo, you would probably also like and trust the people, brands, and companies he knows, likes, and trusts.

Ronaldo happily endorses water for free, but wouldn't endorse Coke for any amount of money. They're not a good fit for each other. Fellow athlete Jessica Ennis-Hill is a brand ambassador for Vitality health insurance (along with Seb Coe, Heather Knight, Jonny Wilkinson, Joe Root, and a plethora of other sports stars). A brand centred around healthy living teaming up with beacons of good health? That's a good fit.

If you're looking for the best quality products, why not take a shortcut and copy the person who sources all the best products? If you want to shop like the Queen of England, then just look on the packet for the Royal Warrant – a seal of approval on products the Royal Family have been buying for at least five years. If you know, like and trust Queen Elizabeth II, then simply look for the words "By Appointment to HM The Queen" to discover who *she* knows, likes, and trusts.

My chosen brand of peanut butter is the "official peanut butter of Team GB" at the 2020 Olympics. George Clooney drinks Nespresso, not

Nescafe. Kevin Bacon's phone is on EE. Whose endorsement would be a good nurture shortcut for you?

NURTURE ASSETS: GOOGLE MY BUSINESS

If you were to research any potential new business relationship, you'd probably google them first, wouldn't you?

Prospective clients are already googling your business. What do you want them to find? Your Companies House registration? Your Facebook page (last updated 18 months ago), and a load of your competitors or unrelated websites?

Google My Business is a free way for you to tell Google important information about your business – your opening hours, location, contact details, photos of your products, reviews from past customers, and even your latest news – so that when people google you, you're in control.

When prospects google you, they want to know:

- Where you're based.
- How to contact you.
- What other customers think of you.
- What you do.
- When you're open.
- How you can help them.

Google My Business puts all of this information at the very top of page one of the Google results for anyone searching for your business. The leverage on this asset is tremendous and it's a proper "do the work once, reap the rewards again and again (and again)" Evergreen Asset.

But, while you can "set it and forget it", there's some nice low-hanging fruit to be had by keeping on top of your GMB listing. Should you change your opening hours, for example, letting prospective customers know prevents them from staring at your "closed" sign in frustration. If you launch a new product range or win an award, write a quick post and publish on GMB to showcase your talent to the people who are actively seeking you out.

Then there are reviews. Probably the most powerful part of GMB is the ability to see what other customers think of you. Most people's attitude to GMB reviews are that "they are what they are" and there's nothing they can do to influence them. I call BS and know that reviews are a highly-leveraged Evergreen Asset that we can collect and improve. And the easiest way to get more reviews? Ask, and ye shall receive. I believe there is no such thing as too many reviews (unless they're all one-star). Don't stop collecting them until you've got at least 1,000.

If I'm researching three companies and one has no reviews, one has seven reviews, and one has 134 reviews, I'm going with the 134 reviews (as long as they're positive). Life's too short to take a chance on someone with no reviews. And only seven? That's not enough data for me. The sheer volume of positive reviews allows us to shortcut our know > like > trust thought process.

Don't just collect reviews either – respond to them. Google itself discovered businesses that respond to reviews are perceived as being 1.7 times more trustworthy than those that don't. A 70 per cent increase in trust? Yes please!

And don't just respond to the negative comments (although, handled well, showing that you do care, listen, and act on negative feedback can turn a negative review into a positive Evergreen Asset). After all, why wouldn't you want to thank your best clients for their glowing five-star review, further cementing your relationship, as well as demonstrating to all future random googlers that you're there for them and you care?

What do people see when they google *your* business?

NURTURE ASSETS: SOCIAL NETWORKS

The best time to dig a well is before you are thirsty. The best time to get your social network to know, like and trust you is before you start selling them stuff.

How long before? In my experience, as long as possible. We've all been subjected to the "connect and pitch" approach and know the horrible taste it leaves in the mouth.

Dig the well before you're thirsty.

Plant the seeds before you're hungry.

Build real connections before you need to make a sale.

Please note, I said *real* connections – actual human-to-human contact where you find out a little about each other, discover things you may have in common, and get a feel for what it would be like to work together. I didn't say, "go and send 100 connection requests a day", "download an automatic 'connect-and-pitch' tool" or buy a bunch of new "friends" on Fiverr.

Remember, Evergreen Assets are not a numbers game. They're a relationships game. And the best relationships are built one person at a time, making that person feel like they're the most important person in your world. You can make more friends (and more true fans) in two months by being interested in other people than you can in two years trying to persuade others to be interested in you.

Everyone's favourite sounds are their own name and their own voice. It's all me, me, me. So, when someone demonstrates a genuine interest in you, wants to hear more about you, and invites you to talk some more about you, you're going to be in your element.

If Dale Carnegie were on LinkedIn, he'd be spending most of his time digging wells. The more time you spend digging your wells, the less time you need to spend prospecting for water. And the less desperate you appear.

Be like Jesse

"What should I post on social networks?"

You don't have to post anything. You could simply join in the conversations your social network is already having. Comment on and engage with their content. And I don't mean typing some bland response like "great post" or "I agree, that's so true" just to cheat the algorithm. I mean truly engage. Be genuinely interested (and therefore interesting). Add value with your opinion or experience if appropriate. But don't make it all about you. Instead, make it all about them. You know, just like a true friend would.

For most people, simply having regular, proper, two-way conversations with the right people in their network digs their well deep enough to give them an evergreen supply of fresh water anytime they need it because their network truly knows, likes, and trusts them.

Those who want to grow their network by posting (broadcasting) themselves can get a minimum effective dose by embracing their inner Jesse. Emerge from your tool shed, shuffle towards the camera and announce: "This week, I 'ave been mostly ___________."

All you need to do to write a great social networking post is fill in that blank and start your own conversation.

What's happened recently that's annoyed you? Upset you? Amused you? Intrigued you? What have you learnt or discovered in the last few weeks? What surprised you? Which clients have made you proud and why? Where have you been and what have you done that has reminded you of the problem you solve for your clients?

Even the mighty Facebook, with its teams of coders, AI-driven algorithms, and everything split-tested to the nth degree, haven't found a more powerful call-to-action that gets people talking than: "What's on your mind?"

So, what *is* on your mind? What *'ave* you mostly been doing this week (or this month, quarter or year)?

Embracing your inner Jesse is the lowest-hanging fruit, minimum effective dose, that will enable you to quickly come up with stories, examples, and anecdotes that are of the moment, but also resonate with the right people in your network. Because there are real people in your network. It's not a numbers game, remember?

Humans buy things from other humans. Especially other humans they know, like, and trust. Other humans they feel they have something in common with. Some form of connection.

If you post personal anecdotes about yourself, your family, your pets, your home, your life, etc., then you will resonate with people, although ultimately, it's still not about *you* – it's about you being the person to help them.

Treat your social network as a two-way communication tool, get to know them and treat them as humans, and you'll be well on the way to them knowing, liking, and trusting you.

You'll have dug wells all over the place. And you need never be thirsty again.

TL/DR:

You don't have to post anything on social networks. Just join in the conversations that are already happening in your network.

Dig the well before you're thirsty, and plant seeds before you're hungry. Remember that humans buy from other humans. To connect with those humans, be more human. Tell them what's on your mind, and what you 'ave been mostly doing this week.

Oh, and to appear more interesting to your social network, try being more *interested* in them first. (It's not about you!)

NURTURE ASSETS: PODCASTS

Can I listen to it on my phone?

After exiting the day-to-day running of our main business in 2016, Jason and I decided we wanted to help other small business owners to design their own ambitious, lifestyle businesses, just as we had. A podcast seemed the natural way to do that and I'd get to scratch an itch from my childhood when I dreamed of being a radio DJ – getting paid to play my favourite tunes and tell jokes in between the songs.

The Ambitious Lifestyle Business Podcast was born to no fanfare whatsoever. Jason and I recorded some truly awful first episodes in my kitchen, capturing them on a laptop that was far too noisy. We had some fancy new business cards printed up and hit the local networking scene in Plymouth:

> *"Hnni, my name's John. I'm a podcaster."*
>
> *"A what?"*
>
> *"A podcaster. I've got my own podcast."*
>
> *"What's a podcast?"*
>
> *"Erm, it's like a radio show but on the internet."*
>
> *"Oh right, I don't listen to internet radio. Could I listen to it on my phone?"*
>
> *"Yep, absolutely. Just open your podcasts app and..."*

"My what?"

"Your podcasts app. Your phone already has a podcasts app built in, you just need to open it and subscribe to our..."

"Oh that sounds far too technical for me. Anyway, nice to meet you..."

This conversation was rinsed and repeated time and time again over soggy bacon sandwiches and crap coffee in every networking event in the area. Eventually, we took the hint and stopped calling ourselves podcasters.

We kept the show going, though, creating a new episode every month without fail. The sound quality got a little better but not much. We still talk over each other, refuse to follow a script and collapse in fits of laughter most episodes. To be honest, that's part of the charm of podcasts – the fact they're not highly polished and edited to within an inch of their life. They're raw. They're real. They're the perfect slow-burn relationship builder.

Be like Terry

Since we started our little show, podcasting has become mainstream, with listening figures reaching record highs every year. At the time of writing, nearly 16million people in the UK listen to podcasts each week – twice as many as two years ago and six times higher than five years ago.

This growth is being driven by the big boys entering the podcasting space. Almost every radio DJ now pumps out a "best of" podcast every week. Peter Crouch used to be famous for being a lanky footballer. Now he's a lanky podcaster, who used to play football. Whatever your favourite TV show is, it's a safe bet you can add the word "podcast" to it and find a show. EastEnders: The Podcast? Check. Love Island: The Morning After? Check.

And those are just the official ones. The big boys of mainstream media are bringing millions of brand new listeners into the wonderful world of podcasts.

Which is great news for us little guys. Sure, the big boys can blow us out of the water with their celebrity hosts, A-lister guests, world-class production quality, and a marketing budget to die for.

But they can't niche like we can.

I'd like to see Chris Evans hosting a podcast about the unusual history of gnomes or Peter Crouch geeking out about his favourite insects. No, let's let the big boys play their big boys' game of creating podcasts for the mass market. We're going to create a podcast for our 1,000 true fans.

The Unusual History of Gnomes? Yep, that's an actual podcast, with a fanatical listenership of gnome aficionados. Dr Tim's Spineless Wonders? Why, that's a monthly examination of real-life insect encounters that encourages listeners to see beyond what "bugs" them.

Whether you want to hear two self-proclaimed "weird sisters" re-reading the Harry Potter books, a show dedicated to helping men talk about divorce issues, or a show "for dentists, by dentists", there's a podcast for you.

Wish there was a talkSPORT-style show that only talked about Plymouth Argyle? There is. If only there were a health radio show that focused entirely on IBS or the menopause or keto? Guess what? There is.

Think of podcasts not as the mass media device that the big boys are using it as but rather as personalised radio where you create a show that, when your target audience hear it, they immediately proclaim: "Wow, it's like that show is made for me!"

Because it is made for them.

As the name suggests, our Ambitious Lifestyle Business podcast is for ambitious, lifestyle business owners – people who want to design their business to work for them, rather than the other way around.

Instead of Jason and I showing off how wonderful we are, and how much we know, we put one of our One Percenters front and centre and make *them* the star of the show:

> *Why Chris Harris walked away from a £5million business.*
>
> *How James Marks became an overnight success (after nine years).*
>
> *Why Dan Harrison doesn't want to be a millionaire anymore.*
>
> *How Tracy Irwin runs a UK business from sunny Spain.*
>
> *Why Paul and Emily Hughes chose sanity over salary.*

Each episode has a similar thread running through it: How the star of the show (our client) designed their business to deliver the lifestyle they truly want and the small part we played in it.

Dedicating our podcast to our clients – truly making heroes of them, putting them on a pedestal, and showcasing the amazing transformations they've made – is a format that works so much better than "we're the experts so you should listen to us".

I love hearing the stories of our most successful One Percenters every month. I love recording the episodes and I love the feedback we get from listeners. Our download numbers are still nothing to write home about (around 1,000 downloads per episode). But that's 1,000 true fans – 1,000 ambitious business owners, who want to design a business that delivers the lifestyle they truly want. I don't need 100,000 downloads a month (or even 10,000) – 1,000 of the right people is all I need.

Sir Terry Wogan was one of the greatest radio broadcasters, with more than eight million listeners a week tuning into his breakfast show on BBC Radio 2. Yet, whenever he spoke directly to them, he always addressed them as "Dear listener..."

Not "Listeners" (plural). Listener (singular).

Sir Terry clearly knew his avatar (his TOGs - "Terry's Old Geezers or Gals"), and spoke directly to each and every one of them, in such a way that they forgot they were one of eight million and instead felt he was talking to them alone. That they were his "dear listener".

If you're going to have a podcast, be like Sir Terry. Embrace your inner Wogan, work out who your TOGs are, and make everything you do all about your "dear listener".

If you're not Terry, be Basil

For most small business owners who want to add podcasting to their Evergreen Assets ecosystem, I advise the 8/800 strategy: either record eight perfect episodes or 800 pretty good ones.

If you choose to record eight, make them top-notch. Record them in a studio with a professional producer. Spend more time planning the scripts and structure of the entire series than you do recording. Ensure that each episode helps listeners to know, like and trust you so that by the end of the series, your "dear listener" will be in no doubt that you are the authority in your niche and perfectly positioned to help someone like them to solve the problem(s) they have.

Treat it as you would a Netflix mini-series. Each episode should build on the previous one. Take your listener on a season-long journey and make them curious about what's next in the story arc. Have a clear call to action at the end of every episode, letting them know the one thing you want them to do next (listen to the next episode, take an online quiz, download a free checklist, call for an appointment, share with a friend, etc.).

You should be proud enough of this single season that you feature it on your website (and optimise it as an SEO Nurture Asset), and add it to your YouTube channel. People should be begging you to record another season and you might want to. But only if you can maintain that level of quality and achieve a similar ROI.

Only 12 episodes of the classic sit-com Fawlty Towers were ever made. How much money do you think John Cleese and Connie Booth have been offered over the years to make another season? They've resisted all offers, because they knew from the beginning that it would be a 12-episode creation. Every minute of every episode was planned and structured to be absolutely perfect and Fawlty Towers works brilliantly as a result.

We get the perfect dose of Basil, Sybil, Manuel, and Polly without the show ever becoming formulaic, the characters turning into caricatures of themselves or "jumping the shark" (when creators try ever-more-desperate attempts to remain popular – named after a scene in the fifth season of US comedy Happy Days in which The Fonz jumps over a shark while on water-skis).

If you're going to create eight episodes of your podcast, then make each one as good as Basil the Rat, The Germans or The Kipper and The Corpse.

If you're not making eight perfect episodes, then aim for 800 pretty good episodes instead. Don't obsess too much over the tech (I use a decent USB mic and not much else), just commit to making a new episode every week or every month. And never stop. Each episode will be far simpler and cheaper to produce than the "8" strategy but what you lose in quality, you gain in consistency.

Sir Terry Wogan hosted thousands of episodes of Wake Up To Wogan from 1993 to 2009 and was renowned for going off-script, making long-winded rambling monologues, and winging it when things went wrong (listeners once thought Terry had died live on air when steam from the gym next door set off the fire alarm, resulting in the "emergency broadcast" tape kicking in).

Every time Sir Terry messed up, collapsed in fits of laughter reading out "Janet and John" stories or described his latest act of TOGiness (a feeling of being old before your time and a fierce resentment of anyone younger than you), he built a bit more know, like and trust kudos and gained yet another "dear listener".

If you want to do the work once and reap the rewards forever, be Fawlty Towers and make a limited number of highly polished, almost-perfect content.

If you want to keep building an audience over time, then be Sir Terry Wogan and embrace consistency as your new best friend.

But if you don't want to create perfect episodes (Basil) and you don't want to keep creating episodes (Terry), then you can always appear as a guest on other people's podcasts, rather than hosting your own. I've appeared on more than 200 shows now. Give me a microphone and I'll happily yap about small businesses, routines, or Evergreen Assets for 30 to 60 minutes. That's the minimum effective dose in action and 200 Evergreen Assets in play.

TL/DR:

Podcasting can be easy or it can be hard. You choose.

Be Basil Fawlty or Terry Wogan. Do eight episodes or 800 (or none and be the guest). Podcasts are the perfect slow-burn relationship builder. They're personalised radio for your "dear listener". Make your clients the star of the show. The big boys are making podcasting mainstream, but don't try to compete with them. Remember why you've got a podcast and who it's for.

Oh, and don't obsess over the tech – unless you're creating Fawlty Towers.

NURTURE ASSETS: BOOKS

"I'm never writing another book again"

Writing a book is hard work. I romanticised the notion of doing it for several years. I loved the idea not of *writing* a book, but having already written one. I wanted the after-effects – the book tours, signing copies for adoring fans, maybe even selling the movie rights (Tom Hardy would make an amazing John Lamerton if he can nail the West Country accent).

What I didn't want to do was spend the best part of a year writing and then months editing, formatting, and promoting the book, not to mention the significant monetary investment required to deliver a book of which I could be proud. Sure, I wanted to reap the rewards again and again. I just wasn't keen on the investment required (a year of my time and several thousand pounds) for the first part of the Evergreen Assets equation: "Do the work once."

But "do the work" I did and as I stood on stage at the *Big Ideas.. For Small Businesses* launch party, I was asked by a journalist if I planned to write a follow-up book.

"Oh hell no!" I proclaimed. "I'm never writing another book again! I had no idea writing one was so much work and so stressful. I've hardly seen my family for the last few months. When I do, all they hear me talk about is 'that bloody book'. So no, I won't be writing another book. Ever."

As you're currently holding my third book in your hands, it's safe to say I rather quickly changed my tune.

So if writing (and editing) books is hard, requires a significant investment of both time and money, and with no prospect of massive royalty cheques landing on most authors' doormats (most books sell fewer than 500 copies), why on earth would you even consider writing a book? And why do *I* continue to write books? I'll tell you.

The best business card I've ever had

Not long after publishing *Big Ideas…*, I started picking up more clients for my coaching business, initially from people I already knew. The book had "tipped them over the edge" and persuaded them that working with me would be a smart thing for them to do. They already knew me. They already liked me. And, thanks to reading my book, they now trusted me too.

A few months later, I started to notice unfamiliar names coming into my world – people I'd never spoken with before. I didn't have a clue who they were, but they knew me, liked me, and trusted me. My book had become the best business card I'd ever had.

Imagine a business card that prospects pay £12.95 to look at, invest a day or two of their time completely immersed in reading, and by the time they've finished all 70,000-plus words of it, they know everything about you and the way you work and are convinced you are the person to help them get what they want. If they feel you are not the person to help them, they'll simply deselect themselves and you'll never hear from them.

It's also a business card that opens up the world's largest retailer (Amazon) as a new Lead Asset and is a low-priced tripwire that can build trust before asking for a bigger commitment.

Respect my authoritah!

We trust doctors more if they're wearing a white coat. We trust a personal trainer more if they've got big muscles and a whistle. And we trust almost anyone more if they've written a book.

Even with the advent of self-publishing, where anyone with a PDF document could technically "publish a book", there's a prestige to having your work published. It tells the world: "I have something to say that people want to hear. I'm worth listening to. I'm an expert in my field."

Writing a book is hard. Most people can't and/or won't do it. Therefore, if you can write a book and you do it well, then the rewards are more than worth the effort.

Once you have published the world's best business card, you can fully leverage that asset. Rather than giving prospects the hard sell on your full product or service (and them risking hundreds or thousands of pounds), you can soft sell them on your book, which only costs them the price of a cup of coffee or two. Ideally, that book will deliver an ROI many, many times what they spent and your "dear reader" will be itching to work closer with you.

Use your book to demonstrate why you're the expert. Tell your story, how you discovered your framework, what life was like for you before, what you learnt (and who/where you learned it from), what mistakes you made along the way and what advice you'd have for your younger self.

As humans, we're hard-wired to respond to stories. So tell stories. Not just your own, but those of your clients – the people you help on a daily basis. In *Building a Storybrand*, Donald Miller shares his Proven Framework for storytelling, which he calls the SB7:

> *"A character who wants something encounters a problem before they can get it. At the peak of their despair, a guide steps into their lives, gives them a plan, and calls them to action. That action helps them avoid failure and ends in success."*

The character is your target market. Your prospect. Your potential customer. The real hero of the story. The problem is what's keeping them awake at night. You are the guide. Your Proven Framework is the plan. Your call to action tells them how to get what they want. And, like any good fairy tale, you'll include some bad guys (failure) to avoid/conquer and ultimately lead your hero to their happy ever after (success).

I told a story earlier about a coach (character), who complained that even though he could help people, no one was buying (problem). I (the guide) chatted to him, explained the Evergreen Assets framework (plan), and told him how to take the first step on the plan (call to action). He told me what failure already looked like for him and, once we agreed what success would look like, we began the next chapter of the story by working together.

I'll bet you've got stories like that from the clients you've helped – reinforcing you as the expert and someone worth listening to.

Public Relations expert Lucy Matthews leveraged storytelling in her 2017 book *A Marvellous Reputation: 10 Lessons From My Life As A PR Insider For Entrepreneurs Who Want To Be Talked About.*

I was in a mastermind group with Lucy at the time, so I know the blood, sweat and tears that went into creating her book. She weaves her story (and that of her clients) into her Proven Framework. She tells you how she fell into PR almost by accident (something most business owners can relate to), and demonstrates the importance of using case studies via a story about getting regular interesting press coverage for a rather uninteresting client who made uninteresting industrial floor cleaning machines.

For those characters who have the problem of "no one will want to write about my business as we don't do anything news-worthy", Lucy (our guide) comes armed with a stories about creating regular press releases for products as unchanging and un-newsworthy as Tabasco sauce and getting them published almost every time (success).

She also tells a story about the importance of proofreading (part of the plan), with an amusing anecdote about a Tabasco sauce recipe that was published in several magazines – stuffed oranges filled with rice, laced with Tabasco sauce. Only the press releases were published with an error and readers complained that Tabasco-stuffed onions (rather than oranges) tasted disgusting.

With her many stories, Lucy demonstrates she really knows her onions (pun intended). Being a published author has positioned her as the go-to person for real-world PR advice for small business owners. She's been asked to speak on stage, appeared on countless podcasts and radio shows, had an absolute ton of press appearances (you would expect nothing less), and launched several products and masterminds off the back of one little book.

A Marvellous Reputation is the best business card that Lucy's ever had.

What, not How

Lawyer-turned-marketer Nick Jervis also leverages his book *The Law Firm Growth Formula: How smart solicitors attract more of the right clients at the right price to grow their law firm quickly.*

There's no doubt what you're getting with that book. A "growth formula" (a Proven Framework – a plan), for "smart solicitors" (characters) to attract "more of the right clients at the right price" (the biggest problem, and a subtle nod to what both success and failure look like), written by "Nick Jervis, Solicitor (Non-Practising)" (your guide).

Nick's entire pipeline of new business comes from this book. He doesn't worry about selling his high-end consultancy services upfront. Instead, Nick focuses on selling his book in which he gives away the secrets of what you need to do to grow your law firm quickly and sustainably, in an inexpensive tripwire product.

Over the course of 250-plus pages, Nick delivers a whistle-stop tour of online marketing for law firms. He explains the importance of always marketing yourself (even when you're busy), how to measure metrics, creating a compelling sales message, optimising the new client conversion process, comparing DIY with DFY (done for you) services – setting up email marketing, overhauling your website, using Google Ads, tracking, and improving referrals, as well as his advice on direct mail, networking, social media, and other paid advertising.

By the time a busy, stressed law firm owner has read Nick's book, and digested the growth formula framework, they're likely to arrive at a couple of conclusions:

1. We need to make a lot of changes to our existing marketing.
2. It would be much easier to have someone do all of this for us.

And guess what? Nick can do all of this for you. He offers a complete done for you service. He's given you the framework and told you exactly what to do to execute that framework. You now know *what* to do but you don't necessarily know *how* to do it yet. That's going to require more learning, more experimentation, and more work. And you're already a busy fool so when are you going to find the time to revolutionise your marketing?

There's a better, easier option that Nick plants as a seed on page 63:

> *"When it comes to marketing your law firm, I promise you that the minute you accept DFY (Done For You) is the only way forward, you will start to attract a steady and consistent flow of new clients.*
>
> *I cannot tell you how sad I am to have seen so many solicitors sabotage their own success by constantly trying to DIY, when if they outsourced their marketing (DFY), everything would*

have been completed faster, more cost-effectively and probably better.

Honestly, stop it. Stop kidding yourself that you are the only person who can do that job. Someone out there is vastly more qualified to do it than you, and the best news is that the hourly rate that you have to pay them is significantly lower than your own hourly rate."

That's great news, isn't it? There is someone out there who can solve this problem for you. I wonder where I might find such a person.

Maybe it's on the final page of Nick's book where it tells us that he is "known as the fast growth marketing consultant to UK law firms"', that he "has a unique insight into what it takes to rapidly and profitably grow a law firm", and that he "works closely with his private clients and Marketing4Solicitors members to rapidly increase their turnover, profits and saleability" before sharing his website (nickjervis.com), LinkedIn and contact details.

In a world full of charlatans and cold callers, how does the average law firm owner choose a marketing consultant? Do they take a chance on that guy they met at the local networking breakfast, the flashy brand with the nice logo that always advertises in the paper or the big firm that's been cold calling for a while now?

Or do they choose the former lawyer, who's already solved their greatest problem (both for himself and for dozens of other law firms), who knows what success and failure looks like for businesses like theirs and who has a Proven Framework that he can guide you through. Oh, and he'll do all the work, cheaper and better than doing it yourself.

It's little wonder that Nick now spends more time selling his book than he does selling his services. Because once law firm owners have read his book, they're beating a path to Nick's door, yelling "shut up and take my money" at him. *The Law Firm Growth Formula* is the best business card Nick's ever had.

My Book Writing Framework

Here's how I approach writing my books. Now, I'm not going to go deep here and share the full how-to (that would be an entire book in itself), but I can share the key points from my Proven Framework (an asset you'll become familiar with soon).

I start by planning my chapters as though I'm writing a 60-minute keynote presentation on the topic. Each slide is a chapter. Sometimes you'll have sub slides with smaller bullet points, relevant stories, examples, and case studies, which will form part of the larger chapters. Eventually, you'll have all your slides ready and you can then go through them in order. Once you've done so, ask yourself what's missing and if the order makes sense – and then fill any holes or adjust the structure (if needed).

Whether you're delivering a 60-minute keynote or writing a 70,000-word book, your audience should be able to answer the following questions (in roughly this order):

1. Is this relevant for me?
2. Who are you?
3. Why should I listen to you?
4. What's the big idea?
5. The Proven Framework: Step 1, Step 2, Step 3.
6. But what about...?
7. To recap…
8. What's the next step?

Straight off the bat, your reader needs to know that you can help them and that you understand their greatest problems or challenges. These *are* the droids you're looking for.

Then, every author's favourite subject – themselves! Hurray, we get to write about ourselves in the third person and make ourselves look like a superhero. Only, as Donald Miller reminds us, *we're* not the hero in this story. The reader is the hero and we are the guide. They're Luke Skywalker and we're Yoda. We need to demonstrate that we're the right guide for them.

Now tell me why. Why should I care about this topic? Why should I change what I'm currently doing? Why should I act now? Why should I give up hours or days of my time to read this book? In other words, what's in it for me?

Next, we unveil the "big idea". This is the overarching concept, the North Star of your book. For Nick Jervis, it was that law firms can use online marketing to rapidly grow in a steady, predictable way. For Lucy Matthews, it was that small business owners can embrace PR as a strategy, regardless of size or budget. This book's "big idea" is that you can do the work once and reap the rewards again and again (and again).

Your Proven Framework should make up the majority of the book. This is where you get to teach, step by step, exactly what to do to achieve the results, solve the problem(s) or make the changes so that your reader can follow along with you.

What exactly should I do? What order should I do it in? How much? When? Where? Who?

You need to prove that your framework works in the real world and that it wasn't just a fluke for you, and you alone. This is where it makes sense to mix in case studies from clients, famous examples, and stories from your own experiences.

Once you've finished walking readers through your Proven Framework, it's only natural that they would have questions:

> "That sounds great, but what about...?"
>
> "How could I do that with...?"
>
> "But my circumstances/business/life is different!"
>
> "Would that still work if...?"

If you were doing a live keynote, you might open up the floor to questions. If you're writing a book, you need to try and second-guess the questions, objections, and queries your readers might have, and try to answer the most common ones, either where relevant in the framework or, at the very least, by the time you've wrapped up your conclusion.

Readers want to finish your book feeling full of motivation and ready to implement what they've learned, so be sure to recap the main points and answer those last few questions. Remind them of your big idea, recap some of the stories from the people who have gone through your Proven Framework, and wrap things up nicely. If you don't recap, you miss a golden opportunity to generate buy-in for your big idea. It would be like ending a keynote presentation with the line, "Oh, it looks like that was the last slide. Well, thanks for listening. Good night!"

And finally – what's next? Don't waste that opportunity when your reader is at their most motivated, most fired up, and most ready to take action. In my last book, *Routine Machine*, I implored readers not to be "one of those people who turns over the final page of this book and then almost immediately picks up the next one," but instead to "try at least one idea from the book, implement one change or at the very least write down your biggest takeaway from the last few hundred pages".

And that's my book-writing framework in a nutshell. It starts with a bunch of slides and a load of notes, bullet points and ideas collected under each one. If you were asked to, you could present a 60-minute keynote tomorrow. If you're feeling brave, why don't you do just that? No one needs ever see it and it'll help you spot where the gaps are and which elements of your presentation need the most work.

I did exactly that for this book and you are more than welcome to watch the 99-minute keynote that I recorded a full 12 months before the release of this book (I'll include a link to it in the resources). You'll notice much of the same structure in this final edition, but a couple of the Proven Framework names have changed, the order of many items shifted, some stories got dropped, and there is (hopefully) a lot less waffling, dogs barking, and cats walking in front of the camera.

Doing that 99-minute keynote helped me plan out my chapter structure and the bullet points for each chapter. They became a brief Google Doc of notes that over several months was expanded into more than 106,000 words of my first draft manuscript. Once you have the structure, it's so much easier to put meat on the bones than simply staring at a blinking cursor.

All the right ideas, but not necessarily in the right order

Finished your manuscript? Great! It's time to stick on some Bon Jovi to celebrate, because "Whoa! We're halfway there!" Good books aren't well-written. They're well-edited.

Routine Machine went through six drafts before it was published (including 25 pairs of eyes going over it) and we still missed a typo! It wasn't until I was listening to the audiobook version of *Big Ideas... for Small Businesses* that I realised I'd got my maths wrong on a crucial section – almost 12 months later! Editing is hard work, but it's where your rough diamond is polished up to become a gleaming gemstone (or your steaming turd is rolled in glitter).

Most books have recurring themes running through them, but these ideas and concepts are often born halfway through writing the first draft.

There are already a thousand and one ideas floating around your head, so when you casually mention a concept in Chapter Four, you need to remember that readers may not be introduced to that concept until Chapter Six or Seven.

Because you started plotting your chapter structure (and tested this structure with slides and a pretend keynote), you should almost be able to write the book in the correct order. Not doing this was the biggest mistake I made with my first book – the chapter structure developed as I was writing, so I ended up moving entire chunks of the book around. Chapter Ten became Chapter 18, 18 became 14, and 14 became Three. I had all the right ideas, but not necessarily in the right order.

The film Pulp Fiction works in a non-linear fashion. Director Quentin Tarantino deliberately crafted his 1994 masterpiece to be consumed out of order. The movie opens and closes with a diner scene that actually takes place about mid-way through the events depicted. John Travolta is gunned down halfway through the movie, only to feature prominently in the finale, which of course actually took place a few hours before his death.

Quentin Tarantino can get away with it. You can't.

Who wants to become a best-written author?

Once you've plotted your structure, written your first draft, and edited it to within an inch of its life, you still need to sell the damn thing. Remember, most books sell fewer than 500 copies in their entire lifetime and I'll wager a bet that most of those are stacked up in the author's garage, gathering dust.

Author Robert Kiyosaki was interviewed by a newspaper reporter after his book *Rich Dad, Poor Dad* had spent a few years camped out on the New York Times bestseller list. The reporter was a highly talented writer and wanted to glean some secrets about how she might make the list too.

Kiyosaki advised her to learn sales and marketing. To attend night classes and seminars and to read books. To make friends with the salesmen in her office and ask them how they present offers and broker deals.

"But I don't want to learn about sales and marketing," she protested. "I'm a professional writer."

Kiyosaki asked her to pick up a copy of his book and read what it said on the front cover.

"New York Times Best Seller," she read aloud.

"Exactly," Kiyosaki retorted. "My book has been praised for being a best seller. It hasn't been praised for being best-written. There's no such thing as the best-written charts – only bestselling. And the reason my book has sold so well isn't because it's so well written. It's not. It's good enough, but I know how to sell, so I've sold a lot of copies."

Decades later, Robert Kiyosaki still works hard making sure *Rich Dad, Poor Dad* remains a constant bestseller. He's created an ecosystem of Evergreen Assets from blog posts and podcast appearances to live seminars, TV and newspaper interviews.

Once you have written your book, you can do the same. Use the other Evergreen Assets to create an ecosystem that continues to sell your masterpiece. Build an email list, leverage Facebook Ads, Google Ads and SEO. Write blog posts about some of the key talking points from your book. Speak regularly with your network – dig the well *before* you're thirsty, and your book will soon form part of the natural conversation.

I've appeared as a guest on more than 200 podcasts, and attended "meet the author" events for dozens of online book clubs, talking about the common themes from my books – lifestyle businesses (*Big Ideas... for Small Businesses*), the amazing power of habits and routines (*Routine Machine*), and, of course, how to create an ecosystem of Evergreen Assets. I'm always selling my books, even years after they were written.

Why you should sell your rivals' books too

My target market is small business owners who want their business to deliver a better lifestyle – small business owners who work on self-improvement and are looking for ways to be better. In short, small business owners who read.

Amazon has a truckload of them, champing at the bit to discover new books and new authors. Even though it's someone else's football, it's still worth the effort to play Amazon's game. I make sure that my Amazon listings are comprehensive, both from an SEO point of view (thinking about the keywords readers use to find books) and a conversion point of view. I want to write compelling copy that inspires potential new readers to think, "This sounds like the book for me!"

I have a system for collecting reviews (see the Viral Assets class for more about that), and I also encourage people who have read my books to read my rival authors' books too. I'm not short-sighted enough to think my readers will only ever read my books and never seek out a contradictory or complementary viewpoint from another author. I know that when I want to learn about a particular topic, I'll often read four or five books from different authors and then forge my own path, based on a balanced viewpoint.

There's a huge benefit in recommending "rival" authors. They're not truly rivals anyway as we're actually on the same team, encouraging readers to learn more about a particular topic. We may well have differing opinions and approach things from our own angle. But by making readers aware of these differing viewpoints, they can find the one that's right for them.

That's why I encourage readers of *Big Ideas... for Small Businesses* to read *Company of One* by Paul Jarvis, or *Work Less, Make More* by James Schramko. It's why fans of *Routine Machine* should also study *Atomic Habits* by James Clear, or *The Slight Edge* by Jeff Olson. And it's why, if after reading this book, you'd like another viewpoint on building a content marketing ecosystem, I'll encourage you to check out *Compound Marketing* by Dan Norris or *24 Assets* by Daniel Priestley.

This practice of recommending "rival" authors is good for the reader and that's ultimately my aim: to provide the best experience I possibly can for you. I don't try to pretend that I'm the only person worth listening to. Instead, I openly acknowledge that there may be a better book out there for you – one that resonates more with you, explains the concepts better than I, or that simply is more engaging for you.

A nice side-effect of recommending other good books on the topic is Amazon's algorithm will soon notice that people who bought your book also buy your rival authors' books and will start to offer *your* book to readers (or potential readers) of *their* book.

Now, I'm not advocating this as a tactic to try and leach sales from prominent authors, rather it's a natural side-effect of a legitimate, heartfelt recommendation. And one worth embracing.

TL/DR:

Writing a book is hard work, but the rewards are worth it.

A well-written, well-edited (and well sold) book could be the best business card you've ever had. It'll give you a level of authority that few other assets can match. Books demonstrate that you are the guide (Yoda) with a plan – a framework that can solve the reader's greatest problems.

Oh, and don't be afraid to recommend your rivals' books. Your readers (and Amazon) will thank you for it.

NURTURE ASSETS: PRINTED NEWSLETTERS

If you don't fancy writing a 200-page, 70,000-word book, how about the minimum effective dose: A four-page, 1,500-word printed newsletter?

Sent regularly (I suggest at least quarterly, but ideally monthly), a printed newsletter serves several key nurture purposes:

1. It reminds people you exist. If they don't know you, they aren't going to like or trust you.
2. It showcases the human side of your business. People like reading about other people and (if what they read is positive) they like the people they read about.
3. It elevates you above all your competitors who don't go to the effort of sending them a monthly printed newsletter. It gives you instant authority and that means more trust.

More know. More like. More trust. That's why printed newsletters make a fantastic Nurture Asset. Whereas an email newsletter is often deleted without ever being opened, a printed newsletter almost always gets read. An email newsletter may be quickly glanced over, before being deleted. A printed newsletter is set aside and read slowly over ten to 15 minutes, cover-to-cover – often accompanied by a cup of coffee (and maybe a slice of cake).

Creating a printed newsletter is harder work and more expensive. But it has one major advantage over its emailed PDF counterpart – it gets read. It gets its readers' full, undivided attention.

"What the hell would I write about?" I hear you ask (again). Imagine you're writing a letter to a pen pal or a friend you haven't seen for a while. What have you been up to? What's new in your world? What interesting tales have you got to tell? What funny things have happened since you last spoke?

People like to read about people. So tell personal stories about the people in your business (demonstrating that "you're a bit like me"), make heroes of your clients and customers through case studies and testimonials (showing that "you help people like me"), and add a little sprinkling of industry news and education (proving that "you're the expert").

The goal is to get your newsletter read cover-to-cover every time and remind readers:

1. You exist.
2. You help [the right people] to [get what they want] by [your Proven Framework].
3. You're bloody good at it.

No one wants to read a sales pitch or a bore fest, so keep the upcoming changes to subsection 34H of the 1945 Watching Paint Dry Act, the fact you've changed the hex code of your logo or that you've decided to move desks in the office to yourself. It may be the most interesting thing in your life, but it's almost certainly not the most interesting thing that your dream client wants to spend their Saturday morning reading while their coffee goes cold.

Don't give it the hard sell either. Instead, tell stories about the people you've helped. Readers will connect the dots and realise you could help *them* too. By all means include a line at the end of the newsletter that says, "We help [*the right people*] to [*get what they want*] by [*your Proven Framework*]. If you'd like to chat about how we can help you, here's our number/email address." (ROI junkies take note: if you use a unique telephone number and email address on your newsletter, you can work out the exact return on investment).

Speaking of ROI, it's worth pointing out that a printed newsletter is a slow-burner. Because it's a nurture tool, it's not going to bring in sales from the first edition. What it will do is ensure you're front of mind when your target market is ready to buy or ready to buy again. Or ready to refer. Or ready to upgrade.

I've seen great success in sending printed newsletters to existing customers of high-margin businesses. A printed newsletter will inevitably be a greater asset for nurturing relationships and picking up repeat customers and referrals than for warming up brand new prospects, but it can be deployed there too if you have sufficient margin to justify it.

Again, I believe sending monthly is optimal, although quarterly also works as a minimum effective dose. Any less frequent than that and you're not going to be front of mind when a potential purchase, repeat purchase or referral is being considered.

I would suggest a minimum of four pages (that's one sheet of A3 folded in half). We've gone as high as 36 pages for a full-on magazine in our sports betting business, but we also leverage a PDF version as The Right Bait to generate leads, as well as sending printed copies to our best customers.

The design should look decent enough, but remember you're not in the magazine business. You don't need to recreate Vogue. Graham Rowan used to produce a glossy mag every month for his Elite Investor Club members, with around 24 pages of editorial content, amazing photography, and all the associated costs that go with it (multiple team members' time, professional design, high-quality print on the best paper, and a couple of quid in postage and packing).

Nowadays, Graham sends a simple four-page monthly letter which has next-to-no design, is written in a much more personal style by Graham himself (it reads like a letter to a friend), and simply printed in black and white, folded in half, stuffed in an envelope, and sent out. I would imagine this takes Graham's team one-tenth of the time to create, costs one-tenth as much, and gets just as much impact. Every month, I'm reminded that Graham exists and how he can help me achieve my financial goals.

And I get to read it with a nice slice of cake too.

TL/DR:

A printed newsletter reminds people that you exist and that you're bloody good at what you do.

It's more expensive and much harder work than creating an email newsletter, but it has one unsurmountable advantage – it'll get read. Monthly is best, quarterly the minimum. Aim for at least four pages, don't be boring, and don't try and pitch – it's not a sales letter! You can track the ROI, but remember that a newsletter is a long-term asset and shouldn't be judged after a handful of issues. Give it at least a year. It's perfect for nurturing repeat business and referrals but only use it for new prospects if you have the margins for it.

Oh, and remember, you're not the editor-in-chief of Vogue magazine.

NURTURE ASSETS: REMARKETING

"Oh my god, these guys are everywhere!"

When the plucky founders of Innocent Smoothies wanted to get into the major supermarkets, they took a rather novel approach to advertising. They found out where the buyers for each supermarket lived, calculated the most likely route they would take to commute to the office, and spent their entire advertising budget on billboards and bus stop ads on those few roads.

What appeared to be blanket, brand-building ads, designed to appeal to the masses were, in fact, laser targeted to a very small demographic – the handful of people who could open the largest doors in the country for them. And it worked, making Innocent appear bigger and more established than they were. The buyers saw the ads again and again every single day as they went about their commute.

There's a psychological phenomenon called the "mere-exposure effect", which makes us prefer images, names, (and brands of smoothie) that we have previously seen even if they've only been seen for a few seconds, and even when we're not consciously aware of having seen them.

In a study by the University of Wisconsin, participants were asked to read an online article. On the webpage, a different banner ad was shown every five seconds and one of those ads was for a camera. After they had been questioned about the article itself, the students were asked which of two cameras (one which had been used in the ads, and one which had not) they recalled seeing. No one could remember.

But, when asked which camera they preferred, the one from the ads won hands down, even though they didn't recall seeing the ad. Interestingly, this preference got even stronger when the ad was shown 20 times rather than five – and they still didn't remember seeing the ad.

And that's where remarketing (sometimes also referred to as retargeting) plays a vital role in your nurture playbook. By leveraging the remarketing capabilities of your email marketing provider, Google Ads, Facebook Ads, and dedicated remarketing platforms such as AdRoll or Criteo, just like the Innocent Smoothie boys, you'll be able to appear to be absolutely everywhere to a very small group of people. And just like the University of Wisconsin study, you'll be able to harness the mere-exposure effect and create an unconscious preference for and affinity with your brand, service, or product.

By laser targeting only those who have entered your ecosystem via your Lead Assets (for example, those who have visited your website, but not yet purchased), you're able to appear to be everywhere they go with banner ads showing up on their favourite news websites, social media feeds and all over the internet dozens of times every day.

In 1885, Thomas Smith wrote a guide called *Successful Advertising* in which he coined the phrase "effective frequency" – a term that is still used and entirely relevant today. Smith said:

> *"The first time people look at any given ad, they don't even see it.*
>
> *The second time, they don't notice it.*
>
> *The third time, they are aware that it is there.*
>
> *The fourth time, they have a fleeting sense that they've seen it somewhere before.*
>
> *The fifth time, they actually read the ad.*
>
> *The sixth time they thumb their nose at it.*
>
> *The seventh time, they start to get a little irritated with it.*
>
> *The eighth time, they start to think, "Here's that confounded ad again."*

The ninth time, they start to wonder if they're missing out on something.

The tenth time, they ask their friends and neighbours if they've tried it.

The eleventh time, they wonder how the company is paying for all these ads.

The twelfth time, they start to think that it must be a good product.

The thirteenth time, they start to feel the product has value.

The fourteenth time, they start to remember wanting a product exactly like this for a long time.

The fifteenth time, they start to yearn for it because they can't afford to buy it.

The sixteenth time, they accept the fact that they will buy it sometime in the future.

The seventeenth time, they make a note to buy the product.

The eighteenth time, they curse their poverty for not allowing them to buy this terrific product.

The nineteenth time, they count their money very carefully.

The twentieth time prospects see the ad, they buy what is being offered."

Twenty times. Thomas Smith said it in 1885. Innocent Smoothies used it to get into Waitrose in the late '90s. And you can leverage it today. Remarketing is the easiest, most cost-effective way to get in front of the right people at least 20 times.

TL/DR:

Remarketing could be the highest-ROI generating, lowest hanging fruit in your nurture arsenal.

It leverages the mere-exposure effect to notch up those 20 (or more) touches that constitute effective frequency. Or, to explain that in plain English, it enables you to appear to be everywhere, and subconsciously build awareness (know), familiarity (like), and preference (trust) over the course of repeated sessions – like driving past the same billboard twice a day, every day for a month – only to discover that this same company have requested a meeting with you…

Oh, and you'll appear to be everywhere, but only to the right people.

NURTURE ASSETS: PR

Making a cow's arse of it

"I need a new phone. My old one's ____________," said Alexander Armstrong.

"Up a cow's bum!" replied Paul Merton.

My jaw dropped open and my social network feed went crazy. It was Friday night and I (along with around five million others) was watching Have I Got News For You, a comedy quiz panel show based around the week's news.

The minute I saw the "I need a new phone" caption appear on the screen, I thought it might be true. But no, surely not? And then Paul Merton confirmed it. They were talking about *me*. My company. My story.

In that week, my little mobile phone insurance website had full-page articles in the Sun, the Daily Mail, the Express, the Metro, the Star, the Times, and the Telegraph, as well as being discussed on LBC, Radio Two, Channel Five's The Wright Stuff, and Loose Women. And now the cherry on top – to be part of the missing words round on Have I Got News For You. Primetime BBC One.

I'd employed a PR agency a few months earlier and each week we'd meet and discuss an angle to send out press releases to journalists in the hope of getting some coverage – some exposure. We'd had some mild successes, with the odd story being picked up here and there and a nice couple of links to our website, which (at the time) helped massively with our SEO assets.

One week, we dug into the old claims forms to see what funny excuses customers had given to explain their damaged or lost mobile phones and collated the top ten most ludicrous – including a pyrotechnician who last saw his mobile attached to a firework as it launched 300ft in the air and exploded, a lady who baked her Nokia 6303i into a Victoria sponge, and a couple who dropped their camera phone into the ocean while trying to recreate the "I'm the king of the world!" scene from Titanic.

But what captured most people's attention was the cow's arse. A farmer was using the torch function of his iPhone to help him birth a calf in the middle of the night. The following morning, he couldn't find his phone, so he called it from the landline. Sure enough, there was a muffled ringing noise coming from inside Daisy and the farmer had to retrieve his phone from the new mother – and it never worked quite the same again.

Within 24 hours of sending out the press release, we'd had full-page stories in every major newspaper, national radio interviews, and TV coverage, culminating in that "missing words" round appearance on HIGNFY. Within a week, the story had gone global, being picked up by media in Australia, Canada, and the US. Reader's Digest asked to include it in their next magazine and our website traffic went through the roof.

On a typical day, we'd get a couple of hundred visitors to the website. At the height of the story, we were close to 50,000 a day. I upgraded the server to cope with demand and waited for the sales to roll in.

After a week and nearly 250,000 visitors to the website, I added up the number of sales that we could directly track back to the PR. It was three. Three hundred? Three thousand? No, it was just three. Three sales, worth a total of about £180.

Oh.

Like any Evergreen Asset, good PR is not a numbers game, it's a relationships game. It's not about 15 minutes of fame. It's about building long-term relationships with the right people, who have access to your target market.

A few years after the cow's bum fiasco, I was trying to get press coverage for my first book, *Big Ideas... for Small Businesses*. There were no national newspapers writing about me this time, Reader's Digest didn't call, I wasn't invited onto Radio 2 and wasn't featured on HIGNFY that week. Instead, I had a few lifestyle bloggers write about the book, a few dozen podcast interviews, a half-page article in the local newspaper, and a 25-minute live interview on BBC Radio Devon.

All in all, a much smaller affair. But not when it came to sales. All these PR assets combined to help propel the book to the bestseller lists in its first week of publication. I sold a lot more books than I did mobile phone insurance policies from a tiny fraction of the media coverage. I can also track several clients with a decent four-figure lifetime value back to that article in the local paper.

How can a half-page in the Plymouth Herald outsell a full-page in The Sun? While The Sun article was an amusing story for the masses, it didn't do anything to convince people that they needed mobile phone insurance or that I was the person to solve that problem for them. I wasn't fishing where the fish were. I was in my tiny little dingy, 20 miles out in the open ocean.

My Plymouth Herald appearance, in contrast, was in their dedicated "Business" pull-out. It has a much smaller readership than The Sun, but almost every one of those readers is my target market – small business owners looking to improve their business.

While The Sun article focused on cow's bums, Titanic FUBARs and pyrotechnic mishaps, the Herald was much more on-message for me, with the headline "Teaching secrets of success comes from thinking big" and the article telling those small business owners what's in it for them by reading the book:

> *"John Lamerton has built a business making a £400,000 annual profit – and written a bestselling book telling you how he did it...*
>
> *Ninety-nine per cent of small business owners aren't living the lifestyle they want. They're working harder than they want to, for less money than they want. They don't enjoy their work, and they don't get to spend quality time with their family.*
>
> *This book is a how-to guide for anyone who strives for that perfect work/life balance... Big Ideas for Small Businesses is available to buy on Amazon, priced £5.99 for the Kindle version, and £12.99 for the paperback."*

The Sun gave me lots of "exposure" with a vague, fun angle, while the Plymouth Herald put my key sales message in front of my target market.

Press Releases are NOT Evergreen Assets

What do you call an email that's sent to a bunch of people you don't know in the vain hope that some of them might read it (and one of them may even take action on it)?

a. A press release?
b. Spam?

Journalists receive a never-ending flood of generic, unsolicited, unfocused pitches, dressed up as important press releases every hour of every day. Most of them don't even get opened, let alone considered. If you want to get a journalist's attention, why would you do the same as everyone else? Why would you think the best strategy would be to throw enough shit at the wall and hope that some of it sticks?

PR is not a numbers game. It's a relationships game. Build relationships with the right people, the right journalists, working for the right media outlets, who have the ear of your target market. Find out what they (the journalists) want. This could be eyeballs on their articles, a quote, a particular people story, a case study, or some research. Go and get it, and give it to them.

Press releases are not Evergreen Assets, but relationships with the right journalists certainly are. Build evergreen relationships with a handful of the right people.

Since my appearance on BBC Radio Devon, I've been invited back onto the same show a dozen times because we've created a win-win situation. I get to position myself as the expert and the producer of the show can fill anything from 20 to 45 minutes of programming with a guest who won't freeze on live radio, has some interesting stories to tell, and who will only occasionally prattle on for so long that they're late for the 11am news.

What do they want? Good, entertaining, light-hearted content for their listeners. Not a sales pitch. Sure, I'm there to talk about my books and will, of course, mention once or twice that my books are available to buy if listeners are interested. But first, I've got to make them interested. And that means being interesting and leaving the sales pitch at home. Find out what they want. Go and get it. Give it to them.

That half-page article in the local paper came about after I had lunch with the business editor. I regularly comment on and share his LinkedIn posts (what does he want? More eyeballs for his articles), we discuss local business issues any time we meet up (where I can demonstrate my knowledge and passion for small businesses) and I remind him anytime he needs a quick article (or even a 15-word quote) on work/life balance, lifestyle businesses, working from home, routines or anything affecting small businesses that I'm his man.

Again, what does he want? Half a page for Wednesday's pull-out? Another 25 words for this article? A contrasting viewpoint for that article? Some stats about business books? I can help him with all of those things. Most people fire off a press release, only ever thinking about themself. Stop spamming the entire media industry and build genuine win-win relationships with the handful of the right people for you.

Making a silk purse from a cow's arse

You may think my foray into PR with the "cow's bum" story was an epic failure. And in terms of the immediate ROI (three sales from a ton of national and international coverage), you'd be right. But there's another hidden nurture benefit of PR that many neglect to count – the huge amount of trust that comes from having been featured in the Press.

In the weeks after the cow's bum story, we noticed our SEO rankings had improved considerably. This was back in the days when Google treated a link *to* your website as a vote *for* your website. The more links you had, and the better quality these links were, the higher you could climb the rankings. Over the course of three or four weeks, we picked up dozens of new links and all from massive media websites, newspapers, radio stations, prominent industry blogs, you name it.

We also updated our own website with a little "as seen on" section and included the logos of the media who had written (or spoken) about us. This enables the human brain to create a shortcut. I trust Radio 2, therefore if Radio 2 are talking about you, I trust you too.

When we add "as seen on" sections to any of our websites, it increases conversions without fail. Once you've had some coverage, you'll make more sales and get a greater ROI by proudly displaying it on your website for years to come, turning tomorrow's chip paper into an Evergreen Asset.

TL/DR:

Very few things increase trust quicker or more reliably than press coverage.

PR is not a numbers game, it's a relationships game. It's about building long-term relationships with the right people, who have your future customer's eyes and ears. Spewing out crappy press releases isn't a PR strategy – it's spam. Find the right people. Find out what they want. Give it to them. When you get coverage, proudly display it for all potential customers to see. That's how you turn PR from 15 minutes of fame into an Evergreen Asset.

Oh, and don't make a cow's arse of it.

NURTURE ASSETS: VIDEO

How to be a YouTuber

Video is a tremendous Nurture Asset because it allows people to see you, your emotion, and your passion. They can tell whether you're winging it or truly know your shit. When it comes to video, there's nowhere to hide. And that's what makes it so powerful.

Video enables prospective customers to see behind the scenes. If they want to, they can find out how the sausage is made. They can watch the journey they themselves would go on if they were to become a customer by walking in current customers' shoes, watching their stories, and their experiences. They can feel like they know you, like you, and trust you – all from watching enough of your video content.

YouTube is the world's second largest search engine. You may not have thought of it as a search engine before, but it receives more than three billion searches per month – more than Bing, Yahoo, AOL and Ask.com combined. A large proportion of those searches begin with one word: how.

> How to draw.
>
> How to tie a tie.
>
> How to lose weight fast.
>
> How to cut your own hair.
>
> How to assemble a trampoline.
>
> How do you cook scallops?
>
> How should you clean your ears? (I'm not sure I want to watch that particular video).

If your target market wants to know *how* to do anything, then YouTube could be the perfect platform for you to demonstrate *how* you can help solve their problem.

Video isn't just YouTube, though

I've just looked and I have 201 subscribers on YouTube. Only another 999,799 until I get my golden play button. Most of my videos get fewer than 100 views. I'm not going to be a famous YouTuber anytime soon.

But I do produce regular video content that takes people through the nurture process. I've got a welcome video on the homepage of my website to explain who I am, what I do, and (most importantly) how I can help you. That video has been viewed tens of thousands of times.

The video recording of every episode of the ALB podcast is also uploaded every month to my website, social networks, and YouTube.

Where video properly kicks the arse of anything else, though, is one-to-one communication. Often, I'll reply to an email or a message not with text, but with a video. I use a piece of software called Loom, which enables me to record short videos with one click from my Gmail inbox. I often find this easier and quicker than manually typing a reply and the impact is ten times that of a text reply. It saves my fingers and gets responses like, "Wow, didn't expect that", "That made my day!" and "Really powerful – thanks for the video". Responses I wouldn't have had if I'd said the exact same words in an email.

When everyone else says "Happy Birthday Neil!" on Facebook, I send Neil a 30-second video, expressing my best wishes for his big day, sharing some inside jokes, and asking him (fairly) tongue in cheek to save me some cake.

Thirty seconds to record and ten seconds to send via direct message. About the same time it would take me and my sausage-like fingers to tap out "Happy Birthday Neil!" on my phone but it has so much more of an impact.

When was the last time one of your Facebook friends posted about your "Happy Birthday!" comment? Here's what happened when I sent a video recently:

"Just got sent a little video from the legend that is John Lamerton. Made me realise how out of the loop I've become about keeping in contact with people. Was a lovely surprise and very thoughtful. Top work John!"

Include some video in your Never-Ending Nurture Sequence. Ninety per cent of my "30-day routine challenge" from my last book was delivered via pre-recorded short videos. All rough and ready, mostly recorded in one-take and full of "umms" and "ahhs".

In my opinion, rough and ready wins the day when it comes to video. Good really is good enough. Use your phone. Record it in one take (unless you say anything stupid or libellous) – people love the authenticity of umms, ahhs, getting words wrong, mind-blanks, and going off on tangents. It's genuine, and builds relationships in a way that a highly-polished, perfectly-scripted, too-good-to-be-true, Spielberg-esque version could never do.

Also, lose the script and leave the autocue to Ron Burgundy. I was asked to critique a video that Dave, a One Percenter, had recorded. He'd written a great script, framed the shot brilliantly, dressed in his best branded clothing, combed his hair, and then delivered the most wooden performance since Nicolas Cage's last movie.

"Dave, lose the script mate. Be you. Imagine you're talking to me, not to a camera. You know what you want to say, so stop trying to be word-perfect, and just talk to me."

Once Dave did this, he was able to be himself – full of his natural character, charm, and wit – and spent his time looking into the camera (making eye contact with his audience) rather than at his script.

Just about every platform – websites, email, WhatsApp, Facebook, Twitter, LinkedIn, Instant Messenger, etc – has embraced video content. Isn't it about time you did?

TL/DR:

Deliver the same content via video and it can have ten times the impact.

Video conveys tone, especially passion and emotion. It's a great way for prospective customers to peek behind the scenes and see how the sausage is made. YouTube is the world's second largest search engine, especially for "how to" searches, but video is about so much more than YouTube – and can be leveraged just about everywhere for a greater impact.

Oh, just remember to lose the script, and keep it rough and ready.

NURTURE ASSETS SUMMARY

I don't know who you are. I don't know your company. I don't know your company's product. I don't know what your company stands for. I don't know your company's customers. I don't know your company's record. I don't know your company's reputation. Now, what was it you wanted to sell me?

What's Joe bloody Wicks MBE got that you haven't? Millions of people who know, like and trust him, that's what. Send weekly emails (but don't sell in them and don't be a dickhead). Find out what they want and start two-way conversations.

Your website is not about you. It's about the problems you can solve for people like us, who buy things like this – and the world's worst website is still better than yours. Awards are a shortcut to trust (if you can trust the awards organiser).

Be in control of what people see when they google your business. Dig the social networking well before you get thirsty. If you want your own podcast, be Sir Terry Wogan or Basil Fawlty. If you want the minimum effective dose, be a guest on someone else's show.

Writing (and selling) a book could be the best business card you ever had, while a printed newsletter reminds people that you exist and that you're bloody good at what you do. Remarketing could be the highest-ROI generating, lowest hanging fruit in your nurture arsenal. PR is not a numbers game, it's a relationships game – and don't forget to turn your 15 minutes of fame into an Evergreen Asset. Video is a great way for people to know, like and trust you, because they can see whether you know your shit or know you're shit. Lose the script and be you.

With enough Nurture Assets in place, I now know who you are. I know your company. I know your company's product. I know what your company stands for. I know your company's customers. I know your company's record. I know your company's reputation. I know, like and trust you. Now, what was it you wanted to sell me?

5. SALES ASSETS

Once you've captured a lead and that prospect knows, likes, and trusts you, they should (in theory) be ready to whip their credit card out, yelling "shut up and take my money" as they eagerly devour your product or service. Of course, in reality, it's not quite that simple, but if you've worked hard on your Nurture Assets, it'll be a hell of a lot easier to ask for the sale than if you haven't.

There's a balance to be struck. Too much nurture and not enough asking for the sale, and you're going to be a busy fool, creating content for content's sake, and still not making any money. Not enough nurture and too much asking for the sale and people will label you as a slimy salesman and start avoiding your calls.

Nurture and Sales Assets are like salt and pepper. If you're cooking a meal, you'll add some seasoning. If you don't, you end up with a bland, tasteless mess. Add too much, and you'll make people gag. Either way, no one's coming back to your restaurant anytime soon.

Hungry, Sir?

Most years, we go for a family holiday in Tenerife. It's hot and sunny, the beaches are great, and the kids love racing each other up and down the long seaside promenades.

There's just one thing that niggles me about Tenerife – the restaurant owners. We've not had any stand-up rows with any of them, we've not had food poisoning and they've not caused any real distress. They've just added too much "sales salt" to their recipe and no nurture seasoning whatsoever.

Indeed, it would appear that the only weapon they have in their "marketing for restaurants" arsenal is desperately trying to drag people in against their will, so they spend all day doing that.

"Hungry sir?"

"No, thanks mate," I reply, flashing my all-inclusive band, and pointing to the hotel from which I've just emerged. "We're all-inclusive at the hotel just there."

"Maybe just a burger then?"

"No thanks mate."

"Beer? Cocktail? Coffee? Ice Cream?"

"No, thank you."

"Come back tonight! We have the best steaks in town!"

He continues shouting after me as I keep walking. Three seconds later, the next restaurant owner on the strip is waving his menu in my face.

"Welcome family. Something to eat? Lunch? Beer?"

Grrr...

When you haven't added any nurture salt to your recipe (like our Tenerifian restaurant-owning friends), you join the race to the bottom with discounted prices ("€1 pint of beer"), and a salesperson every bit as talented as Old Gil from The Simpsons ("How many can I put 'ya down for? A lot? Please say a lot. I need this. The wolf's at Old Gil's door...") scaring potential customers away with their sheer desperation.

If you've ever walked down the strip in Playa de Las Americas, you'll know just how many bars and restaurants are taking part in that race to the bottom. While there one day, I was stopped in my tracks by a bustling, almost-full restaurant, where everyone seemed to be enjoying a relaxing drink, ice cream or the best steaks in town – and no Old Gil in sight.

What did this establishment have that the desperate owner in the bar next door didn't? A welcoming atmosphere, for one. Plus lots of repeat customers, good branding and, as it turned out, a good online presence (Google My Business, social networks, TripAdvisor reviews, etc). They had a marketing plan. They had enough nurture seasoning in the recipe to complement their sales salt, and make the whole recipe work perfectly.

We considered stopping there for a coffee, but couldn't because they were full. Not a spare seat in the house and not a "€1 pint of beer" in sight.

Ready to add a little sales salt to your Evergreen Assets recipe?

ONE SALES ASSET TO RULE THEM ALL: AN OFFER THEY CAN'T REFUSE

> *Michael: "My father went to see this bandleader and offered him $10,000 to let Johnny go, but the bandleader said no. So the next day, my father went back, only this time with Luca Brasi. Within an hour, he had a signed release for a certified check of $1,000."*
>
> *Kay: "How did he do that?"*
>
> *Michael: "My father made him an offer he couldn't refuse."*
>
> *Kay: "What was that?"*
>
> *Michael: "Luca Brasi held a gun to his head, and my father assured him that either his brains or his signature would be on the contract."*

That scene from The Godfather remains one of the most memorable in movie history and the line, "I'm gonna make him an offer he can't refuse" uttered by Marlon Brando's character later in the movie was voted the second most-quoted line of all time. (First was Gone With The Wind's "Frankly, my dear, I don't give a damn!", which ironically represents most prospects' response to your current marketing efforts).

Unlike Don Vito Corleone, we're looking to make a different type of no-brainer offer that's infinitely more appealing to the recipient – an Offer They Can't Refuse because it's so good, not because the alternative is so bad.

In order to make an Offer They Can't Refuse, we first need to know why they would refuse. After all, you're awesome at what you do and you know, beyond a shadow of a doubt, that you can get results for your clients. If only they would give you a fair crack of the whip.

You know that but they don't. They know that they've only just met you. They know that they've made mistakes in the past. They know they've bought stuff and then immediately wished they hadn't. They know that most companies they've worked with before over-promised and under-delivered. They know that they might look foolish if they get this buying decision wrong.

With everything that could go wrong if they go ahead and purchase, it's little wonder that the default, safe answer is always going to be "No". Not buying and just staying where you are is ultimately safer than taking a chance and running the risk of making a mistake.

This emotional fear can be resolved by designing an Offer They Can't Refuse based on the actual reasons your customers might refuse to buy. When their primitive brain is trying to keep them safe and prevent them from making a mistake, your Offer They Can't Refuse must be a true no-brainer – one that quietens down the automatic "fight or flight" response (and when it comes to buying decisions, it's almost always flight).

Many of the Sales Assets that follow will do battle with specific objections. In order to make your sales salt as effective as it can be (so you just need a pinch, rather than tablespoons of the stuff), you should first brainstorm why your prospective customers are refusing to buy from you and then tailor your Offer They Can't Refuse specifically for *your* prospects and *their* objections. One size fits all, this ain't.

The best marketers in the world do one simple thing, over and over again. They find out the exact reasons people aren't buying from them and then counter those objections. They don't guess – they find out the real reasons, from real prospects, and then use that information to improve their assets.

If prospects don't know what your product or service does, then explain it to them. If they know what it does, but aren't sure why they'd ever need it then explain the benefits. If they don't believe that it'll do what you claim, add proof (or a guarantee). If they think it's too expensive, justify the price (or guarantee the results). If they don't trust you, direct them to your Nurture Assets. If they "want to think about it", find out exactly what they're thinking about (what objections you haven't yet overcome) and give them a deadline.

Make them an Offer They Can't Refuse. If they reply with "Frankly, my dear, I don't give a damn!", then go back to the drawing board. Eventually, you should be able to negate their greatest fears and objections and present them with a "no brainer" offer they simply cannot refuse, where their natural reaction will be "shut up and take my money".

Let's look at some of the Sales Assets that could be part of your Offer They Can't Refuse.

SALES ASSETS: A PROVEN FRAMEWORK

Why aren't people buying? Because they're afraid. Afraid they might make a mistake. Afraid that it might not work. Afraid that it might not be suitable for them. Something doesn't feel right and they're afraid of looking foolish, losing money, or having wasted their time.

In your Nurture Assets, you demonstrated you can deliver what they want through case studies, testimonials, awards, and reviews. But for a prospect to buy into the end result, it still requires quite a large leap of faith – a leap too far for many people, who will take the easy option and do nothing.

A personal trainer can showcase all the client case studies they want, proudly showing off the client who lost 70lbs, the lady who dropped three dress sizes, and the gent who completely reversed his type-two diabetes. But prospective clients will still be afraid: "Losing 70lbs must have been hard work. I'm not sure I could do what they did. I bet they had to stick rigidly to a rabbit food diet for months on end. There's no way that would work for me."

Meanwhile, you *know* it would work for them. How do you know? Because you've got a Proven Framework. The step-by-step pathway that you take all clients through. A process that you know if they do step one, followed by step two, and then step three, they'll get a consistent, predictable result. If they continue on the pathway, they'll continue their progress, and end up at their desired destination – 70lbs lighter, a new wardrobe, and no more insulin injections.

If you try to take your prospects from Step 0 (where they are today) to Step 157 (where they ultimately want to be) with no explanation of how they're going to get there, they will automatically fill that gap with "I can't do that".

Like Back To The Future's Dr Emmett Brown, you must take your prospects on a journey in time to show them what to expect when they work with you. If you take them too far into the future, you create too large a gap, their brain will spot the huge disconnect, and they'll call BS: "What do you mean 'flying cars, hoverboards and self-lacing shoes?'."

But if you show them their future step-by-step-by-step along a Proven Framework, their brain will look at each small step and think: "Yep, that sounds doable. I can close that gap."

Remember Joe bloody Wicks MBE? He's got a Proven Framework for closing that gap. He calls it the Body Coach 90 Day Plan. That gap just narrowed – it's now just 90 days wide. He then explains the 90 days consist of three, 30-day cycles. Narrower still. Joe tells you what to expect and counters objections left, right and centre along the way:

> *"This is not a low calorie, restrictive diet..."*
>
> *"...you won't be going hungry."*
>
> *"Includes burgers, curries, pancakes and other favourites."*
>
> *"Train between 25-35 minutes."*
>
> *"Work out when and where it suits you."*

Could I do a few workouts and eat burgers, curries, and pancakes for the next 30 days? Hell yeah, I could! Having put me in that frame of mind and countering all my objections, what Joe does next is genius.

> *"How it works:*
>
> 1. *Start with a questionnaire.*
> 2. *We'll tailor your plan.*
> 3. *Training and nutrition cycles.*
> 4. *Graduation and sustaining results."*

Or to put that another way:

1. *Tell us what you want.*
2. *We'll go and get it.*
3. *You follow the Proven Framework.*
4. *You'll get what you want.*

If I hit the "get started" button on Joe's website, I take the first step on his Proven Framework, which is simply filling out a questionnaire. Brilliant! There's no Lycra or steamed broccoli required for this first step. The gap to step two is just as small and easily made, and I now have momentum behind me.

A Proven Framework provides the step-by-step pathway. "Do this, then do that. Many others (just like you) have followed this framework before. Just follow me to this next step."

It's a lot less scary than taking a punt on the unknown.

A Mickey Mouse Framework

A few years ago, we went on a family holiday to Orlando, Florida. We'd spent a lot of money on this trip, would only be there for 16 days and wanted to do everything – Magic Kingdom, Epcot, Universal Studios, Animal Kingdom, Islands of Adventure, Disney Springs, SeaWorld, International Drive, Blizzard Beach, Hollywood Studios, Kennedy Space Center – you name it, it was on our list.

To help us avoid mistakes, we bought a book, *The Brit Guide to Orlando 2017* by Simon and Susan Veness. Talk about an Evergreen Asset, Simon and Susan have been producing the *Brit Guide to Orlando* book every year since 1996. Every year, it receives rave reviews, sells tens of thousands of copies, and delivers a Proven Framework to enjoy the holiday of a lifetime.

A family holiday to Orlando requires something bordering on a military operation. As the Venesses say in their latest *Brit Guide to Orlando*:

> *"In simple terms, there are eight major theme parks, and several need two days to enjoy fully. Add a day at a water park, a trip to one of the nature attractions and the lure of the*

Kennedy Space Center, and you already have two full weeks of pure adventure mania.

Mix in the night-time fun of Disney Springs, Universal's Citywalk and a host of dinner shows, plus superb shopping, and you start to understand the awesome scope of the place. Even with two weeks, something has to give – just make sure it isn't your patience, wallet – or sanity.

The key to all this is planning. On pages 345-46 is a handy outline guide for a typical two-week stay."

That outline guide is Simon and Susan's Proven Framework. They've been planning trips to Orlando for themselves, and for thousands of other Brits, for decades now. They know what works and what doesn't. They know what makes a holiday memorable and what makes one miserable. When you buy their book, you get a blank version of that Proven Framework, so that you won't make a mistake when planning your trip to Orlando.

By including a blank DIY template in a relatively cheap book, they're again leveraging a tripwire to better position themselves to sell their core service – a full, Done For You version of their Proven Framework.

"If you want to make sure you get the most out of your holiday without wasting time or money, let us help with our unique Touring Plans," they cheerfully announce in the introduction.

We did just that when planning our trip to Orlando and it made things much easier following a Proven Framework. We knew our time was optimised. We were visiting each park on its typically quietest day of the week, when crowds (aka queues) were smaller. We factored in rest days, shopping days, and minimised travelling. As a result of following Simon and Susan's Proven Framework, we spent less time driving and queuing, and more time riding roller coasters and meeting Mickey and Donald.

What a brilliant lifestyle business Simon and Susan have created. They love Disney and they love Florida, so they built a business around their passion. They're effectively selling a spreadsheet but it's a spreadsheet that leverages their quarter of a century of Florida holidays, delivering a Proven Framework.

If you're going to spend a huge sum of money on a once-in-a-lifetime family holiday, you don't want to get it wrong. So buying a Proven Framework that thousands of families just like you have used before takes away most, if not all, of that risk.

SALES ASSETS: A GUARANTEE

If you are as good as you say you are, why not take the risk away from your customer and put it on yourself? Put your money where your mouth is and guarantee the results your customers want.

Guarantees do two things:

1. Reduce risk for the customer. If your product or service doesn't do what you say it will, they will be compensated. They won't lose out.
2. Demonstrate your confidence in your product or service. After all, you'll be out of pocket if you fail to deliver on your promises and out of business if you had to consistently pay out on guarantees.

A *really* strong guarantee also does a third thing:

3. It promises the customer that if they don't get the specific results they want, they'll not only not be out of pocket but be better off.

This is the difference between "we offer a money-back guarantee" and the following, which I used to increase sales of a product in my sports betting business:

> *"If you can't honestly say that my Inner Circle has made you a more professional punter, more astute, and better equipped to make more informed strategic betting decisions – all within the first 100 days of your membership, then I'll happily refund TWICE what you've paid me.*
>
> *If you don't enjoy results every bit as good as the testimonials on this page, then frankly, I don't deserve to keep your money. You have every right to ask for a full, no-questions-asked, on-the-spot refund of DOUBLE what you've paid me.*
>
> *Furthermore, if you do decide you want a refund at any point in the first 100 days of your Inner Circle membership, there'll be absolutely no questions asked, and no hard feelings whatsoever on my part."*

Heads you win, tails you don't lose (and still double your money).

It's got nothing to do with Vorsprung durch Technik, you know?

My wife bought a second-hand car online…from a dealer 215 miles away…without test driving it.

She's never bought a car this way before. She doesn't buy huge, expensive items like cars, unseen over the internet. Not a chance. There's just too much risk. What if it's a lemon? What if the seats are uncomfortable? What if something goes wrong?

Well, the dealer offered a 14-day, no-questions-asked, money-back guarantee. Mrs L enquired and, sure enough, she can hand the car back for any reason whatsoever. Just changed her mind? Not a problem, we'll come and pick it up. Don't like the colour? Simply hand the keys back.

Boom! The sale was closed. A sale that absolutely would not have happened without the guarantee and, more importantly, without further clarification on that guarantee.

I'd bet you the value of a second-hand Audi A4 that they could increase sales by changing the words "14-day money-back guarantee" to "If you're not completely in love with your new car, if it doesn't make you beam with pride every time you jump in the driver's seat, then simply let us know, and we'll come and pick it up and either swap it for another one or give you a full refund. We want you to love your new wheels, so take it for a two-week test drive and if you don't love it – for any reason whatsoever – just let us know and we'll hand your money back. Every penny of it."

Due to remote selling regulations, they're obliged to give a 14-day "cooling off" period whereby customers can cancel for any reason, but surely they genuinely want their customers to love their new cars and to return again to buy their next one? By shouting about the guarantee, highlighting the specific outcome that buyers want, and making clear that the company will be out of pocket if they fail to deliver on that specific promise, they shift all the risk of this transaction from the customer to themselves.

And they wouldn't do that unless they were confident about delivering on that result, would they?

If you're dropping a serious amount of money on a car, a guarantee is a must and will definitely increase conversions. But what about a lower value product, like a milkshake? You wouldn't expect a guarantee on a milkshake, would you?

How about a £20 milkshake? Suddenly, risk comes into play now, doesn't it? You don't want to lose twenty quid on a crap shake. But you're also curious and I'll bet a "best milkshake you've ever tasted or it's on the house" guarantee would help seal the deal.

The more risk you ask customers to take, trusting you to deliver on your promises, the more beneficial a specific, more-than-your-money-back guarantee will be. Keep the milkshake *and* your money.

But what if people claim?

Well, firstly, the uplift in conversions should far outweigh the number of guarantee claims. Fifty to 100 per cent increases in conversions are typical, with an increased refund rate of two to three per cent.

Secondly, you're only going to pay out on unhappy customers. If you didn't have a guarantee in place, those customers would still be unhappy! Why wouldn't you want the chance to make things right with them? If your product or service really is that good, then you shouldn't need to worry about refunds or claims.

Putting my money where my mouth is

Remember our sports coach who said: "I know I can help people, but no one's buying"? Well, guess what? He doesn't have a guarantee. If he did, more people would buy and if he truly can help them as he claims, it won't cost him a penny.

I put a similar "more-than-your-money-back" guarantee in place for my group coaching business and it increased conversions by around 25 per cent. Not only that, but (at the time of writing), I haven't had a single person claim their money back. Here's what I said in my guarantee:

> *"I'm confident that the One Percent Way principles will create a more effective, less stressful way of growing your business.*
>
> *They've worked for me. They've worked for Jason. They've worked for hundreds of One Percenters.*

> *And I believe they'll work for you.*
>
> *My belief is that strong, that I'm willing to put my money where my mouth is (and risk taking food off my children's plates), and offer a rather unique guarantee:*
>
> *If you join the One Percent Club and after three months feel that your business and/or lifestyle isn't in a significantly better place, then I'll refund every single penny you've paid me."*

Note my use of a Proven Framework (the One Percent Way), specifically labelling the results customers can expect (a more effective, less stressful, lifestyle business), pointing out the risk to me (taking food off my children's plates), and offering more-than-your-money-back (they get to attend three months' worth of coaching calls, keep our World Domination planner, download a ton of resources, and get their money back).

I've opted for a 90-day guarantee for the One Percent Club. Sarah's Audi came with a 14-day guarantee, Inner Circle offered 100 days. The coffee cup I'm drinking my flat white from is guaranteed for ten years, while a Zippo lighter I bought 20 years ago is guaranteed for life (I quit smoking before the lighter gave up).

A 100-day guarantee will probably sell more than a 14-day one, but may cost a lot more in claims. There will be a sweet spot unique to your business whereby the number of sales is maximised without being negated by stupidly high refund rates. You can find it by testing different guarantee periods, taking into account three factors:

1. The conversion rate for a sale.
2. The refund rate.
3. The cost of a refund/repair.

Offering a five-year warranty may maximise conversions, but if you know the product is designed to last three to four years, you're creating a ticking time bomb for yourself. Conversely, I've seen plenty of products that are engineered to last for decades, sold with a measly one-year guarantee. These guys could massively increase their conversions with a five-year (or even ten-year) guarantee and it wouldn't cost them a penny.

Many people worry that offering a robust guarantee will cost them more than it will make them. In my experience, this couldn't be further from the truth. Yes, you will have to process more refunds and make things right for more people but only for people who would still be unhappy with your product or service anyway.

Would you rather not know that you've let them down and have the opportunity to put things right? Almost every time I've put a robust, clearly-defined, more-than-your-money-back guarantee in place, I've increased sales at a rate five to ten times that of any increase in refunds and repairs.

Such a guarantee can also act as The Right Bait if you're selling on someone else's platform (Amazon, eBay, Etsy, etc.) and don't get access to your customers' data. Offering an extended warranty or guaranteed results when customers register with you can make sure they're in *your* ecosystem as well as Amazon's or eBay's – allowing you to make repeat sales without the middleman.

TL/DR:

A guarantee puts your money where your mouth is. It reduces risk to the customer and demonstrates your confidence in your product/service.

A good guarantee offers customers more than their money back, promising that if they don't get the specific results they want, you'll be out of pocket while they'll be better off.

A guarantee is a promise to make things right (or more than right) if they go wrong. Without a guarantee, things will still go wrong and customers will still be unhappy. Why wouldn't you want to make things right? A good guarantee should significantly increase conversions, while marginally increasing your refund (or repair) rates. Test different guarantees to find your sweet spot.

Oh, and does anyone know where I can find a £20 milkshake?

SALES ASSETS: A SMALL TASTE

Would you like to try some fudge?

Living in Devon, we're blessed with an abundance of fudge shops (it must be all that clotted cream we've got knocking about the place) and since having children, we seem to now be incapable of walking past a fudge shop without being drawn in. It started when we were offered a free taste of a freshly-made batch. It was so good, we headed straight to the store, armed with a tripwire card (more about that in the next section), and bought several bags of sugary goodness.

My kids can sniff out the sample-givers from half a mile away and chase them down, ensuring they taste every flavour at least twice. As sales tactics go, letting prospects try before they buy is (literally) tried and tested.

Here are some of the comments from our local fudge shop's TripAdvisor reviews:

> *"Lady was very friendly and helpful, letting us taste flavours first."*
>
> *"We stumbled across the shop after a young lad was handing out free samples just down the hill."*
>
> *"A member of staff was on the street handing out samples of their Clotted Cream Fudge and it was delicious! Before*

> *sampling, I really wasn't sure if I wanted to buy any, but couldn't say no after the first taste."*

What happened in that last review from a customer who "wasn't really sure" if they wanted to buy any fudge, but then "couldn't say no" after trying a free sample?

The fudge company took away all the customer's risks, such as:

> *"I might not like the fudge."*
>
> *"I might choose the wrong flavour."*
>
> *"It might be too sweet."*
>
> *"It's quite expensive and I'm not sure if it's worth the money."*

Now, as well as removing risk, those sneaky fudge-pushers are using a known psychological phenomenon called the reciprocity principle to trick you into walking into the shop and purchasing a bag of fudge. If someone does something for you, you feel obligated to return the favour – to reciprocate. And that's how you find yourself munching on 200g of sea salt and honeycomb fudge.

You'd think giving away a free sample would be easy, but I've seen many people get it wrong including a fudge seller here in Plymouth. Their first mistake was that they were focused on the cost of providing samples. They worked especially hard to slice their fudge as thinly as possible, giving each person the smallest possible taste. They were so stingy, they killed the reciprocity effect completely.

The second (and more fatal) blow was that their product simply wasn't very good. The whole point of a free sample is that giving prospects a small taste for free demonstrates your product is so good, so must-have, that they immediately whip out their credit card and demand to buy the full-size version. That simply won't happen if customers aren't impressed with what they taste.

Don't just deliver

This almost seems too obvious, but when customers agree to give you a test drive, take a trial (free or paid), or claim their bonus(es), make sure you deliver on your promise.

In fact, don't just deliver – over deliver. Hold some bonuses back that you don't shout about before people become customers. If they're expecting one free chapter, give them three. If they're expecting a seven-day trial, give them ten.

Things that don't start well, don't tend to end well. You want the customer's first experience of working with you to be pleasurable, enjoyable, and rewarding. There's a reason my local fudge shop isn't dishing out free samples of their Marmite flavour!

Your product or service should be so good that, given a tiny morsel of the full product, customers come rushing back, cash in hand, demanding you take their money. Don't fall at the first hurdle and deliver a "meh" first taste.

Why you should trip your customers up

A word of advice when offering free samples – beware the freeloaders and tyre-kickers who taste every flavour twice, feel no pang of reciprocity whatsoever, and move on to sample the free cheese at the next stall, then the sausages at the next, and the organic cider after that. They're just after a free lunch.

You can separate the potential buyers from the tyre kickers with a tripwire offer, such as a low-cost paid trial.

It may only seem a small step up from charging £0.00 to charging £1 but it's a huge step psychologically. Even if they've only paid you £1, they've still gone past the tipping point of becoming a customer, handing over their credit card or cold, hard cash. They're no longer a prospect – they're now a paying customer.

Your tripwire offer could be the natural next step after a free trial.

Remember what happened when we first enjoyed our free samples of fudge? We were directed to the shop, no further than ten paces away, armed with a voucher that offered a discount on our first purchase. We liked the samples and the natural next step was to become a paying customer. The tripwire offer ensured that happened.

You could offer a tripwire trial instead of a free trial. You won't get anywhere near as many conversions as you would from a free trial, but whereas a free trial captures all prospects (including freeloaders, tyre-kickers, and low-value clients), a tripwire trial only captures paying customers. Once again, test for yourself and find your own sweet spot for your ecosystem.

I deploy various combinations of trials in my businesses. For my group coaching business that might be a free sample chapter of one of my books, free blog posts, free resources and downloads, and free episodes of the Ambitious Lifestyle Business podcast.

In our sports betting business, we offer a free 30-day trial of our entry-level service and then offer a "half-price first month" tripwire trial just to those guys. After their tripwire trial has ended, they go onto the full membership. We go from free trial to tripwire trial to the full offer, turning prospects into customers and customers into loyal members.

TL/DR:

Try before you buy is tried and tested.

Allowing your prospects to take your product or service for a test drive delivers a one-two punch: it massively reduces the perceived risk in the customer's mind and it also creates a reciprocity imbalance. Don't be stingy with your samples and make sure they are good – don't lead with the Marmite fudge! Get rid of freeloaders and tyre-kickers by having a paid tripwire trial.

Oh, and make sure you try the maple and pecan fudge...before you buy!

SALES ASSETS: MAKE IT EASY

After trying that free sample, would I have bought the fudge if the shop was a ten-minute walk away? Of course not. It's too hard. Too much effort. Too much friction.

If you want to sell more, make it easier for people to buy more.

The Bucket List Company is a travel agent with a difference. Instead of flogging a fortnight's all-inclusive in the Costa Del Sol, The Bucket List Company organises once-in-a-lifetime trips to places like Mount Everest Base Camp, Easter Island, and Machu Picchu.

Can you imagine the level of organisation that goes into planning a trek along the Great Wall of China, climbing Mount Kilimanjaro or white water rafting in Morocco?

The Bucket List Company takes something that is incredibly hard and scary and makes it seem easy and effortless. You pay £200 to secure your spot on any of their trips. Then the balance can be paid monthly, interest-free, over up to two years (depending on the date of your trip). They give you a list of everything you need to pack (and everything to leave at home), how to prepare for your adventure and how to make the most of it.

But more than anything, they take away all the fears, worries, and niggling doubts that could cause people not to buy. And they do that using just three words: "We do everything."

"Don't worry about it. We'll take care of everything. Sit back, relax. We'll take it from here. For £200, and a monthly Direct Debit, you're going to have the adventure of a lifetime."

The Bucket List Company has made it easy.

What can *you* do to make it easy for people to buy?

SALES ASSETS: A DEADLINE

> *"'Too late! Too late!' will be the cry, when the man with the bargains has passed you by," – Bacon (played by Jason Statham), Lock, Stock and Two Smoking Barrels.*

The humble deadline is one of my favourite Sales Assets because it gets people off the fence. Deadlines make us decide. They don't magically make people say yes, but they do make people say yes or no. Without a deadline, we'd never get around to doing anything.

We have to get our kids to school by 8:45am, our letters to Santa before Christmas, and our tax returns to HMRC by January 31st. Despite having ten months in which to submit a self-assessment return, Her Majesty's Revenue and Customs receives 45 per cent of returns (some 5.4million) in the final two weeks of January thanks to a rigid deadline, coupled with the threat of a minimum £100 fine, plus interest on anything you owe if you miss it.

What's the opposite of the taxman's set-in-stone, no-exceptions, once-a-year, January 31st deadline? Ladies and gentlemen of the jury, I present to you – the DFS sale.

"Hurry! Sale ends Monday!" the adverts proclaim. Yeah right, only so the next sale can start on Tuesday. We all know it's not a real deadline. Some might say it's not even a real sale. So why does DFS keep doing it?

Because it works. When DFS tells us that the sale ends on Monday, FOMO (Fear of Missing Out) kicks in and enough people spend their weekend trying-before-they-buy at their local retail park.

Laugh all you like at the "our Christmas Sale must end...so our January sale can begin" deadline. It works. DFS has a fantastic ecosystem of Evergreen Assets that it has honed and perfected over several years, so stop laughing and start taking notes.

Exclusive sofas in partnership with Grand Designs? That's The Right Bait to get you through the front door. Up to half price sale? That's an Offer You Can't Refuse. A showroom where you can sit on the sofa is try before you buy. Four years interest free with no deposit to pay is making it easy. Sale ends Monday is a deadline.

You can even deploy multiple deadlines. Often, I'll include "first-responder" deadlines (the first ten people to buy get a bonus), a "halfway" deadline (buy before a fixed date, midway through the campaign, and get an extra bonus), and a final deadline (like Cinderella's coach, all bonuses and special offers disappear at midnight).

It's designed so that there's always a reason to "act now". The people who buy straight out of the gate get the best deal, while for everyone else, there's never going to be a better time to buy than right now.

SALES ASSETS: EMAILS

The People's Elbow. Sweet Chin Music. Stone Cold Stunner.

You can't end a WWE wrestling match without a finisher – a signature move. Every superstar on the roster has one. Even Scotty Too Hotty, whose signature move "The Worm" somehow consisted of 30 seconds of breakdancing, culminating in a single chop that would inexplicably render his opponent unconscious for the three-count.

Your Signature Move will be much more powerful than The Worm. Your Signature Move is a piece of copy that you attach at the end of every email you send – including on your Never-Ending Nurture Sequence. It signposts your most popular products or services and enables anyone ready to buy to bypass your nurture sequence and kick things off immediately. It's an easy way for them to raise their hand and say: "Shut up and take my money."

Here's my Signature Move from our sports betting business:

> *"PLUS: Whenever you're ready, here are four ways you can make better betting decisions by having direct access to a team of in-form professional horse racing tipsters:*
>
> 1. *Check out today's tips. Our website is updated daily from Monday to Saturday with the Little Beauty, Premium Tip, Lucky 15, ITV Racing tips, and bonus tips for VIP members.*
> 2. *Unlock our best bet for the day – for free. The Premium Tip is our NAP or best bet of the day. Our super-secret, hush-hush, members only tip, for those who know a good strike rate when they see it. And you can get free lifetime access!*
> 3. *Get our daily Lucky 15. Our most popular, most exciting, fun-filled service ever – wild and unpredictable, it's a proper rollercoaster ride.*
> 4. *Check our results. We don't just sing when we're winning! Want to see every horse we've tipped – with full profit/loss?"*

I include links to all of the mentioned services, as well as contact details (email and telephone numbers for sales and support). Reading the copy, you'd be forgiven for thinking that it's an ad. But it's not treated as such, for a number of reasons.

1. It's included *after* the main body of the email, including after the "sign-off" where I include my closing salutations, my name, any relevant P.S., and the company logo. At a glance, the Signature Move is just part of the standard email footer.

2. Those opening three words – "Whenever you're ready..." completely disarm the reader, effectively saying "only read the following if and when you want to. If you're not ready to take

things further, this information isn't for you. If you're thinking 'shut up and take my money', here's what to do".

3. "Here are four ways you can..." It's not about us. It's about them *getting what they want.* I then label what they want and my Proven Framework for achieving that result.

Well-executed, your Signature Move can be every bit as devastating as a Stone Cold Stunner and it'll look a damn sight better than The Worm, too.

Milking the GOAT

In *Big Ideas... for Small Businesses*, I shared my Proven Framework for "the best email marketing campaign I ever ran". Five years later, I've turned it into an Evergreen Asset, sending the same tried-and-tested campaign to a new audience two or three times a year.

What started off as a well-executed email sales campaign turned into the Greatest Of All Time – especially when I review and improve the campaign every time. By sending up to three times a year, I'm well and truly milking the GOAT.

Here's a summary of the original Proven Framework, as described in greater detail in *Big Ideas...*:

1. Proper planning. Get the entire campaign on paper first.
2. Have a reason for the campaign. Your birthday. A relaunch. National Pie Week.
3. Add value, don't discount.
4. Multiple deadlines. Oh look, another Sales Asset!
5. Follow up – lots.
6. Counter objections and offer social proof (build nurture).
7. Use Multiple media. Online and offline.

8. Follow up some more.
9. Debrief the campaign and improve for next time.

Every time I get to Step 9 (debrief), I write down what I've learned from this campaign, what I want to do differently next time, any missed opportunities or things that worked especially well (or especially poorly) this time – and that almost automatically ticks off Step 1 (planning) for the next time I run the campaign.

For example, here are the bullet points from my debrief the last time I sent this asset out:

- Don't skip the warm-up. We paid extra attention to our Nurture Assets in the months leading up to the sales campaign and it paid dividends.
- We forgot to be multimedia. Our social networks had no nurture attention, so weren't warmed up and didn't buy. We didn't dig the well before we were thirsty.
- Military precision required. There are lots of moving parts in this campaign and sometimes two emails got sent out at the same time, team members stepped on each other's toes, and it required a little more "who's doing what and when" thinking (an Admin Asset).
- Adapt and improvise. Our horse racing tipster hit an 80/1 winner on day one of the campaign, so we very quickly dropped the planned copy to react to this good news.
- Keep an eye on the numbers. In the past, we'd focused so hard on achieving a particular cost per lead that we failed to bring in a reasonable number of leads. We might have hit our £1.50 CPL target, but we only had a few thousand leads, rather than the 20,000 we were hoping for.
- Have fun! Many of our members commented on how much fun they had during the campaign. We also had some friendly

banter and competition among the team. Just because it's a sales campaign, it doesn't mean your prospects can't enjoy being sold to.

- Hmm... that's strange! Keep an eye out for things that don't look right, places where customers don't behave as they should. We created an "ugly duckling" product that was deliberately designed to be unattractive in comparison to the product we wanted to sell. And we sold over 100 ugly ducks. Turns out these "unattractive" products countered a key objection we'd missed – so next time, we'll turn those ugly birds into an Evergreen Asset swan.
- Don't reinvent the wheel. This campaign was almost a carbon copy of the prior one. Why waste energy starting again when you can rinse and repeat what works? That's the power of Evergreen Assets.

I will run this campaign again every five months. Thanks to the debrief, I've already completed Step 1 of my next campaign (planning). All I need to do is to dust off my Google Doc a few weeks ahead of time and update it with any changes.

Use a SPEAR to capture sales

You've got your Never-ending Nurture Sequence in place together with your Signature Move. You've perfected a sales campaign using the Proven Framework above. With this combination, you will nurture better relationships with your prospects, giving them the option to yell "shut up and take my money", and present them with a gift-wrapped opportunity via a sales campaign.

But what if you want to make some sales right now? Like, today? Well, if you plant a coconut tree, feed it, water it, nurture it for long enough, and wait for the right time, eventually you'll have a steady stream of coconuts. Enough for a daily pina colada.

But, one day, disaster strikes and you don't have any coconuts. What can you do? Well, it's quite simple. You give the tree a shake.

If a sale or two is the missing ingredient from your pina colada then, as long as you've nurtured your tree sufficiently, you can give it a little shake and a coconut (or customer) or two will drop into your hands.

The SPEAR email is a great way to shake that tree. SPEAR emails are:

- Short
- Personal.
- Expecting A Reply.

Whereas your nurture or sales campaign emails may have quite a lot of copy in them, telling stories, countering objections, and highlighting the benefits of your product or service, SPEAR emails are short – typically a couple of sentences at most.

They also look as though they're sent from a real person, rather than a company, so "John Smith" rather than "Smith and Sons Accountants".

And, crucially, they're crafted in a way that indicates a reply is expected.

> *Hi Laura, are you OK?*
>
> *I haven't heard from you in a while.*
>
> *All the best,*
>
> *John*

Or:

> *Hi Matthew,*
>
> *Did you have any questions for me about ________?*
>
> *Cheers,*
>
> *John*

SPEAR emails start (or resume) buying conversations. They shake the tree and speak directly to those people who are ready to progress – and boy do they get replies. I typically see a 20 per cent reply rate from SPEAR emails. Most people would be happy with a 20 per cent open rate.

Of course, not all replies will be from potential buyers. Some will tell you they're not ready yet (in which case you can keep the conversation going and find out when they might be) or you'll discover they've already bought elsewhere or no longer require your product/service (in which case you can quietly remove them from your sales funnel).

The Eight-Word Email

The most powerful SPEAR within your arsenal is the Eight-Word Email.

Sent *only* to prospects who have expressed an interest of some kind in your product/service, it's a way of directly asking them the rude question you're desperate to know the answer to:

> *"Are you gonna buy my stuff or not?"*

Now, clearly, we need to word it a little more subtly than that but that *is* the question we want answered. And I reckon we can do that using just eight words:

> *"Hi NAME,*
>
> *Are you still looking for ___________?"*

That's it. No links to products. No Signature Move. No fancy follow-up sequence. Remove all your usual branding and make it look like a real email, sent from one person to another, asking a very simple question.

Send an eight-word email and you'll soon start getting replies:

> *"I've changed my mind and no longer want ___________."*

"I bought __________ from someone else."

"I'm still interested in __________, but haven't made a decision yet."

"I've been meaning to buy __________, but haven't got around to it yet."

And my personal favourite:

"Yes, I do – shut up and take my money!"

The Eight-Word Email resumes buying conversations with people who have shown an interest in your product or service, finding out exactly where they are on the buying journey and picking up the sales conversation from there.

You'll be able to stop marketing to people who've already bought or are no longer interested. You'll be able to ask people who bought from your competitors why they chose them over you. And you'll make sales.

Every time I send an Eight-Word Email, I shake the tree and make sales.

For my coaching business, it's as simple as: "Are you still interested in joining the One Percent Club?" For my sports betting business, I might ask: "Are you still betting on the horses?"

This is so simple to adapt for your business:

"Are you still looking for a mortgage?"

"Are you still looking to improve your golf swing?"

"Do you still want to learn Spanish?"

"Are you still looking for a cleaner?"

Shake that tree with an eight-word SPEAR.

TL/DR:

Your Signature Move enables prospects to bypass your Never-Ending Nurture Sequence and buy when *they're* ready to.

Milk the GOAT by following my Proven Framework for the best sales campaign I ever ran. Use a SPEAR to shake the tree and get coconuts for your pina colada.

Oh, and eight words are all you need to find out if people are gonna buy your stuff or not.

SALES ASSETS: WEBSITES

Let me take you behind the scenes on a recent coaching call, enabling you to eavesdrop on my conversation with a client as I audited his website:

> *Me: "So I'm on your homepage. How do I buy product x?"*
>
> *Client: "Erm. Well… Erm... You... Let's see... You need to scroll to the bottom and there's an image there."*
>
> *Me: "Yep, that's not clickable."*
>
> *Client: "Oh. Right then, well if you click on the 'blog' tab, and then navigate to Page 5, there's a blog post called 'I May Be Exaggerating This Story To Make A Point'. Halfway through there, there's a link to the product page."*
>
> *Me: "OK, I'm on the product page. Where's the 'buy now' button?"*
>
> *Client: "It's at the bottom of the page. Scroll down."*
>
> *Me: *scrolls**
>
> *Client: "Keep scrolling…"*
>
> *Me: "Found it!" *clicks* "OK, now I just have to fill in these 28 fields, including my dog's middle name, my inside-leg*

> *measurement, and choose a password (with uppercase, lowercase, special characters and numbers of course) – which I have to type in twice?"*

Do you really think people want to go through all that hassle to buy from you? Of course they don't. And most people *won't*. The average conversion rate for a website in the UK is 1.8 per cent. That means that 98.2 per cent of people don't buy and a big reason for that is most websites make it hard to buy.

If you want to turn your website into an Evergreen Sales Asset, you need to design it for what the conversion rate experts call "busy, lazy, drunk, amnesiac idiots", which covers most of those 98.2 per cent of people who found the back button far easier to locate than your "buy now" button.

> *"We need something to make the ordering system frictionless. We need to make it so the customer can order products with the least amount of effort. They should be able to click on one thing, and it's done."*

So said Amazon founder Jeff Bezos in 1997, briefing programmer Peri Hartman and head of software development Shel Kaphan.

Shel, Peri, and the team came up with Amazon's famous 1-Click buying process – a process they patented in 1999, licensed to Apple for $1million a year later and protected fiercely with lawsuits and settlements until the patent's expiry in 2017, by which point Jeff Bezos had turned that frictionless ordering system into a business that had earned him $72.8billion and made him the third richest man on the planet.

Your website is scarier than Doctor Who

Go to your homepage and count how many clicks it takes to buy something. Look at how much you need to scroll, how hard you need to hunt for the information you're looking for, how well hidden you've made the "buy now" button, and how many hurdles you've put in the customer's way in order to do business with you.

Then, consider that you already know your way around your own site.

Imagine you're a brand new potential customer who's never been here before and doesn't know that your "platinum range" is where you keep the "green widgets". It's little wonder that 98.2 per cent of busy, lazy, drunk, amnesiac idiots choose to bugger off and try someone else, is it?

Here are seven of the most common conversion killers that I see on my travels:

1. Poor navigation. Where am I? Where's the product? How do I get back to that page I saw earlier?
2. No clear next step. How do I buy this? How do I book an appointment? Where do I call?
3. Too many options. We sell this, and that. Oh, and these. And we also do x, y and z. Click here. No, click here. No, don't click there, click here!
4. Not enough words. Eight words is not enough for a product description.
5. Too many words. 800 words is probably too many, especially when you've put them in one single block of text.
6. Not mobile optimised. Most web traffic now happens on a mobile or tablet device. Time and again, I see "mobile-friendly" sites that are anything but. They're hard to navigate, hard to use, and almost impossible to buy from.
7. Making things too hard. Web usability expert Steve Krug, author of *Don't Make Me Think*, says: "If something requires a large investment of time – or looks like it will – it's less likely to

> be used." Do I fill in your 28-field registration form or buy with 1-Click from Amazon? What do you think?

To put yourself into your customers' shoes, try the I'm Feeling Lucky test. Go to Google.com and type in a keyword related to your sector or industry. Now, hit the "I'm Feeling Lucky" button, and you'll be taken to a random webpage relevant to that search.

Can you answer the following three questions about that site?

1. **Where are you?** Whose website is this? Can you easily find your way to the homepage? Once you're on the homepage, can you easily navigate your way back to the page you landed on (without using the back button)?
2. **Is it clear what this page is about?** Is it easy to read and digest or a confusing mess? Could you accurately describe the product or service (including what's in it for you) based purely on this page and within 30 seconds?
3. **What's the next step?** And how hard do you have to work to take it?

If you're feeling brave, send a link to a random page from *your* website to someone who doesn't know your business and ask them to answer those three questions. For extra points, record their reactions. But be warned, watching other people trying to find their way around your website can be scarier viewing than Doctor Who was for me as a kid.

To turn any webpage into an Evergreen Sales Asset, remember those three questions, and design your content around this simple, Proven Framework:

You are here > WIIFM > Call to action > Easily Digestible Content > Next Step.

You are here: Accurately describe and label your pages. If I perform the I'm Feeling Lucky test, I'd instantly know where I am, what the page is about, and how to get back on track if I'm lost.

WIIFM: What's In It For Me? That's all busy, lazy, drunk, amnesiac idiots want to know, so tell them upfront – ideally in the page's "big idea" headline. That's how they'll *know* they're in the right place.

Call to action: Above the fold (prominently visible without scrolling). Book a call. Buy now. Schedule an appointment. This is what you want people to do, so why hide it?

Easily digestible content: Enough words, but not too many. No big walls of text. Use bullet points to easily convey the main points. Most of what you write won't be read anyway. Busy, lazy, drunk, amnesiac idiots skim-read, guess, and forget approximately 96.2 per cent of what they do read.

Next step: This could involve repeating your call to action or signposting more information. Put yourself in your browser's shoes and ask what the next logical step would be for them to take.

Don't just apply this framework to your product or sales pages. Every page on your website has the potential to generate sales or move people along the buying journey. There's nothing worse than landing on a blog post, deciding it's the perfect product/service for you, and then having to work hard to figure out how to buy. If the logical next step for someone reading that blog post is to make a purchase, then give them the option to do so!

TL/DR:

A well-designed website is an Evergreen Asset that allows people to buy from you in their pyjamas at 3am.

Some 98.2 per cent of website visitors don't buy but we can easily change that. We just need to make it easier for busy, lazy, drunk, amnesiac idiots to do so. Stop hiding the "buy now" button. Stop trying to fit everything you do onto your homepage. Stop using too many (or too few) words. Stop making things too hard.

Remember: You are here > WIIFM > Call to action > Easily Digestible Content > Next Step.

Oh, and do the I'm Feeling Lucky test, but watch from behind the sofa. It's scary stuff!

SALES ASSETS: FUNNELS

A sales funnel is a way of narrowing down the field, ignoring 80 per cent of your prospects who are not ready or able to buy right now and identifying the 20 per cent with whom it's worth having a conversation. Twenty per cent of those people (that's just four per cent of your prospects) are ready to buy.

And 20 per cent of those ready-to-buy people (a mere 0.8 per cent of those who entered the funnel) are ready to buy right now, and will have their credit card in hand if you just call them. These percentages aren't set in stone – simply know that the majority of people going into your funnel will not buy, and there's a small minority that are worth talking to.

Where most people go wrong with a funnel is they picture the sort you might use in the kitchen – wide at the top, narrow at the bottom, and designed with one key feature that everything you put in the top will come out the bottom.

Sales funnels aren't like that; they are a *de-selection* process. Rather than trying to force everyone who enters the funnel into becoming a paying customer, they're designed to remove incompatible prospects (either popping them back into your Never-Ending Nurture Sequence if they're not ready to buy yet or removing them from your ecosystem completely if they're a bad fit).

Using lead scoring, you can easily discover who's worth talking to. Who opens *all* of your emails? Who opens them *multiple* times? Who *always* likes and comments on your social networking posts? Who are you *already* talking to? If I asked you to name five hot prospects right now, who are they? You're looking for the handful of people who are disproportionately more engaged than everyone else.

You might send 12,000 emails a week, but with lead scoring you can uncover the five or six people your sales team should get on the phone right now or the 25 people you should send an Offer They Can't Refuse. It's a de-selection process to discover who's worth investing your finite resources of time, energy, headspace, and money into.

"Would you like a cup of tea?"

Good funnels are not about hounding people with constant "till they buy or till they die" follow-up. Rather, it's about asking a few questions to ascertain where people are on the buying journey. If they're totally unsuitable for you or your product/service can't help them, then you should wish them well as they exit the funnel (and your ecosystem) completely.

If they're simply not in the right place to make a decision at the moment or it's not the right time for them to buy, a well-designed funnel will allow them to leave temporarily and go back into the Never-Ending Nurture Sequence until they *are* ready to have a sales conversation. (Remember they can always skip the nurture sequence and the sales funnel by booking a call via your Signature Move, and if you think they might be ready to talk shop in the future, you can always send them the world's simplest funnel – the Eight-Word Email).

I want to repeat this point. Good funnels are used to deselect unsuitable prospects, allowing you to focus more attention on the good fits, ensuring high-quality, consistent follow-up happens with those guys, rather than trying to squeeze everyone down the funnel, converting every person into a paying customer, whether it's the right thing for them (and you!) or not.

I made this mistake once, plotting out a truly amazing sales funnel, and then automating it using Facebook Messenger bots. It looked great on a whiteboard, reminiscent of the London Underground map with dozens of *if this > then that* variables, diverging pathways based on users responses and countering every possible objection under the sun.

It might have looked great on a whiteboard but, in reality, it resulted in me being called a spammer, being told to "f*** off" several times a day and close to zero sales. I tried to convert everyone into a customer. My funnel was too aggressive and refused to take no for an answer. I dubbed it the "Mrs Doyle Funnel" after the housekeeper from Father Ted, who was rather keen on brewing cups of tea.

If I were to create an automated funnel for Mrs Doyle to ascertain whether someone might like a cup of tea, it would look something like this:

> Ask: "Would you like a cup of tea?"
>
> If yes > pour tea.
>
> If no > ask: "Are you sure?"
>
> If no > pour tea.
>
> If yes > declare: "Ah you will!"
>
> If yes > pour tea.
>
> If no > ask: "Ah go on!"
>
> If yes > pour tea.
>
> If no > ask: "Just the one little cup?"

If yes > pour tea.

If no > ask: "Go on! Go on! Go on! Go on! Go on! Go on! Go on!"

If yes > pour tea.

If no > pour tea anyway announcing: "Well, I'll pour you one anyway, just in case."

Take it from someone who's tried the Mrs Doyle approach, it doesn't work and the responses you'll get will be similar to Father Jack Hackett:

Mrs Doyle: "And what do you say to a cup?"

Father Jack: "Feck off, cup!"

Nice and Simple

Before you get your whiteboard out and draw something resembling a Tube map, try capturing the basics on a single piece of paper. You can leverage your entire Evergreen Assets ecosystem to convert cold traffic who have never heard of you into raving fans, shouting about you to all of their friends, with a nice simple six-step funnel: Capture Leads > Nurture > Convert > Fulfil > Optimise > Replicate.

The eagle-eyed among you will have noticed the similarity to the six Evergreen Asset classes, which complement this simple funnel nicely. In fact, you could simply fill in the blanks on this funnel with the "One Asset to Rule Them All" from each asset class:

Capture Leads (The Right Bait) > Build Nurture (Weekly Emails) > Convert (Offer They Can't Refuse) > Fulfil (The Quick Win) > Optimise (Company Culture) > Replicate (Bring Your Friends).

You may then want a separate funnel for each step. For example, a Convert funnel:

Introduce Offer They Can't Refuse > Counter Objections > Follow Up > Social Proof > Deadline > Follow Up Again.

Just remember to keep it simple and don't slip into Mrs Doyle mode.

TL/DR:

Funnels are a deselection process, using lead scoring to narrow the field of potential prospects to those worth talking to. They're *not* about forcing *everyone* through to a sale.

They're a great way to ensure that the optimum path to a sale is followed every time but be careful not to overdo the optimisation (and automation), otherwise you'll enter Mrs Doyle territory.

Oh, and I don't want a cup of tea, thanks.

SALES ASSETS: DIRECT MAIL

It's the year 2000 and your letterbox rattles. Thump! A huge pile of junk mail lands on your doormat. You sigh, pick up the lot and dump it straight into the bin without even reading them. As you do so, you hear an announcement from your computer: "You've got mail!" A hit of dopamine floods your brain and you excitedly skip back to your desk, eagerly opening your email inbox, keen to discover what interesting new message(s) awaits.

Fast forward to the present day and you're sitting at your desk working. You glance at your email inbox: 129 emails (107 unread). You sigh, tick (almost) the lot, and put them straight in the bin, without even reading them. As you do so, your letterbox rattles. A single piece of mail lands on your doormat. A hit of dopamine floods your brain and you excitedly skip to the front door, eagerly picking up the brightly coloured envelope, keen to discover what interesting new message(s) awaits.

This is why Direct Mail still works. The cost of sending physical stuff in the mail has become a barrier to entry, making it easier to cut through the noise and get attention. There are very few better ways to get your message in front of the right people.

Not your average Joe

Most car salesmen sell four or five cars a month. Joe Girard sold six a day for 15 years.

Joe's secret weapon? A greetings card. Every month, he'd send a handwritten card to everyone in his Rolodex – past customers, new prospects, suppliers, even rival dealers. Joe would link each card to a particular event that month – Valentine's Day, Fourth of July, Halloween, etc. – while his underlying message each month was simply: "I'm thinking of you."

While Joe sent a lot of cards over the years, eventually employing two full-time assistants to send 13,000 handwritten cards every month, there's one important distinction that Joe made: It's not a numbers game, it's a relationships game.

Joe didn't just send lots of cards telling people he cared. He genuinely *did* care. It's the difference between an automated voice telling us our call is important versus someone demonstrating that our call really *does* matter to them. Joe would overdeliver for the customer, including free services and car washes to make sure they were happy. He would take all the mechanics out for lunch once a month to make sure they were happy (and looking after his customers).

When it came time to buy your next car, why would you trust anyone but Joe? When a friend says they're looking for a new car, who do you recommend? The guy who you know is going to look after them for years to come.

More than four decades later, Joe Girard still holds the Guinness world record for the highest number of cars sold in one year (1,425 in 1973).

The Bloody-Minded Farmer's Greatest Crop

Joe wasn't sending 13,000 pieces of junk mail every month. He sent his monthly "I'm thinking of you" cards to people who already knew him – including those who had already bought from him. For most of us, that's where Direct Mail is going to provide us with the greatest ROI. Sending to existing (or previous) customers means they should already know, like and trust you.

Giving existing customers an opportunity to buy again or to buy more often produces a far higher ROI than going out cold to a large audience. Evergreen Assets is not a numbers game, it's a relationships game. People who know, like and trust you are more likely to buy from you. People who know, like and trust you, and who have bought from you before, are even more likely to buy.

It's worth remembering, though, that if you are sending Direct Mail to lapsed customers (whether they've cancelled a membership or simply not bought for a long period of time), you may need to acknowledge why they haven't bought for a while and why they might want to again.

A few months after I stopped ordering from Riverford Organic Farms, I received a fantastic piece of Direct Mail from them. Here's a brief extract:

> *"Dear one-time Riverford veg eater,*
>
> *Our (sometimes dodgy) records suggest you once bought veg from us, but not lately. Maybe your garden has been bountiful;*

maybe you simply fell out of the habit. Or perhaps we were just a bit too inflexible.

We've changed, hopefully in the right places.

For some of you, perhaps it was more like a bloody-minded farmer dumping a load of unidentifiable veg on your doorstep. This farmer has turned over a new leaf."

Straight off the bat, Riverford acknowledges me as a previous customer and offers up a few explanations why I'm not still buying from them (one of which hits the nail on the head – I simply fell out of the habit). They attach zero blame to me for this. It's not you, it's me is the vibe.

They let me know they've changed. They've listened to feedback. They also assure me the bits I love about them *haven't* changed. They counter objections galore and remind me of all those wonderful benefits I bought into when I first became a customer. They close the letter with a clear call to action, making an Offer I Can't Refuse. I've been a regular Riverford customer ever since.

If they hadn't sent that letter, I might never have bought from them again. But by successfully reactivating me (and turning me into a raving fan) Riverford's ROI from that one Evergreen Asset is off the charts.

They're certainly reaping what they sow.

Insert Trojan Horse here

Printed newsletters are primarily a Nurture Asset and should not be used to overtly sell. They can, however, be the perfect Trojan horse for a Sales Asset in the form of an insert.

Including a sales letter with (but still clearly separate from) the newsletter can be devastatingly effective. Once you've sent the newsletter for several months, readers will look forward to its arrival and pop the kettle on, settling down to read it cover to cover, as they always do, when suddenly: "What's this? There's an extra sheet of paper in this month's edition that isn't usually there. It's brightly coloured and with an engaging headline that makes me want to read more. Do you know what? This is new, different, and interesting. I might actually read this *before* I read the newsletter."

Clearly, you can't perform this trick every month and expect stellar results every time (the Greeks were only able to use their Trojan horse once, after all) but it's great to have up your sleeve for special occasions. It's the element of surprise that makes the difference.

The "oooh!" pile

I've already spoken about the three-pile sorting process for the post waiting for you on your return from a fortnight's holiday.

The first pile is for the junk – pizza menus, leaflets for blinds and sofas and all the "clearly trying to sell me something" crap. Everything goes straight in the bin.

The second is the "meh" pile. Bank statements, bills, and letters with franked addresses. The boring stuff you'll need to open and read, but will leave until later.

And the third pile is where the exciting stuff goes. The bright pink envelope with handwritten address and a real stamp. The large A4 envelope, which contains something lumpy. This is the "oooh!" pile and gets opened first.

The first objective of any piece of Direct Mail you send is to get it opened. If it doesn't get opened, it doesn't get read. If it doesn't get read, it can't generate an ROI. If it can't generate an ROI, it's not an

Evergreen Asset. The surest way to get your Direct Mail opened is to make sure it's in the "oooh!" pile.

Use brightly coloured envelopes. Handwrite the addresses (in your best handwriting and with a nice pen). Stick a real stamp on it. In most cases, that alone will get you in the "oooh!" pile. You can go further by adding scribbles or doodles to the envelope or including "lumps" inside so it's clear there's more than just a piece of paper in the envelope.

For our horse racing tips business, we sometimes include some PG Tips teabags (Tips? Get it?). Others have had success sticking in a chocolate bar or a keyring. Many charities included a free pen in their sales letters and saw a big rise in the number of donations. One chap who wanted to have a chat with a key decision maker started sending his sales letters out with a wind-up "chattering teeth" toy and more than trebled his conversion rate.

But be careful that your lumps aren't "too lumpy". I once sent a reactivation letter to lapsed One Percenters. Emulating the Riverford campaign, I wrote a piece of copy absolving them of blame for the lack of purchase and taking complete responsibility myself. I acknowledged why they might have left and what I'd done to change things since. Of course, I also pointed out all the things they previously loved that hadn't changed.

I wrote a headline that summed all of this up, while generating curiosity to ensure the rest of the letter got read: "I screwed up!"

I then turned this single piece of A4 into a piece of lumpy mail (and linked it to the headline) by screwing it into a ball, and popping it into a bright pink envelope with handwritten address and a first class stamp on it – and waited for the sales to roll in.

Three days later – nothing. Not a sausage.

Five days later – nada.

Finally, after seven days, I got my first response: "Just had to pay £1.50 to get your sales letter. WTF?"

That's strange, I thought. And then I got another, and another, and another – each one angrier than the last. It turns out my screwed up piece of paper became too lumpy for a single first class stamp, so my lapsed customers had to pay to receive a letter trying to flog them something.

Oops. I really had screwed up.

TL/DR:

Direct Mail cuts through the noise and gets attention. Its barrier to entry (cost) is also its greatest asset.

Done well, it can make you a world record-holding salesman or generate an off-the-charts ROI for a bloody-minded farmer. Its greatest ROI usually comes from sending to existing or lapsed customers (or highly qualified prospects). You can include a sales Trojan horse in your nurture newsletter, but don't pull the same trick too often. Make sure you're in the "oooh!" pile.

Oh, and don't screw it up (without checking the postage).

SALES ASSETS: GOOGLE ADS

Someone googling for an "emergency plumber" doesn't want a 12-email nurture sequence to warm them up. They want someone to remove the water feature from their living room carpet.

Google Ads enable you to laser-target people who are further along the buying journey, enabling you to find the 20 per cent of people who are ready to talk about buying, as well as the 20 per cent of those people ready to buy right now.

You can target different keywords such as "plumber near me" versus "emergency plumber near me" and send visitors to different sales pages, different funnels, different members of your sales team. You can put a different Offer They Can't Refuse in front of different people to counter different objections and highlight different benefits.

Rather than having a "one size fits all" campaign, a well-optimised Google Ads account is a Sales Asset that allows you to fish where the fish are *and* to start shooting fish in a barrel. In my sports betting business, I can divert traffic to different landing pages based on where prospects are on the buying journey. People searching for "horse racing tips" will go into my standard funnel, whereas those searching for "Royal Ascot Day 1 Tips" will enter my Royal Ascot sales funnel where there's a lot less nurture and a lot more Sales Assets.

It's worth noting that Google Ads on their own are not an Evergreen Asset (after all, if you want more clicks from Google, you're going to have to pay again), but they can become a source of highly targeted, buying-intent-focused traffic for your entire Evergreen Assets ecosystem.

Playing with Google Ads also gives you tremendous insight into the world of SEO, effectively giving you the chance to pay to be on the first page of results for any keyword, work out whether it's worthwhile doing so (assuming you're tracking conversions) and help to shape your SEO Assets with a buy-before-you-try approach. Do some paid ads, see what works, and then go after what works with your SEO.

SALES ASSETS: VIDEO

"If I'm in front of a prospect, they almost always buy."

So why aren't you getting in front of a prospect every time?

Rand Fishkin, the founder of SEO service Moz, had no problem selling the service face-to-face at conferences, but his website just wasn't performing. He approached conversion rate experts, who asked him to pretend they were one of his prospects and go through his usual in-person presentation.

While Rand did this, the conversion rate experts also filmed him. They dissected every aspect of his face-to-face approach and replicated it on his website. Crucially, they also edited the actual footage of Rand's presentation and put *that* on the website too.

The result? A 52 per cent increase in sales and an extra $1million a year in new subscribers.

A good video is like having your best sales rep deliver a perfect presentation to your prospect every time. A sales rep who never gets tired, never sleeps, never complains, and who can deliver five pitch-perfect presentations *at the same time*!

Prospects will also happily watch (or at least start to watch) a sales pitch when delivered by video. People who won't take your call, and certainly won't let a sales rep in the door, will engage with video content in order to do their own research and make their own decision.

People buy from people and video adds personality and warmth. Tonality and sincerity that's lost in text are plain as day on a video. Where could you add a sprinkling of video into your Evergreen Assets ecosystem?

Could you add video presentations to your sales pages? Video testimonials from satisfied clients? How about a video walkthrough showing me what to expect when I become a customer? Don't just tell me what happens next – show me. Demonstrate your product or service in action. Let me meet your team face to face (without being face to face).

You could include a short, personalised video when sending quotes through, detailing:

1. Exactly what the client asked for. (I know what you want).
2. Stories of similar clients you've helped (If you've got video testimonials to drop in here, even better).
3. An introduction to the people who will be making the product/servicing the client.
4. The price. Recap again their requirements (I really know what you want), and reveal the price. If necessary, explain how your pricing works ("The ultra-rare blue widget you asked for has to be handmade by a team of master craftsmen").
5. Go through the FAQs. If 60 per cent of people reply to a quote with a question, answer those questions in your video.
6. Explain (and show me) what happens next. How do I place an order? How long will it take? When can I expect it? (Note, these are all questions, so flow nicely from the FAQs).
7. Ask for the sale. Don't go out with a whimper – go out with a sale. Ask and ye shall receive.

Most people don't send a seven-step personalised video. They send a crappy Word document with the price scribbled on it and no detail about what to expect or what happens next. They email it over, don't ask for the sale, and often don't follow up.

For the sake of a few minutes on a shaky camera phone (and maybe a little editing), prospects could feel a connection with the people behind the quote, can see the results they can expect, and are clear on what happens next.

Which one do you think will convert? After all, if you can get in front of a customer, they'll probably buy.

Webinars

For decades, the Jim Rohns and Brian Tracys of this world sold from the stage. They'd travel the world, putting on seminars in city after city. Put them in front of 300 people and 75 of them would buy something.

Then the internet came along, enabling people to host a seminar on the web (a webinar). A webinar is a great way of converting prospects to sales, especially if your product or service involves some kind of education.

Using The Right Bait ("I know a secret and I'll tell you about it on Tuesday at 7pm"), you can use a webinar to generate leads, send a couple of emails to kickstart the nurture process, walk prospects through your Proven Framework, make them an Offer They Can't Refuse, and – bish, bash, bosh – make the sale.

Of course, it's not quite that easy. But webinars are devastatingly effective when done well. Over the course of 60 to 90 minutes, you can usually whizz prospects through your entire Evergreen Assets ecosystem and almost always make a good number of sales.

Be under no illusions, this is a sales pitch disguised as education.

Why would people want to sit through a 90-minute pitch? Well, clearly there has to be some value. Viewers have to believe that you're the person to solve their problem and the Proven Framework you're presenting can help them get what they want.

You don't need to be on camera, so don't fret. Just create some slides and share your screen. There are dedicated webinar software platforms you can use, but I like the minimum effective dose of Google Slides, which is free, and then recording over Zoom, which also has a free option.

Your first slide should answer two questions for viewers:

1. What are we going to learn today?
2. What's in it for me?

Ideally, the answer to those two questions will be the same. What we're going to learn today just so happens to be the greatest thing viewers want to discover/learn/implement.

There's a Proven Framework I use on my first slide that answers both questions:

> *"I am going to teach ________________ how to ___________________, without ________________________"*

Let's delve into that a bit more.

"I am going to teach ________________". This is where we label our target market and hopefully get them nodding along saying, "Hey, that sounds like me!"

"...how to ___________________". What do they want? Label it. "Hey, that's exactly what I'm looking for!"

"...without ________________________". What are they afraid of? What are their preconceived misconceptions? "Hey, that's what I was worried about!"

Here are a couple of fleshed out examples:

1. I am going to teach brand new property investors how to buy apartment buildings, without putting any of their own money in.
2. I am going to teach professional men in their 40s how to lose belly fat, without doing hours of cardio.

This "What's in it for me?" slide hooks viewers in for a 60 to 90-minute journey towards getting what they want. That journey involves:

- Demonstrating that you know what they want.
- Making them believe that what they want is possible and that you're the person to deliver it.
- Building a nurture rapport with your audience.
- Introducing (and teaching) your Proven Framework.
- Telling stories to build social proof.
- Countering objections and false beliefs.
- Telling them what's in it for them.
- Making them an Offer They Can't Refuse.
- Calling them to action.

For an in-depth walkthrough of a Proven Framework for creating the rest of the slides, I recommend the book *Expert Secrets* by ClickFunnels co-founder Russell Brunson. While I have recorded a 74-minute webinars masterclass (which I'll include in the resources), I'd advise you to swipe and deploy Russell's "Perfect Webinar Script" straight out of his book.

TL/DR:

Video enables you to sell face to face, without being face to face.

It's your best sales rep, delivering their best pitch every time. Video speaks directly to your prospects, making a personal connection.

Video sales letters and webinars enable you to whizz prospects through your Nurture and Sales Assets ecosystem in a matter of minutes.

Oh, and you look fine on camera. Stop overthinking it, and just film the bloody thing.

SALES ASSETS: REMARKETING

Remarketing allows you to repeatedly show ads across a variety of media platforms to a tiny group of highly-targeted people. You'll appear everywhere they go online – and putting your Offer They Can't Refuse in front of these highly-targeted prospects (and no one else), creates a devastatingly effective Sales Asset.

Remember Thomas Smith's effective frequency framework we covered earlier in the book?

> *"The fourteenth time, they start to remember wanting a product exactly like this for a long time.*
>
> *The fifteenth time, they start to yearn for it because they can't afford to buy it.*
>
> *The sixteenth time, they accept the fact that they will buy it sometime in the future.*
>
> *The seventeenth time, they make a note to buy the product.*
>
> *The eighteenth time, they curse their poverty for not allowing them to buy this terrific product.*
>
> *The nineteenth time, they count their money very carefully.*
>
> *The twentieth time prospects see the ad, they buy what is offered."*

Having excluded unqualified leads, dead leads, tyre kickers, time wasters and those who have already bought, your ads are now shown again and again and again - but only to your hottest, highly-qualified prospects (which could be opt-ins, manually qualified by a sales team, or automatically tagged as having visited a sales page, or added a product to their basket). This is where your remarketing ROI skyrockets.

Using effective frequency, remarketing keeps providing prospects with the opportunity to purchase until they no longer indicate any interest (they've stopped visiting your website, opening your emails, clicking on your ads or – the ideal scenario – they've bought your product or service).

Please make sure you do exclude buyers from your remarketing campaigns. So many people seem to enjoy wasting their hard-earned cash targeting me with remarketing ads after I've already purchased. That's like producing a dessert menu at the end of a pie-eating competition.

A nice side-effect of running remarketing campaigns is being able to download the list of URLs (website addresses) that your remarketing ads appeared on.

This tells you which websites your target market visits – which can be very helpful in identifying your ideal client demographics, as well as planning joint ventures, banner campaigns, or display network ads on Google Ads – turning your existing remarketing Nurture and Sales Assets into a Lead Asset as well.

SALES ASSETS: SOCIAL NETWORKS

Can anyone recommend a ____________?

This question is asked fifty gazillion times a day on social networks. And I'll bet at least a handful of them are asking for people to recommend someone who does what you do.

If you've been digging your well and nurtured a strong network, you'll know it because you'll start to be tagged in all these posts without needing to ask anyone to do so. Of course, this only happens when you dig the well before you're thirsty, and you focus on the quality of relationships, not the quantity. Remember, it's not a numbers game. It's a relationships game.

You don't need to rely on that mythical "word of mouth", though, as you can add fuel to the fire and leverage your network as part of a sales campaign. Ask your existing clients to comment on a sales post, sharing their experience of working with you and adding some much needed third-party social proof.

Unless they're looking for recommendations, people don't tend to go on social networking sites to buy. That doesn't mean you can't leverage social platforms to make sales, especially as part of a multimedia campaign. Where most people go wrong selling on social platforms is they haven't nurtured an audience of the right people, who know, like and trust them. They've spent all their time broadcasting *to* social media, rather than chatting *with* their social network.

They don't know what their network wants. They've not dug the well, and now they're thirsty.

If the right people know, like and trust you – and if you can successfully demonstrate that you know what they want, are the ideal person to give them what they want, and present them with an Offer They Can't Refuse – then, of course, you can sell on social networking platforms.

I've described myself as anti-social media, yet Facebook and LinkedIn generate a significant number of sales for me because that's where my network is. I don't broadcast *to* them five times a day but I do chat *with* them several times a week. I dig the well before I'm thirsty. Then, when I'm thirsty, I lower my bucket and ask for the sale.

SALES ASSETS: SUMMARY

Sales Assets are like salt. You need a little, but not too much.

Embrace your inner Don Vito Corleone, and make them an Offer They Can't Refuse. Show them a glimpse of their future, as they travel along your Proven Framework. If you are as good as you say, why not put your money where your mouth is and guarantee the results your customers want?

Let them try before they buy – but make sure you deliver! Make it easy for them to buy. Give them a deadline to get them off the fence. "'Too late! too late!' will be the cry, when the man with the bargains has passed you by."

Deploy your Signature Move in your nurture emails, so prospects can tell you to "shut up and take my money". Milk the GOAT, and SPEAR the best prospects using as few as eight words.

Your website lets people buy from you in their pyjamas at 3am, but 98.2 per cent of busy, lazy, drunk, amnesiac idiots won't and that's *your* fault. Funnels are a deselection process, not forcing everyone to buy (or drink tea).

Direct Mail cuts through the noise and gets attention. Its greatest ROI usually comes from sending to existing or lapsed customers (or highly qualified prospects). Google Ads enable you to laser target people who are further along the buying journey, allowing you to fish where the fish are and to start shooting those fish in a barrel.

Video enables your best salesman to get in front of a prospect and deliver a perfect pitch every time – 24 hours a day, seven days a week.

Remarketing Sales Assets truly skyrocket your ROI, because you've excluded all the unqualified, dead leads, tyre-kickers, time wasters, and those who've already bought, leaving nothing but qualified prospects for whom you appear to be everywhere.

If you've been digging the well, you should be able to lower the bucket.

By now, our recipe should be nicely seasoned. We've captured leads. Those prospects know, like and trust us. We've demonstrated we're the person to give them what they want and they've bought. Hurray!

Now, all we have to do is *deliver* on our promises.

6. FULFILMENT ASSETS

Fulfil (fʊlˈfɪl). Verb, meaning to:

1. Achieve or realise (something desired, promised or predicted).
2. Carry out (a duty or role) as required, promised, or expected.

The Evergreen Assets ecosystem is built around a single promise: "I can get you what you want." Well, now it's time to deliver on that promise. It's time to give them what they want.

Unfulfilled, unhappy customers are the result of a disconnect between what was promised and what was delivered. It's when the burger you're served doesn't look like the one in the picture.

Fulfilment Assets are not about giving them what they want; they're about making damn sure they've *got* what they want. Your customers will never cast a lustful eye elsewhere if they're truly fulfilled – if they're achieving or realising what was desired, promised or predicted.

When I was a kid, there was a TV show called Knightmare. Teams of four children would play a virtual reality choose your own adventure game. One would take on the role of "Dungeoneer" and don the "Helmet of Justice" (basically an upside-down bucket with some horns stuck on) so they couldn't see. The other team members would guide the Dungeoneer through quests, avoiding computer-generated dragons, fire traps and rickety bridges.

Most weeks, the Dungeoneer would inevitably plummet to their death, be eaten by a dragon, or burned alive (virtually, of course, this was pre-watershed). Because the Dungeoneer's field of vision was impaired, he or she would stumble around trying to follow instructions from the others. It went a bit like this:

"Turn left. No, the other left." (The Dungeoneer spends the next minute and a half of prime-time kids' TV walking in a circle).

"Walk forward." (Ten seconds later, the Dungeoneer walks straight into a fiery grave because he wasn't told to *stop* walking).

"Jump!" "Crouch!" "Duck!" (All three teammates give conflicting advice at the same time, leading to the Dungeoneer attempting some kind of jumping, crouching, ducking combo).

"Look out!" (An instruction the Dungeoneer simply cannot follow with a bucket on their head, standing in front of a blank green screen).

All of this made for amusing telly, watching Dungeoneers walk blindly into traps, run themselves off cliffs, and impale themselves on swords. But it's not so amusing when you realise this is the experience you're giving your newest customers.

Yep, the first thing your new client does is don the Helmet of Justice and blindly await your instruction. They don't know what to expect or what's supposed to happen next. They're completely unfamiliar with their new surroundings and how your business works – so they're waiting for you to help them.

With a few select Fulfilment Assets, you can do what those kids on Knightmare couldn't – you can hold your customer's hand and lead them to their desired outcome, sidestepping the goblins, trolls, and pitfalls along the way. Less "do this, do that" and more "follow me, let me show you".

How do your customers feel when they first buy from you? Nervous? Excited? Worried? Confused?

Good Fulfilment Assets meet customers right here – acknowledging how they're likely to be feeling and taking them by the hand to carefully guide them to the first step on your Proven Framework.

Once the honeymoon's over, it's common for buyer's remorse to creep in. The buyer's high wears off and your customers are left with niggling doubts:

> *"Have I made a mistake?"*
>
> *"Will this really work for me?"*
>
> *"Did I pay too much?"*
>
> *"Have I chosen the wrong level/size/colour/model?"*

This will be especially true if there's a disconnect between what was promised and what is delivered in the first few days. Does your burger look like the one in the picture?

If your Lead, Nurture and Sales Assets are built around that single promise ("*I can get you what you want*"), then your Fulfilment Assets should be built around the following promise:

> *"I'm here for you and I care. I'm going to help you to get what you want. And I'm not going to stop until I'm damn sure you've got what you want. Your success matters to me."*

Let's start delivering on that promise, shall we?

ONE FULFILMENT ASSET TO RULE THEM ALL: THE QUICK WIN.

Your clients will be much more confident you can give them the big results they want in the long term if you can deliver a small win in the short term – and the quicker the better.

Things that don't start well don't tend to end well. But things that do start well tend to keep going well. Newton's first law of motion in action. That's why I've included these "one asset to rule them all" sections. They're the quick wins. The disproportionate return on your investment, helping you get a result straight off the bat.

By the time you've finished reading this book, I'd love for you to have already implemented a couple of quick wins and generated a significant positive return on your investment in this book.

If I can persuade you to take some action, and you see some results, then you're much more likely to keep taking action, knowing that you'll keep getting results. If the first step on the Proven Framework gives you a quick win, you'll be itching to take the second step.

On the other hand, if I make the first step difficult, you're unlikely to be motivated to do it and even less likely to want to progress to step two. Likewise, if it's simple but you don't get a win or see any results, you'll again lose motivation to move on.

If you're a health and fitness coach, you wouldn't make the first step of your programme running a 5k. Instead, you'd make it a quick win – one that's going to flood your clients with endorphins and get them fired up, enthusiastic about taking the second step. That could be something as simple as drinking an extra litre of water, getting a full eight hours' sleep, or walking around the block. Something easily achievable with minimal effort, but which will deliver a noticeable effect.

FULFILMENT ASSETS: THE KICK-OFF CALL

For years, my onboarding process for the One Percent Club consisted of fitting our new One Percenters with their Helmet of Justice and sending them on their merry way. Most people found their way around, despite bumping into a few walls and falling down a couple of wells. But we also lost far too many clients and kept hearing the same reasons over and over again:

"I don't know where to start."

"It's overwhelming."

"There's too much stuff. I haven't got time to look at it all."

"It's not quite what I was expecting."

Clearly, there was a disconnect between what was promised (or what was expected) and what was delivered. Our burger didn't look like the one in the picture.

I'm a marketer at heart, so I've nailed my Lead, Nurture and Sales Assets. But I'm not so good at operations.

I can fill the bucket with customers, but I'm not the best choice to fix the bucket if any holes appear. That's why I need a strong team around me to do the things that I can't do. To be brilliant at the things I'm terrible at. I focus on Leads, Nurture and Sales, and my team looks after Fulfilment, Admin, and Viral Assets. I fill the bucket and they fix any holes.

To start plugging those holes, the team made sure new One Percenters had plenty of quick wins in their first few weeks. They created a Proven Framework, leveraged personal onboarding videos, and created a "First 100 days" checklist – all of which you'll learn about in this section. But one of the most powerful new assets added into the ecosystem was the kick-off call.

This is a 30-minute one-to-one Zoom call with my business partner Jason, who can spend that half-hour getting to know our newest client, finding out what they want, telling them how they can get it, and ensuring we've created the systems to make damn sure they get what they want.

Jason's aim on this call is to find out where clients want to go and take them by the hand to step one of our Proven Framework, deliver a quick win, and get things off to a flying start. He will ask questions to discover what the burger looks like in each client's head and then set them on the path to deliver that burger.

It's also an opportunity for Jason to discover if new clients have any unrealistic expectations in their heads – where their burger doesn't look like the ones we make at all.

> *"When do I get a one-to-one with John?"*
>
> *"Erm, you don't. It's a group coaching platform. John hosts the coaching calls three times a month, but it's not one-to-one."*

If what they want isn't what we do, it's better Jason explains so on the kick-off call. It means we can go our separate ways now, rather than months down the line when the customer has become more and more frustrated that the group coaching burgers we keep serving are not the one-to-one burger they pictured in their head.

Jason can't remove their Helmet of Justice during these kick-off calls, but he can take our Dungeoneers by the hand and lead them where they want to go – giving them a quick win by showing them how to stack up their first few one per cent gains. He can also warn them of the pitfalls that lie just off the Proven Framework path and assure them:

> *"I'm here for you and I care. I'm going to help you to get what you want. And I'm not going to stop until I'm damn sure you've got what you want. Your success matters to me."*

Different clients want different things. Those who want to be held accountable are led to the weekly one-to-ones with Jason. Those who want to hang around with like-minded business owners are directed to the thrice-monthly group coaching calls and vibrant One Percent Club community. Those who want to learn marketing strategies and tactics from me are signposted towards The One Percent Way, my Proven Framework of more than 250 "one per cent gains".

Find out what they want, go and get it, give it to them.

A kick-off call is going to be most useful for service businesses. But if you sell a product with good margins, why not offer this too? When you're delivering a brand new car to a happy customer, why not spend an hour showing them how to use all the buttons and gadgets, where the dipstick is (not in the driver's seat, hopefully), how to access the four-wheel drive or sport mode?

Make sure that their burger matches the one in the picture before you drive away.

FULFILMENT ASSETS: THE HANDOVER

A burger/reality disconnect often results from the handover from sales and marketing to operations. People read my books and blog posts, listen to my podcasts and radio appearances, digest my Never-Ending Nurture Sequence, see me speak on stage, get my sales campaigns, watch my videos, visit my sales page, and buy into me and my story.

And then they get a kick-off call... with Jason. The natural reaction could be: "Who the hell is this guy? Where's John?"

Imagine Bob and Sue fall in love, get engaged, and eventually decide to tie the knot. On their wedding day, Bob and Sue declare their eternal, undying love for each other, vow to remain together till death they do part, and whisper "I do" while gazing lovingly into each other's eyes.

"I now pronounce you husband and wife," says the vicar. "Now, Sue… I'd like you to meet Terry. Terry will be looking after you from here on in. Terry – you may now kiss the bride!"

Sue would understandably be miffed by this turn of events and so would your clients. Like me, you may need to hand new clients over to your operations team. You can't do everything yourself, and your ops guys may be better than you at onboarding, logistics and operations. But that handover must be handled delicately.

Rather than surprising new One Percenters with Jason *after* we've exchanged vows, he's included in much of the courtship. Jase is mentioned many times in all of my books, he co-hosts the ALB podcast, I refer to him throughout the Never-Ending Nurture Sequence, my sales pages and web copy contain photos of both of us, and make it clear that we come as a duo – Morecambe and Wise, Ant and Dec, John and Jason.

When onboarding new clients, I remind them that Jason is my business partner of almost 20 years and that he's much better than I am at looking after their needs. I signpost them to a quick win, the first step on the Proven Framework, which is their kick-off call with Jason.

I swiped and deployed this approach from One Percenter Tracy Irwin. Tracy owns an accountancy, payroll, and bookkeeping company in the Lake District, but lives in sunny Spain. She's fully systemised her business and delegated all the day-to-day tasks to her team, leaving her free to focus on what she does best – winning new clients and serving as a virtual finance director for her dream clients.

Prospects buy from Tracy. They read her emails, they meet her at networking events, they get great value from her blogs, website, and videos. Tracy is the reason prospects come on board, but she hands over to her team brilliantly. Tracy makes it clear from day one that she doesn't get involved with the day-to-day, and that you, the client, are better served by someone else in her team.

If I've got a question about the tax implications of a particular strategy I'm exploring, Tracy will say: "Lucy knows so much more than me about the tax rules. I'll get her to give you a call." If I want to know whether a particular invoice has been paid or the Statutory Sick Pay rules for part-time workers, Tracy will defer to Sarah who "knows this stuff inside out".

Just like John "Hannibal" Smith in the '80s TV show, Tracy has assembled her own A-Team, with each member an expert in their specific niche. If you have an accountancy or payroll problem, if no one else can help, and if you can find them (it shouldn't be difficult as Tracy's optimised her Google My Business listing), maybe you can hire… TI Accountancy.

At no point do I feel that I'm being fobbed off or foisted onto a junior member of staff. Tracy signposts me to the best team member to help me get what I want, meaning I benefit from the team as a whole, while she is free to get to know my business inside-out as a financial director should.

I love it when a plan comes together.

FULFILMENT ASSETS: FIRST 100 DAYS CHECKLIST

> *"How can smart people so often be wrong? They don't do what I'm telling you to do: use a checklist."*
>
> *– Charlie Munger.*

I absolutely adore checklists. There are few things more satisfying to a former civil servant than ticking a box. But what really floats my boat when it comes to checklists is the ROI. When I follow a well-thought-out checklist to the letter, the results are pretty much guaranteed. Nothing gets missed. Nothing gets overlooked. Nothing gets half-arsed.

Customer experience expert Joey Coleman, author of *Never Lose A Customer Again,* says losing customers is the biggest threat facing businesses today and estimates most companies lose 20 to 70 per cent of new customers within the first 100 days.

"I like to emphasize the first 100 days after the sale as a critical window for securing customer loyalty. Not because it is an exact time limit, but because it is easy to remember, short enough to maintain focus, and long enough to deliver value. This 100-day time period gives you the opportunity to form a relationship, impress the customer several times, and deliver consistently so they trust and like you... If you get these first 100 days of the relationship right, you can keep a customer for life."

As someone who runs a couple of membership businesses, the importance of those first 100 days is obvious. We know that getting members to stay for the first 100 days is far harder than getting them to stay for the next 200, 300, or even 1,000 days.

If you order a pizza from Domino's via their app, you'll see their checkpoints:

- Order received.
- Pizza prepped.
- Baking.
- Quality check.
- Out for delivery.

That's an accelerated checklist to deliver a simple, one-off pizza order. Your first 100 days milestones could include:

- Celebrate the buying decision with your new customer.
- A personal interaction (phone call, rough video, handwritten note).
- Handover (Sue, meet Terry).
- Reaffirm your guarantee. Remind them they can't lose.
- Kick-off call.

- Set expectations.
- Achieve the first step on your Proven Framework.
- Deliver a quick win.
- Deliver an unexpected treat/bonus.
- Follow-up from the support team (I'm here and I care).
- Deliver a starter kit (tools to help them get started and enjoy the process).
- Arrange a welcoming committee (other customers who can show them how things work).
- Deliver another unexpected bonus. Continue to surprise and delight.
- Design evergreen content to keep them on track (via your Proven Framework).
- Make a follow-up call. (Hunt for problems and make damn sure you fix them. Does their burger look like the one in the picture?).
- Set up a slipping away system. (People going quiet is a red flag that they aren't getting what they want. Spot the red flags before they're lost forever).
- Deliver unexpected tools to help them succeed.
- Celebrate their wins. (Show how far they've come, especially if they've stacked up a few quick wins and are starting to get what they want).
- Send a milestone gift to keep celebrating those landmarks with them (a bottle of wine, box of chocolates, or – better – something that means something to them).
- Figure out what's next. (How can we help you now? How can we make things even better? I'm still here and I still care).

Your checklist may look very different, depending on your customer journey, but whether you're just getting started after 100 days or have everything wrapped up in 20 minutes like Domino's, having (and using!) an onboarding checklist will give you a distinct advantage over your rivals.

I've found that shorter, simpler checklists get followed, while longer, more complex ones don't. If I asked my team to follow a 20-step checklist for the first 100 days of every customer's journey, I can guarantee a handful of those steps would be skipped and the checklist itself would soon gather dust in a drawer somewhere.

What would a six-step first 100 days checklist look like? Which steps matter most?

As Joey Coleman says: "Most companies barely do any onboarding of new customers, let alone taking them through a strategically designed process that creates a feeling of welcome."

Consistently delivering a strategically designed onboarding process fixes the holes in your bucket in the short term and can deliver an astronomical ROI in the long term – long after those first 100 days are a distant memory.

TL/DR:

Most companies will lose 20 to 70 per cent of their customers in the first 100 days.

Get those first 100 days right though and you can keep a customer for life. Plan out the key milestones for your customer's perfect journey from complete newbie to 100-day-old-raving-fan. Put them in a checklist and tick them off. Check!

Oh, and keep it simple – a six-step checklist gets followed, while a 20-step one gets filed in a drawer.

FULFILMENT ASSETS: PROVEN FRAMEWORK

As a Sales Asset, our Proven Framework gave prospects a glimpse into their future, showing them what to expect as a paying customer. We can turn our Proven Framework into a Fulfilment Asset by putting the guard rails up and simply keeping customers on track.

At every step on your first 100 days checklist, ask yourself: "Are they on track?" When you've got a Proven Framework, you know that:

1. People who are on track are on course to get what they want.
2. People who aren't on track are off course to get what they want.

I own a horse racing Software as a Service (SaaS) business. It's extremely powerful and tracks hundreds of data points for every racehorse in the UK, then compares each horse against the rest of the field in every race. It's a fantastic product for those members who know how to use it.

Once members figure out how it works, they usually end up staying with us for years. But for those new to the service, it can seem a bit scary and overwhelming. When they log in for the first time, with their Helmet of Justice on, they see a load of numbers and tables, and don't know what the hell they're looking at or what they're supposed to do with the data. It just seems like random ones and zeros to them.

Each month, we review member cancellation requests and look for patterns. We don't have to look far to find the holes in this bucket:

> *"I don't understand it."*
>
> *"It's too complicated."*
>
> *"I don't know what I'm looking at!"*

New members told us they were confused, overwhelmed, and scared by the perceived difficulty in learning how the service works. I didn't get it. On the one hand, we've got overwhelmed newbies cancelling in their droves. And on the other hand, lifelong advocates of the exact same service who love everything about it.

The only difference? The lifelong users simply stuck with it. They made it past those crucial first 100 days and figured out how it worked, with a little hand-holding from the team. There wasn't a Proven Framework to show them, so *they* created one. They carved their own path. Sure, they met a few dead ends and took many wrong turns but they got there in the end.

While our most successful, lifelong members had created (and were still following) their own Proven Framework, we were still expecting newbies to figure it out by themselves and, unsurprisingly, most didn't.

In the movie Independence Day, the humans threw everything they had at the invading aliens – fighter jets, RPGs, nukes – and nothing worked. Humanity as we knew it was doomed until Randy Quaid flew a bomb directly into the mothership on a kamikaze mission (cue lots of CGI explosions as somehow all the alien warships implode).

Meanwhile, the President of the United States, who happened to be flying past in his own fighter jet, sees this unfold and issues a decree: "Now we know how to take them out... gentlemen, spread the word!"

Maybe you don't have a Proven Framework yet but your most successful customers will find one. They'll create their own. Speak to them and find out what they did, step by step. And then simplify it as much as possible. When your best customers tell you how they got the results they wanted, you can simply don your aviators, gaze ruggedly into the distance, and declare: "Now we know how to give them what they want... gentlemen, spread the word!"

This is what we did with our SaaS business. We spoke to those who were crushing it and asked how they did it. We simplified their answers, condensed them to a handful of steps and gave our new Proven Framework a catchy name – the Simple Six. Then, we "spread the word, gentlemen" with the newbies.

We also provided some training, taking clients through the Simple Six framework, one step at a time. We delivered a quick win and held our members' hands to ensure they made it to the first step. Once they're at the first step, we guide them to the second. It's as simple as that.

Note that the actual SaaS product didn't change at all, but breaking down the steps required to learn how to use it into a Proven Framework and giving it a disarming name, instantly made it less scary in new customers' minds. If you recall, that was the main reason members were cancelling – they were confused, overwhelmed, and scared. But no longer.

By breaking things down into a simple, step-by-step framework, holding members' hands all the way, and demonstrating via the use of case studies that many of their fellow members were succeeding using this Proven Framework, we massively reduced churn and are well on our way towards keeping them past those crucial first 100 days – and beyond.

TL/DR:

A Proven Framework is the guard rail that keeps customers on track to getting what they want.

People who are on track are on course to get what they want. People who aren't on track are off course and unlikely to get what they want. If you don't think you have a Proven Framework, just speak to your most successful clients and ask them how they got there, step-by-step. They'll tell you how they carved their own path. Then: "Gentlemen, spread the word".

Oh, and Independence Day is still a cracking movie.

FULFILMENT ASSETS: VIDEO

"That was amazing, John! So much more useful, with much more detail than a text response!"

I'd sent a client a four-minute video answering their questions and explaining something that would have taken me 15 minutes to type out a crappier text version. I do almost all my onboarding and a great deal of my fulfilment via video. It's quicker for me and much more impactful for my clients.

I can get across tone, sincerity, and explain quite complex things much easier than with text. I can tell jokes (and smile, so people know I'm joking). I can demonstrate how hard something is for me to convey. I can use my hands to emphasise key points.

I follow a checklist of the key points I need to make (including celebrating the sale with them, reaffirming they've made a great choice, introducing Jason and Vicky, preparing them for the handover, etc.), future pacing the Proven Framework and holding their hand while we move to the first step of the Proven Framework – the kick-off call.

None of this is scripted, so I just chat away for anything from three to five minutes, including some personal references and inside jokes if appropriate, and then hit send. It's still quicker than typing, editing, and sending a text version and at least ten times as impactful.

I have a "one take" rule, so if I stumble over my words and mess up (believe me, this happens a *lot*!), then I apologise, and carry on regardless. I imagine the client is on the other side of the camera and I'm talking directly to *them*, not to the camera. I'm not aiming for perfection, I'm aiming for genuine. That means no scripts, no do-overs, and very much what-you-see-is-what-you-get.

People buy from people, so use video to show yourself as you truly are. Show your team as they truly are. Show us what happens behind the scenes (warts and all). Don't just tell me how something works – *show* me. Grab your product and do a live demo for me. Share your screen and walk me through what happens next. Take me around the office on your camera phone. Show me how to use your software or my brand new car being waxed and polished before it gets delivered to me. Let me see a 20-second video of my dog playing happily at the kennels.

Meet your customers' levels of passion and excitement about their latest purchase. And don't just tell me how excited you are to work with me – show me.

FULFILMENT ASSETS: EMAIL

If you want your burgers to look like the one in the picture, you must resist the temptation to stick with the boring "product delivery" emails that often come out of the box.

Your onboarding sequence should contain just as much razzmatazz as your Nurture and Sales emails. Keep the energy going. Otherwise, your customers will notice that their burger looks different from the one in the picture.

You created a Never-Ending Nurture Sequence for your prospects, so why not do the same for your paying clients? Make them feel even more loved, even more nurtured, as you continue to hold their hand, reminding them: "I'm here for you and I care. I'm going to help you to get what you want. And I'm not going to stop until I'm damn sure you've got what you want. Your success matters to me."

Sometimes, I'll send a random "surprise and delight" email that isn't automated or part of the Never-Ending Nurture Sequence. Most times, I'll include a personal video, as described in the last section, within this email. It shows I'm here and I really care. You're not just a number in the machine. This isn't a numbers game, it's a relationships game.

Here's a reply I received to one of those emails recently: "Thanks John, really appreciate the personal touch. I was waiting for the pre-recorded section to kick in on the video, but it was all live. So impressed with that, and also really inspired."

It's also time to add a new Signature Move because the one used for clients should be different from that for your prospects. Rather than continuing to sell, you can now signpost your Proven Framework(s), tell people what they should do if they get lost/stuck, and showcase those success stories and case studies that will help them to get what they want.

Once prospects turn into clients, each email you send becomes an opportunity to demonstrate:

1. I'm here for you.
2. I care about you.
3. I'm not going to stop until you've got what you want.

FULFILMENT ASSETS: WEBSITE

As with your emails, your website should keep the pizazz going! Your membership area, product download/delivery pages or "what happens next" confirmation page post-sale should be every bit as good as your sales page – if not better!

Here's what most people do:

> *"Thanks for your order. We'll be in touch."*

Compare that with the following:

> *"Thanks for your order, John!*
>
> *I really appreciate you putting your faith in [insert your company name]. I'm so looking forward to helping you get what you want.*
>
> *Here's what's going to happen next.*
>
> *I've sent you an email with the first step on our Proven Framework. This will help you achieve your first quick win. Now, I know you're probably itching to get started, and just play with the product – so if you want to, you can do so here [insert link to step one of your Proven Framework].*
>
> *We've designed the product/service to be really user-friendly, so you should be able to get to grips with it in no time. That being said, we do have some amazing how-to videos. You can find them in the members' area here [insert link to members' area].*
>
> *And if you ever get stuck, are unsure how anything works, or have any questions whatsoever, you can give me a call on 01234 567890 (that's my direct line), or you can email me yourname@yourcompanyname.com. I'm here for you, and I care about you. I won't rest until you've got what you want.*
>
> *And don't forget... that's guaranteed. If this isn't the best quality [insert goal-focused outcome] you've ever had, I'll personally put my hand in my pocket, and send you back twice what you've paid me, no questions asked. I'm really looking forward to working with you, and helping you achieve [insert what they want]. Here's that first step of the Proven Framework again to help you get a quick win under your belt..."*

Which one looks like the burger in the picture?

A while back, I was reviewing our customer support logs when I spotted this line in an email sent to all new clients:

> *"Hopefully, you should have everything you need."*

First of all, how does a new customer (wearing the Helmet of Justice) know *what* they need, let alone whether they *have* everything they need?

Secondly, how about we remove "hoping" as a strategy for getting what they want? If ever there's a word to stoke the fires of buyer's remorse, it's "hopefully".

Thirdly, do they have everything they need? What do they need? When do they need it? What's the easiest way for them to find it when they need it? Do they need product walkthroughs, FAQs, video tutorials, assembly guides, specifications? A little signposting, a simple checklist or a quick chat with a team member?

Write down everything your clients may need and then make sure it can all be easily accessed from your website.

If your customer service team find themselves answering the same questions and dishing out the same advice several times a week, then your clients clearly *don't* have everything they need. So, find a way to put it in their hands *before* they need it or so they at least know where to look for it.

Your website is more than likely the first place they'll look. Will they find it there or just a message saying, "Hopefully you have everything you need"?

FULFILMENT ASSETS: EVERGREEN PRODUCTS

In 2011, I cancelled my Netflix subscription. I could never find anything to watch on there. It was full of awful straight-to-video, bargain-bucket movies such as Dumb and Dumberer, Son of the Mask and most of

Nicolas Cage's back catalogue. It was a long way from the Netflix we know and love today.

In the last three years, Netflix has spent more than £30billion producing its own content. Every movie and TV series that Netflix creates is another Evergreen Asset added to its ecosystem, attracting new viewers and retaining existing ones. Netflix is doing the work of creating the programme once, and reaping the rewards of having subscribers pay for access to the ecosystem again and again (and again).

Could you be the Netflix of your niche?

Creating Evergreen Products means that *you* are no longer the product, selling live access to you by the hour. Instead, people can pay to access the information, knowledge, and expertise in your head or share the assets you own.

Dean Samed used to be a freelance digital artist, specialising in creating amazing bespoke book covers for the horror sector including commissions for the likes of Stephen King. Frustrated with selling his time for money, and the "don't work, don't earn" nature of freelancing, Dean started building his own Evergreen Products – a digital library of stock images that people could license from him.

Now, Dean could do the work (a photoshoot) once, and reap the rewards (license the images) again and again (and again). It wasn't long before Dean realised it cost him money to accept the freelance roles, and that creating Evergreen Products was infinitely more scalable. He now focuses entirely on his Evergreen Products ecosystem, constantly creating more digital assets, as well as branching out into other Evergreen Products such as Earn With Your Art – a guide for fellow freelancers and a core skills Photoshop training system.

Dean removed himself as the product and turned himself into Netflix for digital artists.

Pivoting from live work to creating Evergreen Products has one major drawback. When you're creating, you're not earning. In many cases, you'd have to turn away paid work to carve out the time needed to create the Evergreen Products. Do an hour of live work and you get paid for that hour. Do an hour of Evergreen Product creation and you'll only get paid if and when you sell that product.

After one hour, you've sold nothing and earned diddly squat. After a month, you might have sold one product and your hourly rate (for that same solitary hour of creation) might be £10 or £25. But imagine if after six months you've sold £200 worth, a year later it's £500, and after a few years, your total earnings from one hour of creation could be several thousand pounds.

With Evergreen Products, the return on investment is delayed.

Netflix isn't going to recoup its £30billion investment in Evergreen Products in a quarter or two – although with more than 200million subscribers paying up to £13.99 a month, it isn't going to take long.

You're going to turn away paid work in the short term, earn very little in the medium term, and reap the rewards again and again (and again) in the long term.

Why is Netflix continuing to invest so heavily in original content? Because it understands the larger its library of original content, the greater ROI it can expect over the long term. Netflix knows the lifetime value of subscribers will continue to rise (I returned in 2013 and can't see me leaving anytime soon as I've got a "to watch" list of at least 20 shows) even if they put the prices up (as they did last year by 20 per cent). The more Evergreen Products Netflix adds to its ecosystem, the more valuable my membership becomes to me.

During the Covid-19 pandemic, One Percenter Rupert Bassadone was unable to work. His company used computer-aided design (CAD) to provide site plans, floorplans, and GPS surveys for major events such as Badminton Horse Trials, WOMAD Festival, and Red Bull Soapbox. May 2020 was lining up to be Rupert's busiest month ever but it became his quietest. Everything got cancelled.

With his hand forced, Rupert decided it was the perfect time to create his Evergreen Product side-project that had been on the back burner for the best part of three years. Thus, AutoCAD for Events was born. It is an evergreen course, teaching event professionals how to use AutoCAD – a specific piece of computer-aided design software.

With event professionals also suddenly finding themselves with a lot of time on their hands, many of them decided to upskill and finally get around to learning how to use that new-fangled software they've been "meaning to get to grips with".

Rupert created Netflix for AutoCAD users.

Information products such as courses, ebooks, downloadable resources, guides and how-to manuals can easily be converted into an Evergreen Product ecosystem. If you can create them yourself and deliver them digitally, then even better. You'll have no suppliers to deal with, no inventory sitting on your shelves tying up your cash flow, low (to no) overheads, and much less customer service. You can deliver your products anywhere in the world instantly.

And, best of all, you'll enjoy the freedom of time. You choose when to create your products and your customers can buy them whenever it suits them. You can create your Evergreen Products in your pyjamas at 3am if you like (unless you're recording a video course… that could be a bit weird… or a new niche?), and your customers can buy it weeks, months or even years later, in *their* pyjamas at 3am.

TL/DR:

Evergreen Products enable you to be the Netflix of your niche.

They remove "you" as live produce, being sold by the hour and instead license the information, ideas, and experience in your head as replicable digital assets. The more assets you can add to your Evergreen Products library, the more valuable the entire library will be.

Oh, and Evergreen Products can be created – and consumed – at 3am in your PJs.

FULFILMENT ASSETS: MEMBERSHIP MODEL

Memberships are by far my favourite business model. They're notoriously hard to get going, but just like the world's largest merry-go-round, also very hard to stop once you've got momentum. They offer predictable, steady income without too many peaks and troughs.

Knowing you're not starting each calendar month from £0, leaving you free to invest the majority of your time, energy, focus and attention on delivering value to existing paying members (rather than constantly chasing new ones), really appeals to me.

Next time you look at your bank statement, check out the Direct Debits and you'll see some great examples of membership sites – your gym, Amazon Prime, Netflix, etc.

But memberships aren't just for the big boys. They can work for anyone with a clearly defined audience – coaches, therapists, nutritionists, accountants, Forex traders, property investors, personal trainers, tutors, and teachers of any description. If you train, teach, or advise, memberships could work for you.

Many of the most successful businesses I've been involved in over the last two decades have been membership sites:

- Net Free Stuff: A freebies website with 125,000 free members (advertising supported).

- Free Racing Tips: A horse racing tips business; currently 37,000 members (mix of paid and ad-supported).
- Easy Content Units: An affiliate SaaS business with 300 paying members.
- One Percent Club: Group coaching for small business owners with 90 paying members.
- Form Ratings: Horse racing data SaaS business with 450 paying members.

Memberships work brilliantly with Evergreen Assets because the more assets you create, the more value there is for members. That ever-increasing value means members stick around for longer, leading to a higher Lifetime Value (LTV).

The higher your LTV, the more you can spend to get and keep members, which pushes your LTV even higher – leveraging the immense power of compounding. The more members you have, the more value you can create, attracting more members and keeping them longer.

It's a virtuous circle, especially if you implement the feedback loop from the next section. Find out what they want > Give them what they want. Each month, we create new Evergreen Assets for our existing members, based on what they've told us they want:

- New deep-dive training "Masterclasses" for our One Percenters.
- New systems and strategies for our horse racing SaaS business.
- New predictions and custom bets for our sports betting members.

The more we listen to our members, the more value we give. The more value we give, the more valuable they become, enabling us to invest further and create even more assets.

Evergreen Assets you could create for your members include:

- Downloadable resources.
- Checklists and cheat sheets.
- Private chat groups, forums, or communities.
- Training videos, walkthroughs, and how-to guides.
- Email coaching.
- Group mastermind calls.
- One-to-one calls.
- Opportunities to follow/copy what you do.
- Members-only strategies and systems.
- Software.

Once you have a good collection of assets, recruiting new members becomes easier because you can simply throw some meat over the fence and show non-members what they're missing out on by giving them a small taste of membership. I give prospects free access to a handful of our One Percent Club Masterclasses. However, the full Netflix-style library of more than 60 Masterclasses is only available to paying members.

Move the paywall slightly, lower the velvet rope for a while, and allow prospects to see what's behind the curtain (even if just for a few minutes). We all want to know what it's like to turn left on a plane.

Memberships aren't just for service-based businesses, either. You can even turn a product into a membership model, as wine retailer Naked Wines has done. Instead of buying bottles of vino as and when you feel like it, you become a member and pay £20 a month into your account which gives you £20 of credit towards some booze.

Before long, Rowan (the founder of the club) will send you an email telling you how guilty he feels that he's "got your money and the wine", so how about he sends you some wine? Just choose what you'd like. "Oh, and here is a particularly good offer," he says – making an Offer You Can't Refuse.

It's a great way to pretty much guarantee a £240 a year spend per customer. And before I gave up the booze, I would often top up my Naked Wine account with a few quid here and there.

Because it's a membership club, it's not just about the product. Instead, it's the feeling of belonging to a tribe championing the same cause – helping independent vineyards and refusing to settle for crap supermarket wine ever again.

TL/DR:

Memberships offer predictable, steady income without too many peaks and troughs.

If you train, teach, or advise, memberships could work for you. Memberships compound with Evergreen Assets – the more you create, the more valuable your membership becomes. Once you have assets, recruit members by throwing meat over the fence. Once you have members, focus all your attention on giving them what they want and creating assets just for them.

Oh, and memberships aren't just for service business.

FULFILMENT ASSETS: FEEDBACK LOOP

To know that your clients are getting what they want – that their burger looks like the one in the picture – you need feedback and lots of it.

If your clients are deliriously happy then, brilliant, ask for a referral (Viral Asset) or make heroes of them for a case study (which could be deployed as a Nurture, Sales or Fulfilment Asset).

If they're not happy, then that's good news too because you can now course-correct (improve the machine) and ask again, ensuring you not only give this client what *they* want, but improve the experience for every client who follows in their footsteps.

When you have an eye test, the optician uses a constant feedback loop – "is this better or worse?" – to ensure you get the right prescription. Likewise, asking your clients a few simple questions could be the perfect prescription for your business.

The problem with Net Promoter Score

A widely-accepted Proven Framework for customer feedback is the Net Promoter Score, which is calculated by asking clients the following question:

> *On a scale of 0-10, how likely is it that you would recommend us to a friend or colleague?*

Respondents are then grouped as follows:

Those who answer 9 or 10 are classed as Promoters, your most loyal clients, who will buy again and again – and refer others.

The 7s and 8s are classed as Passives – satisfied customers, but with no real loyalty to you or your brand. Their heads could easily be turned by a competitor with a half-decent offer.

Anyone answering 0 to 6 is tagged as a Detractor – an unhappy customer who not only is unlikely to buy again, but may also spread negative word of mouth about you or your brand.

Subtracting the percentage of Detractors from the percentage of Promoters gives you your official Net Promoter Score, which can range from a low of minus-100 (if every customer is a Detractor) to a high of 100 (if every customer is a Promoter).

Using NPS as a feedback tool is great in theory. Simply ask your Promoters for a referral, testimonial, or case study. Ask the Passives what you could do to improve, and get on the phone to find out what's gone wrong with the Detractors.

But it doesn't work like that. In reality, when you send out the NPS question, you get loads of 8-10 responses, some 1 or 2s and not much else. Happy people (Promoters) tell you they're happy. Really unhappy people (Detractors) tell you they're unhappy.

But the mildly disgruntled people – the Passives who are a "tad miffed", underwhelmed, and ever-so-slightly disappointed – generally won't say anything. Even though this group may make up the largest section of your customers, you get very few responses from them. The Passives are more likely to ignore the survey altogether, telling themselves: "Well, they didn't listen to my support request, so what's the point in telling them I'm mildly annoyed now?" or "I don't want to rock the boat" or "I don't want to get anyone in trouble".

The likelihood of clients providing feedback is 100 per cent correlated with their perceived impression that it'll make any difference whatsoever. If they don't feel they'll be listened to and their feedback used to make things better, they won't respond.

It's more likely that the Passives will demonstrate their contempt in the most passive-aggressive British way they can possibly think of – by quietly taking their business elsewhere and vowing to never buy from you ever again (but not telling you).

If you don't hear negative feedback from your customers, don't assume for one minute that everything is rosy.

"They haven't complained therefore they must be happy..." – BZZZZ! Wrong answer! Their burger still doesn't match the one in the picture, but they don't see the point in complaining about it, so they'll just buy their burgers elsewhere in future.

Getting feedback from the Passives might be like getting blood out of a stone, but this is where you'll find the highest ROI. By fixing the problems and issues this group has – the small, niggling annoyances – you can prevent Passives from becoming Detractors, and increase the likelihood of them becoming Promoters in the future. You improve the machine for everyone.

This is why I always attach some copy to my feedback requests, letting clients know how much I *truly* want to know what's going on and imploring them to find fault with my product or service. I also ask them to be as brutal as possible because I want to be better. The best way I can deliver a burger that looks like the picture is for you to let me know when it doesn't.

If I'm the person delivering the service, I also get someone else to ask for the feedback, because what if I'm the problem? The Passives aren't going to gripe about me to me, are they?

So I get someone else to say: "John's asked me to drop you a quick line with a couple of questions about your experience so far. He thinks you'll be far too nice if he asks you himself, and wants to know what you *really* think. I've got tough skin, so please be as brutal as you like and let me know the good, the bad, and the ugly. Seriously, I can take it, and you'll be doing us a huge favour, helping us to improve [product or service name] not only for you, but for all of our clients."

That gives them permission to complain about me and highlights how much importance I place on feedback.

To get relevant, actionable feedback, I like to ask four open-ended questions:

1. What should I stop doing? (This lets clients rant about the stuff that annoys them).
2. What should I keep doing? (This helps you find the hidden gems – the stuff you do that clients value above all else).
3. What should I start doing? (This puts the clients into "if this were your business, what would you do?" mode and can provide great inspiration for new features or products).
4. Is there anything else I should know? (The Columbo question. This is where the Passives get their chance to tell you about their mild annoyances. The "no biggies". The broken link on your website. The segmentation that's gone wrong. The support request where we could have been a little more helpful. The fact that their burger doesn't quite look like the one in the picture).

Clearly, asking four open-ended questions is harder for customers to complete than a single "rate us from 0-10 with one click" Net Promoter Score question. But while you may get fewer responses (hence the need to highlight the importance you place on feedback), you'll get real-world, actionable feedback rather than an arbitrary NPS score of 38.7.

You'll know what works and what doesn't. You'll know what to fix. You'll know *why* your customers feel their burger doesn't look like the one in the picture and what to do to make it right. You'll also know what they love. You'll have a feedback loop.

If you want some quick, actionable feedback today, you don't even need to send all four questions. You can kick-start the world's simplest feedback loop. Just pick up the phone, take a client for coffee, or send an email. Here's your script:

> "Hi NAME, how's it going?
>
> How are you getting on with ________?

Cheers,

John"

That's it. How are you getting on? How's it going? Then, shut up and listen. Don't talk. Don't interrupt. Don't defend. Just listen. Make notes. You want feedback? This will give you feedback.

If you're running a membership model, watch out for people going quiet. That's when you should start to worry about them slipping away. Set up a system; some form of trigger that nudges you when members are starting to slip away. Perhaps they haven't opened an email for a few weeks or haven't logged into their member area.

One of the simplest "slipping away systems" I've seen is a simple whiteboard with every client's name on it. When you speak to a client, rub his or her name off the top of the whiteboard and move it to the bottom. Then, simply work your way down the whiteboard every day and the ones most likely to slip away suddenly stand out – marooned on their own on the whiteboard, highlighting the fact they've gone quiet and need some attention.

Once you identify these people, you can send the world's simplest slipping away SPEAR email to re-engage them:

"Subject Line: Are you OK?

Hi NAME, are you OK?

I haven't heard from you in a while.

Cheers,

John"

That email normally gets a 60 to 70 per cent reply rate. It shows you care about them and their wellbeing.

What are you gonna do about it?

Getting feedback is only one part of the equation, though. You need to listen to and act on the feedback. That's what makes it a loop, otherwise it's a feedback black hole (which pretty accurately describes most businesses' feedback systems and is why Passives don't bother with feedback as a rule).

I recently emailed the MD of a company I've been working with for a few years with "a bit of a rant". Standards had been slipping, communication was all over the place, and his team were letting him down. His response was quite simply brilliant.

He thanked me for bringing these issues to his attention. He told me: "Without your feedback, I would have been in the dark. Now all our clients will benefit from the changes made, so I really appreciate you reaching out."

He acknowledged there had been issues, and accepted personal liability for those issues. He told me what I could expect from him to resolve my issues and exactly what he was going to do to prevent them from happening again.

His business will improve as a result of not just getting feedback, but by acting on it. I also benefit, as my experience of working with his company should improve, as will all of his other clients. That's a proper win-win. He's turned me from a Passive into a Promoter, and improved the machine for all of his clients. That's why a top-notch feedback loop should be part of every business owner's Evergreen Assets ecosystem.

Often, we think that customers demand perfection. But they don't. Most reasonable customers (and yes, I accept there are unreasonable customers) accept that things sometimes go wrong. They don't expect things to be perfect every time. But they do expect you to put things right if and when they *do* go wrong.

And at a bare minimum, they expect you to listen to feedback. I recently signed up my cockapoo Chewie for a dog food subscription service where, for a monthly fee, we'd receive a box full of all his favourite flavours and maybe even the odd treat or two. (There's the membership model in action right there).

After our first delivery, I received an email from the company with the subject line, "Happy with your order?". Great," I thought, "They've got a feedback loop!" They went on to say:

> *"Hi there,*
>
> *We just wanted to follow up and check that everything was great with your order and that your pet has been enjoying their [company name removed to protect the guilty] dog food.*
>
> *Don't forget, you can still get 15% off your next order with us, just use code AB-12-15-PF on our website or over the phone*
>
> *We're here to help however we can. So if you have any questions, please don't hesitate to get in touch. We're open Monday to Friday, between 9am and 5pm on 01234 567890 or at hello@companyname.co.uk.*
>
> *Kind regards,*
>
> *Kate*
>
> *Senior Customer Care Manager"*

Not bad. I'd probably give this a 5/10. There was far too much company branding on the email, so it didn't look personal. They haven't used my name or Chewie's, despite having both.

They seem more focused on getting me to order again (despite the fact I've set up a recurring monthly subscription for all the food we need) rather than telling me how important my feedback is. By dishing out discounts from day one, they're also training me to never pay full price. And who is Kate? There's no surname, photo, bio, or anything to enable me to nurture a relationship with Kate.

But it's not *that* bad. They've sent an email to a new customer a few days after the first delivery, asking how things are going. That's the minimum effective dose. Or at least it would be. Because when I replied to the email, letting Kate know that Chewie has indeed enjoyed his food, but seems to have an allergy to one of the recipes and could we please swap that flavour out for next month's delivery, my email bounced right back to me.

> *"Your message could not be delivered. There is no mailbox by that name (no-reply@companyname.co.uk) on this server."*

I couldn't believe it. I had to double-check. Sure enough, Kate, the "Senior Customer Care Manager" at a major pet food company sends her feedback requests from a "no-reply" email address.

Sorry Kate, but I've downgraded you from a 5/10 to a 1/10. Evergreen Assets is a relationships game, and sending your feedback loop email from a no-reply email address is a cardinal sin. It screams from the rooftops: "I don't *actually* care what you think. I don't *really* want to hear it. I'm just ticking the box."

That's not a feedback loop. That's a feedback black hole. To create a feedback loop, you need to ask for feedback *and* listen to it *and* act on it. Then, ask (and listen and act) again, closing the loop.

Kate is very much in the dog house.

TL/DR:

A feedback loop tells you when customers' burgers don't match the picture and enables you to do something about it.

Getting feedback from very happy (and very unhappy) clients is easy. Squeezing it out of the Passive masses is much harder but much more valuable. The biggest reason people keep their feedback to themself is they don't think you'll listen anyway. Asking for real, honest feedback shows that you care. Acting on that feedback demonstrates you really do care.

Oh, and don't pretend you care about your customers while letting their feedback disappear into a no-reply@ black hole.

FULFILMENT ASSETS: DIRECT MAIL

Keeping customers is a piece of cake

The best ROI from Direct Mail usually comes from sending to current or past clients – people you already have a relationship with. If you've already got a great relationship with your clients, sending them something in the post can be the cherry on top of the cake.

In fact, it could literally *be* a piece of cake. For our sports betting business, we send members a "cake card" (a greetings card with two slices of cake) on their first anniversary. One Percenter and Google Ads expert Tash Conway sends new clients a box of brownies. I've been known to send random clients an entire cake in the post and have received more than a few myself.

While sending new clients something (a bottle of wine at Christmas or a gift on their birthday) makes sense, it can look a bit…calculated. You've paid me £x, so you get a prize. It's Christmas, so I'm expected to send you a present.

Compare that with: "I'm sending this, just because. I'm thinking of you and I care about you. I thought you'd enjoy this."

Remember, Joe Girard sent 13,000 cards a month out to his clients with one single message: "I'm thinking of you." While Joe sold a record-breaking number of cars as a result, no one who received his cards felt he was doing so in order to sell them a car.

Removing any ulterior motive makes sending a gift so much more impactful. It shows you genuinely *do* care about your client and their happiness. Let everyone else send gifts at Christmas or company-branded cards (with a discount voucher) on birthdays. But your clients will know you truly care, because you sent something... *just because.*

For even more impact, send something personal to them and demonstrate how well you know them. When I received an unexpected T-shirt in the post, custom-printed in the style of the *Big Ideas... For Small Businesses* cover, with an added crown and the words "King of Routine" (after I was called this on a podcast), the impact was off the scale. I've written about it in two of my subsequent books and still talk about it years later. It still fits, too!

But be careful of sending a gift that you know someone doesn't like as this can have the opposite effect. Sounds obvious, but it happens, especially when sending out the same thing to a large group. For example, I don't drink alcohol. I quit in 2013 and have spoken and written about it hundreds of times since. Yet, every year I get sent bottles of wine, champagne, gin, crates of beer and so on, many from people who know I don't drink.

When I open my gift to find it's a bottle of booze from someone who knows I'm teetotal, the first thought that enters my head is: "Well, they either don't know me very well or don't care." Without wishing to sound ungrateful, the relationship would have been better served if they hadn't sent me anything.

Direct Mail Fulfilment Assets are about cementing the relationship. They're an opportunity to create some wow moments, demonstrating that you know your clients well and that you genuinely care about them. Remember how many unexpected extras we planned in our first 100 days checklist? Lots of these can be delivered via Direct Mail.

If customers have signed up for a digital product, sending them something physical in the post will be even more unexpected and therefore impactful. We send all new members of our sports betting SaaS business a "starter pack", which contains a printed "how-to" guide, a stick letter (more on that in a moment), an explanation of the Proven Framework, a couple of quick wins for them to get their teeth into and something to *actually* get their teeth into – a small bag of sweets or a chocolate bar.

We don't tell anyone they're going to get this. We don't advertise it as a feature. It's an unexpected bonus. And it's massively impactful. Adding this Direct Mail starter pack into the first 100 days checklist increased the lifetime value of a member by around 35 per cent (and rising).

We're in the renewals business

If your business benefits from repeat custom, you need to sell customers on not leaving. You need to put as much work into persuading them (and demonstrating to them) that they've made a wise decision choosing you, and that you're definitely the person to give them what they want – now and in the future.

As executive vice-president of Boardroom Inc, Brian Kurtz oversaw the mailing of more than 1.3billion pieces of Direct Mail during a 40-year career. In his 2019 book *Overdeliver*, Brian explains his lightbulb moment that enabled him to grow the business to more than $150million in sales.

> *"This slow and steady process started with a one-year bogey, making a new subscription profitable a year after we sold it. Then we moved to a two-year bogey, and eventually a three-year bogey.*

Who would have believed when we launched the publication that we would be willing and able to wait until year three to break even on a new subscriber? The day Marty (Boardroom's chairman Marty Edelston) and I realised we were in the business of renewals was the day I believe we really understood lifetime value...

...calculating this number and basing all our marketing decisions on it was the single biggest reason Boardroom became as large as it did."

Brian Kurtz knew it. Joe Girard knew it. And now you know it. We're *all* in the renewals business.

You should invest just as much of your time, energy, attention, and marketing budget into *keeping* customers as you do into getting customers. The longer each customer stays with you, and the more they buy, the higher their lifetime value, which in turn increases the amount you can spend to acquire a customer in the first place, then invest even more in keeping them, compounding their LTV ever-higher.

Most marketers skimp on Fulfilment Assets. Keeping customers is an afterthought for them because they're far too busy refilling that leaky bucket.

Smart marketers devote time to create Fulfilment Assets, knowing those cogs will compound and make the whole machine work more effectively.

Every piece of fulfilment marketing you send to clients keeps you in the renewals business. A great place to start is with a stick letter. As the name suggests, the sole purpose of this letter is to get your new customer to stick with you, to shut down any hint of buyer's remorse before it can surface, and to reaffirm some key points:

1. You've made a great decision.
2. Remember why you bought this particular product/service.
3. Don't forget I'm going to personally guarantee your success.
4. Here's what you're going to get.
5. Here's our Proven Framework.
6. Here's what to expect next.
7. I care.

That last point – I care – should run through the tone of the entire letter. Every word of this letter should shout from the rooftops: "I'm here for you and I care. I'm going to help you get what you want and I'm not going to stop until I'm damn sure you've got what you want. Your success matters to me."

Now, it may seem strange the first time you write a stick letter, because it can feel as if you're trying to make the sale again when the customer has already bought. In many ways, you are. You're certainly trying to remove any doubts customers may have – any niggling feelings they might have made a mistake.

The stick letter reassures them: "You haven't made a mistake. You've made a great choice. Here's why."

It should motivate your new client, making them even more excited to work with you and inspire them to take the first step on your Proven Framework.

TL/DR:

Keeping customers is a piece of cake – especially when you send cake.

Send stuff because you care, not because it's expected. Put some thought into it and show that you truly know (and care about) your client. We're all in the renewals business. If you want customers to stick, send them a stick letter. Close that sale and remind them what a great decision they've made.

Oh, and please don't send me booze – but I'll happily accept all forms of cake!

FULFILMENT ASSETS: REMARKETING

Now, this may seem to contradict my previous advice to ensure your remarketing excludes existing buyers, but bear with me.

Because I suggest you create a separate remarketing campaign *just* for buyers to follow them around the internet with the sole purpose of making damn sure they are getting what they want. That their burger looks like the one in the picture.

Imagine buying a new car and a few days later spotting an ad on Facebook with your car and the dealer's smiling face, together with the headline "How's the new car?". You'd click on it, wouldn't you? That ad could take you to an online version of a stick letter, combined with a feedback loop.

Or let's say you're a coach who's just signed up a new bunch of clients. You could create a remarketing campaign for them, which features your happy smiling face and the headline "Got any questions about [Proven Framework name]?" or just "I'm really looking forward to working with you". This could link to a video webpage where you genuinely enquire how they're getting on (world's simplest feedback loop), remind them of your guarantee, and tell them what they should do if they need help. Then, have an open-ended text area underneath for them to fill in with the questions: "How are you getting on with [Proven Framework name]? Is there anything else I should know?"

Who else follows new clients around the internet just to make sure they're happy? Done well, this could be a very low-cost, very high-impact asset.

FULFILMENT ASSETS: SOCIAL NETWORKS

As your network evolves, your clients will become part of it and you part of theirs. You could create private groups or roped-off VIP areas for your clients to chat with you (and each other) semi-privately, making it easier to ensure they're getting what they want now and to find out what they want next.

Jason and I have a private Facebook group for our One Percenters (which is the only place I spend any time on Facebook). I'm part of several private WhatsApp groups as a client too. These social networking platforms make it easy for your network to socialise with each other. The clue's in the name – social networking.

If you continue to dig the well (before you're thirsty), once you've given those clients what they want, you can offer to do the same for their friends too (creating a Viral Asset). In the same vein, you can also leverage your existing clients as a welcoming committee for new ones.

Who better to show the newbies around, tell them how things *really* work, and provide a bridge between you and your new clients than those who have already completed your Proven Framework (or are at least a few steps ahead)?

It's also worth thinking about any other problems you can help solve for your newest client by introducing them to people from your existing network. Think about who else can help them. Are they looking for a new accountant? Have they talked about a desire to lose weight? Are they looking to work with a particular target market?

Can you make introductions to others in your network, helping to solve additional problems for your new client beyond your area of expertise and, as an added bonus, deliver even more value to your network as a whole?

FULFILMENT ASSETS: SUMMARY

You've built your entire Evergreen Assets ecosystem around a single promise – *I can get you what you want.*

Well, now it's time to deliver on that promise. It's time to give them what they want. It's time to make sure that their burger looks like the one in the picture.

Things that don't start well, usually don't end well. So give them a quick win and a kick-off call to get things off to a flying start. Make sure you hand over to your A-Team like Hannibal, rather than Bob's wedding to Sue ("Terry, you may now kiss the bride!").

Don't lose 20 to 70 per cent of your customers in the first 100 days. Instead, use a checklist to keep you (and them) on your Proven Framework. Leverage video again to show customers how their new product/service works. Keep the razzmatazz going long after they've bought – no boring product delivery emails or "thanks for your order" web pages.

Just like the world's largest merry-go-round, memberships and subscriptions are hard to stop once you've got momentum. They offer predictable, steady income without too many peaks and troughs. Embrace the feedback loop. Find out when customers' burgers don't match the picture and then do something about it.

Keeping customers is a piece of cake – especially when you send cake. Or T-shirts. Or 13,000 hand-written cards that say "I'm here for you and I care. I'm going to help you to get what you want. And I'm not going to stop until I'm damn sure you've got what you want. Your success matters to me".

We're all in the renewals business. So let's make those burgers look like the one in the picture, shall we?

7. ADMIN ASSETS

Let me be very clear – I hate admin. I'm a former civil servant who would be quite content to never push another pen in my life. I'm a marketer, not an administrator. But you know what? Everything's marketing – even admin.

Every boring invoice, every mundane company policy, every tedious set of accounts and every monotonous forgotten password request is marketing. Every time you answer the phone, it's marketing. Every email you send is marketing. Every word on your website (including the error messages) is marketing. Every time someone uses your product, walks past your premises or chats to one of your team – it's all marketing.

Marketing is something that every person in your business (and every Evergreen Asset you create) is doing 24/7. You can't not market. Everything is marketing – even the boring, beige, vanilla admin.

Now, I'm not going to persuade you to fall in love with admin. Most of the entrepreneurs I've met are truly awful at it. We hate it. But I'm also an investor and I know excellent Admin Assets can deliver a tremendous ROI, especially if you can add a little raspberry-ripple razzmatazz to the boring, beige vanilla.

Time is your most finite of resources. No matter how big a pile of money you amass, you can't buy more time. Evergreen Admin Assets save you time, prevent valuable hours from being wasted, and generate an increased ROI on your time invested. Admin Assets increase your earnings-per-hour by either:

1. Generating more money for the time invested, or
2. Generating the same amount of money, with less time invested.

Either way, your time-ROI is going to skyrocket. I'm aiming to make admin palatable for even the most ardent, fly-by-the-seat-of-their-pants entrepreneurs because everything is marketing. Even the admin. Raspberry-ripple scoops at the ready...

ONE ADMIN ASSET TO RULE THEM ALL: COMPANY CULTURE

Your team is the largest Admin Asset you have at your disposal. If you've got a team of five, that's five people interacting with your customers and doing things that could either wow them or piss them off. Everything is marketing, so everything that these five people do is marketing. Got a team of 12? That's 12 marketers, all out there marketing for (or against) you every hour of every day.

It's probably a good idea to put some thought into what they do each day and to think about your company culture. Designing and creating your ideal company culture gets everyone on the same page and singing from the same hymn sheet.

Creating a great company culture isn't something you *do*, though. It's something you *get*. The culture isn't just a mission statement, pool table or pizza on Fridays. The culture is the by-product – the result of everything you do and the reasoning behind it. Your "why".

Derek Sivers, founder of CD-Baby (a website he started to help his musician friends sell their CD's online) hired his first employee in 2000. A year later, he had eight employees, but says that he was "still doing 'everything else' myself, working 7am to 10pm, seven days a week. Every five minutes, my employees had a question for me. It was hard to get anything done while answering questions all day."

Derek reached a breaking point and decided to stop answering his team's questions. Or, rather, he stopped *just* giving answers.

"Instead of just answering the question, I called everyone together for a minute. I repeated the situation and the question. I answered the question, but more importantly, I explained the thought process and philosophy behind my answer. I asked around to make sure everyone understood the answer. I asked one person to start a manual and write down the answer to this one situation, along with the philosophy behind it.

Then everyone went back to work. Ten minutes later, a new question. Same process:

1. *Gather everyone around.*
2. *Answer the question and explain the philosophy.*
3. *Make sure everyone understands the thought process.*
4. *Ask one person to write it in the manual.*
5. *Let everybody know they can decide this without me next time.*

After two months of this, there were no more questions"

It would have been far quicker in the short term to just give them the answer to their question. But in the long term, once Derek showed his workings (as my maths teacher always insisted), and his team understood *why* and *how* to arrive at the same answer themselves, they could reliably arrive at the "right" answer for almost any decision they needed to make without interrupting the boss every five minutes.

Whether Derek meant to or not, he created a culture based on his principles and ethos. Once his team knew that "helping musicians is our first goal and profit comes second", they could think like Derek. "Make sure everyone who deals with us leaves with a smile," enabled them to act like Derek, and "Do whatever would make the customer happiest as long as it's not outrageous," helped them grow Derek's company from less than £1million to around £15million in four years – and from eight employees to 85.

I'm following Derek's example with my team, telling stories, and giving real-life examples to demonstrate to my guys how I think and how I arrive at decisions. I want my team to think like me. I want them to act like me. So rather than just giving them the answer, I show them my workings. I tell them *why*.

I constantly remind them of our company's core values – not just so they can repeat them, parrot-fashion, but so they can live by them. I tell stories about lifelong fans who were saved by following the core values, as well as cautionary tales about the times I've got it wrong.

I don't just say, "Choose option A over option B," I'll explain my decision-making process, laying bare the frameworks and mental models I use daily to make decisions. Once everyone knows how I think (and *why* I think that way), I should be able to present any conundrum to any member of my team and have them make the right choice 99 per cent of the time.

If you ask my team, "What would John do in this situation?", I'd be confident that you'd get the same answer from all of them. Because they'd know why. And when you know why, what to do and how to do it becomes so much easier.

ADMIN ASSETS: PROVEN PROCESSES

Once you, your team and your clients know *why* you do it, it's time to start thinking about *how* you do it. The good news is that you probably already have processes for everything.

The bad news is that those processes are likely to be different for every member of the team, different every time you do the task and are never questioned or challenged. Worst of all, they're all in your head.

You have a proven process for doing the school run. You have proven processes for driving to work, cleaning your teeth, and getting dressed each morning (hopefully not in that order!).

Cooking the Christmas dinner? I'll bet there's a proven process. (One Percenter Rupert has taken this to the nth degree by creating an interactive Excel spreadsheet with exact timings, oven temperatures, and all roles and responsibilities clearly assigned to all members of the team so there's not a soggy Brussels sprout or a burnt pig in blanket to be found on the big day).

You maybe don't need to go as granular as Rupert's Festive Feast, but you do need clarity on your proven processes. If you know the best way to do something, then that way needs to be documented otherwise people will start "winging it".

In your business, you've spent years perfecting your processes and can do them with your eyes closed. But if you want to scale, and you want your team to work with you, you need to break down the proven processes into step-by-step instructions, so they know what to do and how to do it.

This is what we do. This is how we do it step by step by step. It's a Proven Framework, leading your team members by the hand and gently guiding them to the next step on a journey that many others have taken before, showing them the easiest, least stressful, most reliable, most productive, highly leveraged pathway.

ADMIN ASSETS: THE COMPANY HANDBOOK

Once established, organise all your proven processes into a single resource that makes it easy to find the right one.

Charlie Mullins, the founder of Pimlico Plumbers, London's largest independent plumbing company, wanted his growing team to deliver the same quality of service and attention to detail as when he was on the tools by himself.

> *"People were blown away if you turned up on time, did the job, did it fast, did it right, for the price you'd quoted, and with a smile to boot. Getting and keeping customers was a piece of cake! It's just common sense but the thing about common sense is, it ain't that common."*

Getting a bunch of tradies to turn up on time, do a good job, not overcharge, *and* smile? Charlie must have had his work cut out in those early days. He had started to collect an assortment of rules and standards over the years, leaving notes all over the office, such as, "Do not carry out work on obsolete or unfamiliar appliances", "Uniforms must be clean and worn at all times", and – a reminder of his big why – "Always leave a satisfied customer".

Some followed the rules. Many didn't, as Charlie explains in his 2015 book *Bog-Standard Business – How I Took the Plunge and Became the Millionaire Plumber*:

> *"If you want to build something valuable and unique, something that stands out in the wasteland of mediocrity, you can't expect everybody to jump on the bandwagon or even 'get it'. Getting my plumbers and tradesmen to take those rules seriously proved a constant, uphill battle.*
>
> *The temptation to take shortcuts and fall back into old habits is very strong. They would see every new sign as Charlie's 'new thing', while to me it was another finger in the latest hole in a big, leaky dam."*

Charlie's answer was a bible. Not The Bible, but the Pimlico Bible:

> *"I needed a way to enshrine all this stuff, to turn it from what it seemed to them, a bunch of shifting whims, to what it actually*

was, the framework and philosophy of the business – in other words, the law of the land.

So I ripped down all the notices and put them into a folder. This helped me see what was missing, and I added new pages. Soon it was a couple of inches thick, covering everything from personal appearance (no piercings, tattoos, or extreme hairdos) and customer etiquette to job pricing, forms and complying with regulations. It was a complete 'do's and don'ts' reference book. I made copies and gave everyone one.

A powerful tool, it allowed me to say, 'Here, is what's expected of you. It's not rocket science. It's your job to understand it and follow it. if you don't, you're out'."

The Pimlico Bible is an ever-changing document that Charlie has continued to update as regulations change and best practices evolve. It's a document that guides every aspect of Charlie's business, centred around his philosophy – his *why*.

Pimlico Plumbers is a huge company with around 350 staff members and a turnover of more than £43million. They need the level of formality and structure the Pimlico Bible gives them. What about a smaller business with a handful of staff and a six-figure turnover?

Earlier, you were introduced to Tracy Irwin and her A-Team. While Tracy runs a much smaller operation than Charlie, they share the same issues ("What do our clients want and how do we make sure that we deliver that every time?") and the same solution – a company handbook.

Tracy successfully removed herself from the day-to-day running of her business, TI Accountancy, by first deciding the culture she wanted to create. She gave her team one defining question that they could ask themselves to arrive at the same answer that Tracy would when faced with any question, problem or conundrum: "What would you want us to say/do if it were your business?"

This culture of "we treat your business as if it was our own" shines through in everything Tracy and her team do because she designed it that way.

She has told her team *why* they're doing it. She's given them the proven processes and uses task management software to make sure those processes are done. And she shows her team *how* to follow the proven processes through her company handbook.

It's not a physical handbook like Derek Sivers' manual or the Pimlico Bible. Instead, it's a curated, digital collection of Word documents, spreadsheets, checklists, and how-to videos. It's organised in one spreadsheet, accessible by everyone, and updated regularly.

Got a new client you want to onboard? There's a checklist for that. Not sure how to amend a client's Direct Debit mandate? You can watch the video of Tracy doing it. Ready to tackle an HMRC inquiry for one of your largest clients? Best get a cup of tea because there's a few documents to work through for this one.

Whatever Tracy's team might encounter each day, they'll find the answer in the company handbook.

ADMIN ASSETS: THE HUMBLE CHECKLIST

If your company handbook is your Bible, then the humble checklist is your ten commandments.

"Thou shalt be presentable," the Pimlico Bible says. "Thou shalt turn up on time and do the job right first time."

You can't expect your team to memorise the entire contents of your company handbook. So give them a cheat sheet – a one-pager that ticks off the milestones, just as we did for our new clients with our first 100 days checklist.

How do you make sure more than a thousand teenagers turn up with the equipment they need every day? At my kids' school, they are given a checklist.

> *Students must carry the Super Six. This will be checked daily by tutors and consists of:*
>
> 1. *Blue or black pen.*
> 2. *Green pen.*
> 3. *Pencil.*
> 4. *Ruler.*
> 5. *Knowledge Organiser kit.*
> 6. *Mini whiteboard kit (board, working whiteboard pen, rubber).*

Just like the Pimlico Bible, this tells students what's expected of them. While Charlie Mullins ruthlessly fired people who committed sins against his commandments, my kids' school hands out detentions for any Super Six violations.

In 2001, Peter Pronovost, a critical care specialist at Johns Hopkins Hospital in Baltimore, US, implemented a simple checklist to help prevent infections:

1. Wash your hands with soap.
2. Clean the patient's skin with antiseptic.
3. Put sterile drapes over the patient.
4. Wear a mask, hat, sterile gown, and gloves.
5. Put a sterile dressing over the insertion site.

Nothing ground-breaking there. Just the basics. Surely there was no need for a checklist to remind world-class surgeons to wash their hands and use sterile equipment?

Well, before Pronovost implemented the checklist, he asked the nurses on the team to observe the doctors for a month to see how often they missed a step. Unbelievably, the nurses saw these experienced doctors, with patients' lives in their hands, skip at least one of these five steps in more than a third of operations.

Still think your team does everything right every time? To butcher one of my favourite Warren Buffett quotes, you should make your checklist so simple that an idiot could follow it because, sooner or later, one will.

After implementing the simple five-point checklist, ten-day infection rates at Johns Hopkins ICU went from 11 per cent to zero. Pronovost's team continued to monitor results for the next 15 months, and calculated that the checklist had prevented 43 infections and eight deaths, saving $2million in costs.

Nowadays, most of my businesses run on checklists. In my sports betting business, I created something I called the "Heinz 57", a simple checklist of the 57 things that if we do them (well) when they should be done, the business will not only run itself, but thrive and grow.

Now, I know what you're thinking – 57 things sounds like a lot.

But that's 57 things that need to happen in a *year*. Not all of them are done by me and many are once a week/month/quarter/year tasks.

> *On the first Tuesday of the month, post this offer on Facebook.*
>
> *Every Saturday, send this email.*
>
> *On the last working day of the month, compile this report.*
>
> *Every 12 weeks, let's schedule a meeting.*

57 things.

Check. ☑

Check. ☑

Check. ☑

When the Heinz 57 is followed, the business works like a dream.

When it stops being followed, the business becomes a nightmare.

ADMIN ASSETS: TASK MANAGEMENT SOFTWARE (AKA THE MORE ADVANCED CHECKLIST)

Detailing every step of the proven processes – whether in a company handbook or a simple checklist – makes no difference if nobody follows them.

So how do you get the company handbook used?

Charlie Mullins' tactic was to fire anyone who didn't toe the line.

> *"It's not rocket science. It's your job to understand and follow it. If you don't, you're out. A couple of guys put it to the test and I sacked them. The message stuck then."*

Atul Gawande, a highly acclaimed surgeon and author of *The Checklist Manifesto: How to Get Things Right,* found that having his team create their own checklists rather than being dictated to from above was key.

> *"Simply having the doctors and nurses in the ICU create their own checklists for what they thought should be done each day improved the consistency of care to the point that the average length of patient stay in intensive care dropped by half."*

I've found the sweet spot is a mixture of the two – processes and checklists created by the team and enforced by task management software (TMS), such as Asana, Trello or Monday.com.

If I design the process, it will be 150 steps and perfected to within an inch of its life. And it won't be followed.

But if it is designed by the team member who has to follow the process, they will distil it to its purest form and the chances of it being followed are infinitely higher.

Of course, I will review the team member's version to ensure they've not deviated too far from the proven processes I know work like gangbusters. I reserve the right to veto, edit, and overrule any process design. But nine times out of ten, they get it right anyway.

By allowing the people who have to follow the processes to design them themselves (as well as suggest improvements, update them when they change, and review at least once a year), I get much higher buy-in. They're more likely to do what *they* said they would do, rather than what I said they should do.

But, of course, once the proven processes are agreed, they still need to be enforced. It's not rocket science. It's their job to understand and follow it. Now, I'm not quite as ruthless as Charlie Mullins, so I've yet to fire someone for not following a process but there do need to be consequences (especially when it's a process they designed themselves).

In our task management software, we create tasks for each of our proven processes. Each process (or part thereof) is assigned to the relevant team member and given a deadline. Proven processes that need to be repeated are automatically scheduled to repeat. If This > Then That processes are set up with relevant rules. For example, when the copywriter completes the "Write Article for page 14 of the magazine" task, a new task will be allocated to the designer so they can "Design page 14 of the magazine".

When you complete a task, you get to hit the "task complete" button on the task management software. In the TMS we use, that results in an animation of a confetti cannon and/or a rainbow unicorn flying across the screen. Time to celebrate. Whoop! Well done.

But, be warned. I have a rule about that button. When you hit "task complete", you are publicly declaring to me (and the whole team) that you have completed that task exactly as documented in the company handbook. If I find that you've missed a step, taken a shortcut, or deviated from the proven processes, then woe betide you. No amount of rainbow unicorns or confetti cannons can save you from my wrath.

I include a link to the relevant section of the handbook in the TMS task so the how-to is there if they need it. It's not for them to look at every time, but rather as a resource if needed. If you're not sure about anything, it's all explained in the handbook.

But don't tell me you've done it the right way if you haven't because I have a proven process for checking up on you.

Within the TMS, I have regular "red flag" tasks allocated to me, as well as my head of operations, to do spot checks and mystery shopping. We trust, yet verify. And if we find a completed task hasn't followed the proven processes, it'll be bounced right back to you. We'll mark the task uncomplete and ask you to either:

1. Explain why you didn't follow the proven process.
2. Follow the proven process (either retrospectively for this task or next time you perform the task).
3. Suggest improvements to the proven process.

I may even ask you to do all three!

Remember, the company culture is *why* we do it.

The proven processes are *how* we do it.

Task management software *ensures* we do it.

ADMIN ASSETS: EMAILS

> *"Here's a link to reset your password."*
>
> *"Thanks for your payment."*
>
> *"Your meeting is confirmed."*

Boring! Boring! Boring! Have a look in your inbox right now and see how many of these bland, vanilla emails you've received in the last day alone. Who says these emails have to be boring? Who says they have to be vanilla?

Why choose to be vanilla when you could be locally made raspberry ripple gelato (with real raspberries), served in an M&Ms crusted waffle cone, topped with the finest Devon clotted cream?

When was the last time you received a memorable admin email? Something that was just serving a basic administrative purpose but which made you smile?

It can be as simple as injecting a little personality into a forgotten username ("I can't help you find your keys, the TV remote or your marbles, but I can help you find your account details") or an appointment reminder message ("Just confirming our Zoom call next Thursday at 2:45pm. Please use this time wisely to choose an amazing virtual background!").

Why not include some images of you and your team having some fun? Not professional headshots or a stock image of "team bonding at the office", but real photos from your phone. The stuff that truly gets across what you stand for and why you do it.

What about your customer service emails? Do you send the same copy and pasted reply to everyone who asks question number 13? While you may deal with hundreds or thousands of emails every month, most people end up asking some variation of the same few questions.

To save time writing from scratch each time, you may have created canned responses. Copy, paste, send. Bish, bash, bosh!

But wait. This one-size-fits-all response is a bit one-size-fits-all, isn't it? What if you sent (un)canned responses instead? These are essentially very similar copy and paste templates that do 80 per cent of the work but where a little customisation on the remaining 20 per cent makes the email exponentially better.

I recently sent an email to Derek Sivers, inviting him to speak at an event I was organising. As his book title (*Hell Yeah Or No: What's Worth Doing)* suggests, I knew Derek was likely to say no, but I was more interested in knowing *how* he said no. So I asked him. Here's the reply I received:

> *"Hi John - Thanks for the invitation! So sorry I can't do it yet.*
>
> *I did a bunch of interviews last year, said everything on my mind, so I'm taking a break for a few months and saying no to everything so that I can finish my next book, "HOW TO LIVE".*
>
> *I might take you up on that invite in the future if that's OK. I'll let you know when I'm ready.*
>
> ====
>
> *And since you wanted to know HOW I say no? I hit backslash-P which pulled up that form letter, above, which I have to use about 10 times a day.* ☺
>
> *Derek"*

That's a perfect (un)canned response. The bulk of the email was copied and pasted, and automatically inserted via a keyboard shortcut in less than one second. As Derek's sending (almost) the same reply ten times a day, this makes sense.

But then, Derek's taken another 14 seconds to add some raspberry ripple to the vanilla. There are a few words in the main body of the email that refer specifically to my request and, of course, the final sentence is not part of the canned response and felt 100 per cent personal. The smiley face emoji was the clotted cream on top of the raspberry ripple.

Note that this isn't anything earth-shattering. Derek simply takes a bog-standard reply that he sends ten times a day and gives each one a bit of a polish, a dose of personality, a sprinkling of customisation. Eighty per cent of the message is still purely functional copy and paste, answering my question. The extra 20 per cent is the stuff I remember, though.

Derek's got form when it comes to writing amazing emails. His original "thanks for ordering" email went like this:

> *"Your order has shipped today. Please let us know if it doesn't arrive. Thank you for your business."*

Derek invested 20 minutes tweaking it and turned it into this Evergreen Asset:

> *"Your CD has been gently taken from our CD Baby shelves with sterilized contamination-free gloves and placed onto a satin pillow.*
>
> *A team of 50 employees inspected your CD and polished it to make sure it was in the best possible condition before mailing.*
>
> *Our packing specialist from Japan lit a candle and a hush fell over the crowd as he put your CD into the finest gold-lined box that money can buy.*
>
> *We all had a wonderful celebration afterwards and the whole party marched down the street to the post office where the*

entire town of Portland waved "Bon Voyage!" to your package, on its way to you, in our private CD Baby jet on this day, Friday, June 6th.

I hope you had a wonderful time shopping at CD Baby. We sure did. Your picture is on our wall as "Customer of the Year." We're all exhausted but can't wait for you to come back to cdbaby.com!"

I hope you like raspberry ripple because there's no vanilla in there whatsoever!

ADMIN ASSETS: SELF-SERVE

I'm a technophobe.

My local supermarket replaced all but one of the checkouts with self-service tills, which take up less space and require fewer staff. If they work efficiently, they should result in shorter queues for customers and bigger profits for the supermarket. Win-win.

But not for me. No, every time I attempted to use the damn thing, I'd get the red light and an "unexpected item in the bagging area" announcement for everyone to hear. "I'm really sorry," I'd say, feeling the need to explain myself to the lady with the override key. "I'm not a trained checkout operator, you see."

So now I queue up at the cigarette kiosk, despite quitting the fags in 2006. I talk to a real human, often sharing a joke or at least a smile (apart from that one lady who's *never* cracked a smile in all the years I've been shopping there). I also feel that I'm doing my bit to keep us humans in a job, before robots finally replace us all – Skynet is coming, and they're starting with my local Co-op.

But while I crave the human connection at the supermarket, I avoid it elsewhere. "You'll need to call HMRC and speak to them yourself if you want to pay your VAT in interest-free instalments," my accountant told me. I chose to pay in full instead – using my bank's self-serve online banking facility to do so.

But was I avoiding the humans at HMRC or their automated phone system? "Please press 1 for PAYE, press 2 for Inheritance Tax, etc." Followed by: "You are in a queue. Your call is important to us. Please continue to hold" for at least 25 minutes.

If my call was that important to you, you'd hire some more people to take calls!

It turns out I'm neither for nor against self-serve. I'm for easy and against hard. I avoid self-serve when it's harder than speaking to a human, but use it when that's the easier option.

How easy is it for your customers to change their email address, update their credit card or upgrade/downgrade after they've become a customer? Can they easily self-serve or do they need to speak to a human?

If they want to speak to a human or are unable to self-serve, how easy is it to do so? Too many companies invest heavily in a self-serve process and then remove the human option completely for anyone who doesn't fit neatly into one of their self-serve boxes.

When I changed web hosting companies recently, I received an email from the firm I was leaving letting me know that they'd set up a support ticket with details on how to pay my final bill. I attempted to log on, but found my login no longer worked (because my account was now closed).

I replied to the email only for it to bounce back: "This email address 'noreply@yourbusiness.com' does not exist."

Is there a less customer-focused email address than noreply@yourbusiness.com?

How about wedontgiveashit@yourbusiness.com or notmyproblem@yourbusiness.com?

Eventually, I googled their main switchboard number and sat through several minutes of "your call is important to us" before finally being connected to a real human, who took my card details and sorted the problem within a minute.

One minute with a human versus nearly an hour trying to self-serve. Done right, self-serve can be a tremendous Admin Asset – hitting that sweet spot where it's more convenient and easier for the customer and more profitable for the business. But when it's done wrong, it can be a liability, making once-loyal customers' blood boil and removing revenue from the top line before it has a chance to drop to the bottom.

In his 1977 autobiography *Grinding It Out*, former McDonald's owner Ray Kroc said:

> *"If I listened to the computers and did what they proposed with McDonald's, I'd have a store with a row of vending machines in it. You'd push some buttons and out would come your Big Mac, shake and fries, all prepared automatically. We could do that. I'm sure we could work it out, but we never will.*
>
> *McDonald's is a people business and the smile on that counter girl's face when she takes your order is a vital part of our image."*

I wonder what Ray would make of the self-serve kiosks popping up in every branch and their effect on his *why* – that "McDonald's is a people business".

If the robots *are* coming, let's hope our mechanical overlords are better at designing customer-friendly self-serve options, instead of those used by many businesses, which are more self-serving for shareholders than for customers.

ADMIN ASSETS: VIDEO

Video can add a tremendous dollop of raspberry ripple to even the most vanilla of your admin assets. By using screen-sharing software like Loom or Zoom (other software ending in "oom" is also available), you can *show* your team how something works rather than just telling them as you create an interactive company handbook. They can clearly see which buttons and tables you're talking about, what you're clicking on, and can compare and contrast what's on your screen with what's on theirs.

If your customers are self-serving via your help section or FAQs, don't just tell them how something works, show them with a screen share, whiteboard animation or old school face-to-face explanation.

Remember, one of the main benefits of video is that tone, sincerity, and personality are conveyed much more easily than with text, so if you're looking for an impactful way to sprinkle that extra 20 per cent (for an 80 per cent ROI) on your (un)canned emails, why not add a 30 to 60-second personal video to each one?

"But that doesn't scale," I hear you shout.

Exactly. That's how you build a core of 1,000 true fans – by doing stuff that doesn't scale.

I'm not suggesting you record a personal video for everyone who sends a forgotten password request, but if you're going to spend a minute or two replying to customers anyway, why not invest an extra 20 seconds for five times the impact? As mentioned before, I often find that responding with a video is quicker than typing, making the ROI on time invested even more lucrative.

Personal video *doesn't* scale and that's exactly why it's so damn effective.

ADMIN ASSETS: FINANCE

If there's one area of admin that everyone seems to put their boring hat on for, it's finance. This is great news for the rest of us because it means we don't need to do much to leverage this key asset and get an edge over everyone else.

Invoices are one of the lowest hanging finance fruits. If you think about it, an invoice is a chance to communicate with your best customers (those who pay you) every time they buy something.

On paper, sending an invoice should be a joyous occasion for any business owner. It's the final step before having the customer's money in the bank and a perfect marketing opportunity to inspire the customer to return and buy from you again (and again).

Brewdog founder James Watt said: "With a bit of imagination, you can turn even the dullest of documents such as an invoice into marketing and simultaneously increase your chances of being paid on time."

He adds the following raspberry ripple footnote to Brewdog's invoices:

> *"Please pay this invoice on time. Otherwise, I won't be able to feed my dog. I wish I was kidding. If you're not intending to pay on time, please send dog biscuits to: Simcoe (James' dog), Brewdog, Balmacassie, Ellon, Scotland."*

Everything's marketing. Every invoice you send is marketing, whether you send a boring vanilla "screw it, that'll do" invoice or whether you create a raspberry ripple version, full of creativity, personality, and highly leveraged copy to ensure you get paid on time (or even early).

"But I'm not a numbers person!"

If you've been telling yourself that you're "not a numbers person", then that's all the more reason to deploy Finance Admin Assets to look after the numbers for you because you're clearly not going to look after them yourself.

Make your bookkeeping easier by using cloud-based software such as Xero or QuickBooks. If you outsource your bookkeeping (which I would strongly advise, but even more so if you're "not a numbers person"), your bookkeeper will more than likely already be using such software. And if you insist on doing it yourself, it'll make the task at least 50 per cent quicker.

Instead of a carrier bag or shoebox full of receipts, use apps like Dext (formerly known as ReceiptBank) or AutoEntry to take a quick photo and automatically reconcile the purchase against your bank statement and cloud-based bookkeeping and accountancy software.

You wouldn't get very far driving a car focusing only on the rear-view mirror, yet that's what most "not a numbers person" business owners do. They base their financial and strategic decisions on their previous year-end accounts.

I'm writing this in March. My financial year ends in May, so if I did what most small businesses do, the last set of accounts I would have access to is the year ending the previous May – a period that *started* in April almost two years ago. Do you really want to be making financial decisions that will affect your business for the foreseeable future based on what happened two years ago?

Of course not. Stop driving using the rear-view mirror and let's look out of the windscreen instead.

Speak to your accountant about switching to monthly management accounts – a regular financial review, comparing your financial goals and targets with what's happening in the real world – and have a one-off conversation with them about the numbers that matter most in your business.

But which numbers do matter most to you? This is the magic question to ask your accountant and they should not give you a "one-size-fits-all" answer. You want to know the numbers that matter to you and affect your decisions going forward – decisions that enable you to steer away from trouble and embrace opportunity.

I like to run a lean business with low overheads and predictable income (a membership model run by a small team working from home). The numbers that matter most to me are:

- Net profit margin: I'm looking to maintain a fairly consistent percentage each month and deliver a target margin over the year. This is the most important number for me and the first one I look at every single month.
- Income from various memberships: Here, I'm looking for trends and patterns, both in terms of growth and churn for my membership models.
- Cash Flow: Occasionally, I'll ask for a cashflow forecast. For example, during the Covid crisis, I asked my accountant to show me the forecast for three possible outcomes – a best-case scenario, a worst-case scenario, and a middle ground. This gave me the confidence to make strong decisions (with a high degree of certainty), especially once it became clear which of the three paths we were on.
- Tax report: How much of the cash in my bank is actually mine and how much should I put aside for the taxman? (Then actually put it aside! Set up a standing order to automatically move it out of temptation's way... it's not your money!)
- Total Operating Expenses (Breakeven point): How much do I need to make just to cover the cost of opening the doors? I also like to fully audit all expenses every quarter to ensure they're still necessary and not eating into my net profit margin.
- Cost of Sales (as a percentage of turnover): As I primarily focus on memberships, I achieve a greater profit margin with scale.

> My cost of sale to serve ten members is almost identical to the cost of serving 100 so I want a nice low percentage here.

These are the numbers I focus on every month. I don't necessarily want to know my Non-Current Liabilities, Foreign Currency Gains and Losses or Net VAT movements. But every now and then, something will go wrong in my ecosystem and I'll need to add a new metric to my monthly management report.

For example, because most of my income comes from automatically recurring Direct Debit and debit card subscriptions, as well as self-billing invoices from suppliers, I always get paid on time. Therefore, I never look at the Aged Receivables on my monthly management report. One day I noticed that I hadn't seen a payment from one particular company for a while. I checked my bank statements and, sure enough, they hadn't paid for several months.

The company had changed technology platforms nine months earlier and our account hadn't been migrated properly. We didn't have a self-billing agreement on the new platform, so we didn't get paid. Nine months' worth of unpaid invoices built up in our Accounts Receivable report – a report which I had been ignoring.

Oops.

One new self-billing agreement later and my bank account was several thousand pounds better off. I also had a new Evergreen Finance Asset in place – adding Accounts Receivable and Accounts Payable reports to my monthly management numbers that I need to look at. Never again will I leave getting paid to chance by only looking in the rear-view mirror.

Sending in the heavies (for £1.50+vat)

Unfortunately, not everyone is reliable with payments. Many seem to treat Accounts Payable as a game of "how long can we avoid paying this invoice?". Let's create some Evergreen Finance Assets to win this game, shall we?

First of all, what are your standard payment terms? Cash upfront? Fifty per cent deposit before you start work? Full payment on delivery? Invoices paid within seven days? Or 30? Or 90? (Seriously? Ninety days interest free? Are you a bank? A money lender? A registered charity?).

Anyway, you get to decide what your standard terms are, so make them work for *you*. You can always decide to deviate from these terms if a particularly lucrative supplier insists on different terms. But be clear from the outset.

Next, make sure you send an invoice on time. I can't believe the number of businesses who do a job and then wait several weeks to send an invoice (often with 30 days payment terms or, worse, no deadline at all). This sends a very clear message to the client – getting paid isn't a priority. If you're using cloud-based accounting software such as Xero or QuickBooks to send invoices, you can leverage their automated payment-chasing skills. They can send a copy of the invoice two days before it's due as a reminder and then send statements at set intervals, all of which can be personalised with a little raspberry ripple. Set it up once, reap the rewards again and again (and again).

Don't give poor payers any excuse to delay things further. Make sure you send your invoice on time and include all the relevant information including a description of what the invoice covers, any related purchase orders, your payment terms, and how to pay. Make sure when you send the invoice, you know who approves them, any strange rules they have that might delay payment, and who signs the cheques.

You can also legally charge interest on late payments. So, tell everyone upfront that you will do this. I include this simple line on my invoices:

"We reserve the right to charge interest on late payments. Interest will be calculated daily at the Bank of England Base Rate, plus eight per cent."

Be sure to enforce this and charge interest to your perennial late payers. I used to have one company who would pay so sporadically, I would usually charge them interest on 80 per cent of their invoices and, as the interest compounded over several months (after which they'd eventually settle up in full), it turned into a nice little savings plan.

It was far from predictable cash flow, and thankfully I wasn't relying on their prompt payment to meet payroll or pay the VAT bill, but I was earning far more interest from them than the 0.1 per cent I was getting from having their cash in the bank.

If charging interest doesn't get them paying on time, there's a three-step debt recovery process that you can deploy as an Evergreen Asset:

1. Call them. No one likes chasing people for money on the phone, so we wimp out and email, send passive-aggressive letters or just whinge about them. I find that picking up the phone and saying, "I don't appear to have been paid for the work I did?" works at least 60 per cent of the time.
2. Call in the heavies. For about £1.50+vat, you can get a lawyer to send a threatening letter. I've sent several of these and they usually get the job done. If they don't, the lawyers can take things further, including taking the clients to court and employing bailiffs to enforce the debt.
3. Sack them. This is *your* ecosystem. You get to choose the rules. You choose who to work with and who to fire. So if 20 per cent of your customers are causing 80 per cent of your cash flow problems, sack them. The time, energy, and money you're wasting trying to get paid could be better spent looking after your dream customers, who respect you enough to pay on time.

A few companies I've worked with offer discounts on their invoices for prompt payment. Rather than accepting the standard 30-day terms, I'm happy to pay immediately in exchange for a five per cent discount, which is far more than I'll earn in interest keeping that money in my bank. I get a greater ROI on my spend and they get far improved cash flow. Everyone's a winner.

TL/DR:

You don't need your boring hat to create highly leveraged Finance Assets.

Your invoices are a great opportunity for marketing to people who already buy from you. But they also need to make your expectations crystal clear and be enforced every time.

You don't need to be a full-on "numbers person", but you do need to know the handful of numbers that truly matter to you.

Oh, and stop driving with the rear-view mirror.

ADMIN ASSETS: THE PURGE

Repeat the mantra: Evergreen Assets is not a numbers game, it's a relationships game. So, like the third step of my debt collection process, if there are toxic relationships floating in your ecosystem, it's healthy to have a little purge every now and then to cull some of the people who are hurting you more than they're helping.

If a certain segment of your clients cause a disproportionate amount of stress or contribute disproportionately less to your bottom line, you have the power to purge them. If a particular product range takes up 80 per cent of your time but only produces 20 per cent of your profits, purge it.

There are probably members of your social network to whom you've never spoken. I dare say there are people whose posts make your skin crawl or who you'd cross the street to avoid in real life. If this is the case, hit that unfollow/unconnect/unfriend button. You'll be doing both of you a favour in the long run.

If prospects aren't opening your emails, unsubscribe them. This probably sounds like an alien concept to a lot of old school marketers as surely you want your list to be as big as possible, right? Just because they've not opened your last 15 emails, it doesn't mean they won't open your next one, does it?

Well, Tom Kulzer, founder and CEO of AWeber, the email marketing software that I use to send more than a million emails per month, assures me the evidence is overwhelming – email providers such as Hotmail, Yahoo!, and Gmail only deliver email to their users from sources those users want to hear from.

If half your subscribers don't open your emails, then it becomes more likely that *all* your subscribers will have to hunt in their junk folder to find your emails because you'll be labelled a spammer.

Conversely, if you're getting 30 per cent open rates on most emails, 90 per cent of your subscribers have opened an email in the last few weeks, and they're engaging with those emails – scrolling, reading, clicking, replying, and forwarding – then that's a clear signal to the email providers that your subscribers love hearing from you and your emails will get the green light to land in their inbox.

When I first purged my lists from 74,000 subscribers to 48,000, it was terrifying to remove all those people who had signed up five years earlier and who "might open an email one day", especially as I'd paid for a lot of those leads via Facebook Ads or Google Ads. But they were effectively dead leads.

As Tom Kulzer told me: "Taking the opportunity to prune those who are unengaged feels scary at the time, but you'll get better results in the long run."

Here's a guy who gets paid based on the number of subscribers I have telling me to go and delete half of them. That's going to cost Tom a few hundred dollars a month in the short term, as my bills get lower (at the time of writing, I've culled another 15,000 from the list) but we're both going to benefit in the long run, because my emails will still get delivered in five years, meaning I can still get a great ROI from the channel and keep paying Tom.

I now purge my email lists every month, which keeps my AWeber bills down and my open rates up.

Keep it simple, stupid

If you're anything like me, you've probably amassed a messy tangle of stupid business ideas over the years, with many of them still lying around your ecosystem for no reason other than "we've always done it that way".

How about we give your business model a purge to remove those processes that are more pea-brained than proven?

The first thing Gordon Ramsay does with any failing restaurant on his Kitchen Nightmares TV show is throw out the 14-page Tex-Mex/Chinese/Pizza/Curry/Burgers/Steakhouse menu and replace it with a simple one-pager. Fewer menu options means diners waste fewer decision calories figuring out what to eat and kitchen staff waste less time running around like headless chickens.

Once Gordon's done his stuff, there is now great food, cooked well. No need for microwaved chicken, frozen pizzas and "deep-fried everything". All ingredients are bought (and cooked) fresh, with much less inventory stored "just in case someone orders it".

Simple is beautiful and effective.

I'll bet your business started simple. I know mine did. But as soon as a business shows signs of success, we start adding complexity. People like me (and business books like this) don't help the situation as they constantly tempt you with things you *could* add to your ecosystem.

So before we add stuff, let's create some room. Throw out your 14-page menu. Think about what bloat could you remove from your model. Are there processes, products or features you could purge that wouldn't be missed but could free up your finite resources (time, energy, money) to invest in Evergreen Assets that give you a disproportionately higher ROI?

The simpler your business model is, the easier the admin will be. You won't have to work as hard and fulfilment becomes easier too. Imagine Gordon Ramsey's just walked into your business. Is he throwing up in a bin, waving mouldy chicken at you and asking "how long has this been in the @*%&ing fridge?" or giving you the evil stare after you assured him that, no, of course his "homemade lasagne" hasn't been microwaved from frozen?

Just as Gordon condenses the bloated menu to a simple one-pager, you can do the same with your business model. Remove the superfluous or the unnecessary and keep only the truly essential. If you can't fit your entire Evergreen Assets ecosystem on a single sheet of A4, you've made it too complex.

Here's a one-page template for your entire Evergreen Assets ecosystem. Just fill in the blanks:

> We help _________ [target market) to _________ (what they want) by _________(Proven Framework).
>
> We generate leads by _________ .
>
> We nurture relationships by _________ .
>
> We convert to sales by _________ .
>
> We fulfil clients by _________ .

We get paid by ________ .

We turn 1 customer into 1.2 by ________ .

That's it. The entire process from identifying the right prospects, nurturing relationships with them, making the sale, fulfilling the orders, taking care of the admin, and getting referrals and repeat clients, all on one sheet of A4.

Everything else is bells and whistles. Get this one-page ecosystem happening consistently, every time for every prospect and every client before you start thinking about adding any complexity.

Keep it simple, stupid. (Yeah, I'm talking to you.)

ADMIN ASSETS: SLOPEY SHOULDERS

In his 2010 book *The Rational Optimist: How Prosperity Evolves*, economist and journalist Matt Ridley proclaims that self-sufficiency (doing everything yourself) is a leading indicator of poverty, while "specialisation and exchange" is a leading indicator of wealth and prosperity.

What the hell is "specialisation and exchange"?

Imagine you live in a small village and want to feed your family. To be self-sufficient, you need to grow enough crops for your entire family. You also need to be able to bake, fish, and hunt. Then, you need to prepare and cook that meal. It's a lot of work.

With specialisation and exchange, you specialise in baking bread, for example, while I specialise in catching fish, and an expert huntsman captures our Sunday roast. We all specialise, generate a surplus above our own requirements, and then agree to exchange that surplus with others, meaning we *all* have a meal.

No entrepreneur *wants* to do admin. We're here to put a dent in the universe, not a sheet of paper in the filing cabinet.

But I've got good news. While the admin still needs doing, it doesn't have to be done by you. Embrace specialisation and exchange. Focus on what *you* do best and employ a specialist to do the rest (exchanging your hard-earned money for their specialism). Pass on the tasks you're not good at or, to coin a phrase, develop slopey shoulders.

Other than admin, I can't think of many things worse than ironing. But I know a lady called Lynn who *loves* it. She's a freak of nature. She's got an industrial press in her conservatory and finds it therapeutic to stand there listening to the hiss of the press, feeling the warm steam escape, and turning a basket of crumpled clothes into a neat pile of perfectly-pressed apparel. She's a specialist in ironing and gets paid for the privilege. I know this because I pay her to do my ironing.

Admin, filing, bookkeeping, data entry, minute-typing, research and analysis, transcription, chasing invoices, email management, photocopying – you name it, there is a specialist out there who not only can do it for you, but who can do it better than you.

Yep, believe it or not, there are people in this world who love to do the things you hate and you can hire these people for an hourly fee or a monthly wage. It's usually far less than you could earn in that same hour or month – especially if you invest that time wisely, creating an Evergreen Asset in your area of speciality.

Investing in a specialist gives you leverage. It greases the wheels of your Evergreen Assets machine and can deliver a huge ROI.

I used to mow my lawn. It would take me about an hour and it would look pretty crap once I was finished. Plus, when my lawn mower broke, I had to buy a new one. Now I outsource my lawn mowing needs to a company that specialises in mowing lawns.

It takes them 15 minutes and looks amazing when they're done (stripes and everything). They scarify it in the winter, put new seeds down in the spring and feed it every few months. They charge £19, which might seem a lot for 15 minutes work but, remember, 15 minutes is how long it takes *them*. For £19, they're actually saving *me* an hour and doing a far better job than I ever could, even if I had all day to spend mowing my lawn.

But I don't have all day to spend mowing my lawn because my area of speciality is creating Evergreen Assets for my businesses – writing books, coaching clients, crafting nurture sequences, and making sure our burgers look like the ones in the picture.

I can't do any of those things if I'm mowing lawns, ironing shirts, or doing my own bookkeeping.

So, allow your shoulders to slope and outsource all the stuff that you shouldn't be doing to someone who's better than you at it.

As Berkshire Hathaway vice-chairman Charlie Munger said about the approach employed by him and Warren Buffett: "Warren and I avoid doing anything someone else at Berkshire can do better."

It's a sentiment concurred by Buffett himself, who said: "They do a much better job than I could in running their operations. What can be more logical, in whatever you want done, than finding someone better equipped than you are to do it? Who wouldn't select Tiger Woods to take his place in a high-stakes golf game?"

Let go of the tasks that are far outside your specialism, whether that be bookkeeping, photocopying, or cutting your own grass.

Work out your actual (or desired) hourly rate. Divide the income you actually take from the business (or would like to take), by the number of hours you actually work. So if you earn £60,000 a year, working a 100-hour week, you're on £11.54 an hour, but if you draw £50,000 a year and work 20 hours a week, you're taking home £48.08 an hour.

(Of course, the more holidays you take and time you spend away from your business, the higher your actual hourly rate (AHR) goes).

Working this actual hourly rate out was the key factor in my wife quitting her teaching job. She was on a good headline salary, but worked an extra 40 hours a week for free. When we calculated her AHR, she earned £8.50 an hour as a university graduate with two decades of experience. Discovering she could earn more per hour as an entry-level employee at McDonald's was the final straw and she's now running her own ambitious lifestyle business and in control of her actual hourly rate.

Knowing what tasks to outsource becomes so much easier when you know your AHR. If someone else can do a task to a similar standard (or better) than you for less than your AHR, then it's a no-brainer – especially as freeing up another hour (or more) of your time increases your AHR, either from earning the same amount from fewer hours worked or from reallocating that hour to more income-generating tasks to increase your earnings.

Let go of all jobs which you can outsource for less than your actual hourly rate, so that you can focus on AHR-increasing tasks, as well as those roles that only you can do. Remember that self-sufficiency (doing everything yourself) is a leading indicator of poverty, while "specialisation and exchange" is a leading indicator of wealth and prosperity.

ADMIN ASSETS SUMMARY

Everything is marketing. So let's stop putting all the razzmatazz and all the shiny things before the sale, shall we?

"People don't buy what you do, they buy why you do it," so let's get the whole company on board with why we do it. Once we know why, our proven processes document *how* we do it, and our company handbook makes finding the right proven process easy.

A checklist defines what matters most and in what order it should be done. Task management software looks after your proven processes, managing who does what and when. It can also be used to enforce the processes, ensuring they happen on time, and to the required level, through the use of mystery shopping and red flags.

Add some raspberry ripple to your boring, bland beige vanilla emails, invoices, documents, and packaging. Embrace self-serve if it helps your customers, not because it helps your bottom line. Personal video doesn't scale and that's why it's so damn effective.

You don't need your boring hat to create highly leveraged Finance Assets, just stop driving with the rear-view mirror and don't tell me you're "not a numbers person". The Purge might be a crap movie (current IMDb rating 5.7/10), but it's also a great way of culling some of the people who are hurting your business more than they're helping.

No entrepreneur wants to do admin, so embrace your slopey shoulders and outsource all the stuff you shouldn't be doing to a specialist who's better at it than you and can do it for less than your actual hourly rate.

We've greased the wheels, optimised the machine, and added some locally made raspberry ripple gelato (with real raspberries), served in an M&Ms crusted waffle cone, topped with the finest Devon clotted cream. Because everything's marketing. Yes, even the admin.

8. VIRAL ASSETS

During the Covid-19 pandemic, we became familiar with the R rate: the basic reproduction number of a virus. This term was previously only of concern to epidemiologists studying patterns and causes of diseases for preventative healthcare. But during the pandemic, it became important enough to be reported daily alongside the pollen count, FTSE 100, and then-US President Donald Trump's latest tweet.

Suddenly, Karen from Facebook became the world's leading expert on epidemiology and discussions over the R rate even overtook the great British weather as the main topic de jour on those rare occasions you spoke to another human.

The R rate is the number of people on average that one infected person will pass a virus to. For example, in communities without immunity, measles has an R rate of 15, meaning, on average, one person will spread measles to 15 others.

Without interventions, Covid-19 had an R rate of around three, meaning each person with the coronavirus would pass it to three others, on average. Interventions such as hand washing advice, lockdowns, masks, social distancing, track and trace, PPE, vaccinations, etc., were all designed to bring the R rate under 1.0, meaning the spread of the virus would start to slow. If the R rate was above 1.0, the virus would continue to spread exponentially.

The higher the R rate goes above 1.0, the faster the spread accelerates, and the further below 1.0 it falls, the more dramatic the slow is – from 0.9 (gently touching the brakes) to 0.1 (pulling on the handbrake).

Here's the effect the R rate would have on 1,000 infections after 60 days:

R rate	Number of infections after 60 days (approx.)
1.1	25,000
1.0	13,000
0.9	7,000
0.5	2,500

Because viruses are, erm, viral, they replicate. Therefore any growth (or slowdown) is not linear, it's exponential, meaning the growth itself is accelerating. A mere ten per cent increase in the R rate (from 1.0 to 1.1) results in an exponential 92 per cent increase in the number of infections after 60 days.

Exponential growth is how 1p doubled every day for a month turns into more than £10million. The growth in the first few days is literally a few pence. A third of the way into the month and you've got £5.12 in the bank. Twenty days in and you're up to £5,242.88. It's only in the last few days that things get interesting – from £671,088 to £1.3million to £2.7million to £5.4million to £10,737,418.24.

One pence, plus exponential growth.

What's the R rate of your business?

Is your business viral enough to infect your clients and get them to spread the word for you? Can you turn one customer into 1.2? If so, for every ten sales your Lead, Nurture and Sales Assets generate, those ten customers will spread the word and bring in another two sales completely of their own accord. This isn't "word of mouth", but predictable, scalable exponential growth that *you* control.

With an R rate of 1.2, if you make 1,000 sales, your Viral Assets will add another 200. Those 200 bring in another 40 viral customers (because they go through the same ecosystem and the same Viral Assets), who in turn spread the word to another eight. Even those eight will introduce another 1.6 customers (although I'm not quite sure what 0.6 of a customer looks like).

Your Viral Assets turn 1,000 customers into 1,250 customers. The following table shows the effect of exponential growth on 1,000 customers entering your ecosystem with slightly different R rates.

Business R rate	Number of customers (approx.)
1.5	1,999
1.4	1,666
1.3	1,428
1.2	1,250
1.1	1,111
1.0	1,000

If none of your customers ever bring another customer to your door, your business R rate is 1.0 and you turn one customer into exactly one customer. Viral Assets help you turn one customer into more than one. The more Viral Assets you add to your ecosystem, the higher your R rate, and the more exponential growth you can look forward to. Just a 1.1 R rate (every ten customers bring you one for free) generates an extra 111 sales for every 1,000 you have to work for. If you can ramp up your business's R rate to 1.5, it's "buy-one-get-one-free" on customers.

So what *can* you do to increase the R rate of your business? Why *do* people tell their friends about stuff?

Jonah Berger, author of *Contagious: Why Things Catch On*, says there are six reasons why people share things (ideas, stories, businesses referrals, etc.):

1. **Social Currency.** People share things that make them look good.
2. **Triggers.** Top of mind is tip of tongue.
3. **Emotion.** People share things that arouse strong feelings in them.
4. **Public.** People naturally imitate what they see others doing.
5. **Practical Value.** People like to share useful information that can help others.
6. **Stories.** Information can be embedded into stories because people find them easy to remember and share.

We're going to bake all six reasons into our Viral Assets, giving us the greatest chance possible of turning one customer into 1.2.

We're going to give our customers what they want so consistently that they know their friends will get what they want too, ensuring they look good in the process.

We're going to bake the Viral Assets into our ecosystem so well that the triggers appear natural and unforced.

We're going to play a relationships game, not a numbers game – generating high levels of positive emotion.

We're going to make it easy to imitate what others are doing (and what others are doing is referring their friends).

We'll create huge amounts of practical value, so people can rely on us to help others.

And finally, we'll wrap all of the above up in story form and embed those stories throughout our entire Evergreen Assets ecosystem.

ONE VIRAL ASSET TO RULE THEM ALL: BRING YOUR FRIENDS

Seeing other people do something makes us more likely to do it ourselves, whether that's smoking cigarettes, dropping litter, or making referrals. If we want to create a referral culture where our customers bring their friends along too, then we should shine a light on every referral, making it clear:

> *"Our customers refer their friends and colleagues to us. That's what happens around here. That's what we do. That's what you should do too – but only if I deliver on my promises."*

How do we shine a light on referrals? You could add a few lines such as, "Did you know that 74 per cent of our business comes from referrals?" or "Who do you know who would make a good client?" into your Signature Move.

You could publicly thank everyone who makes a referral. You could even send the referrer a small gift to show your appreciation. Why not ask successful clients if they can think of anyone looking for similar results?

You could even insist on a referral as a condition of working together. Direct response marketer Jay Abraham achieved a 50 per cent referral rate (yep, 50 out of 100 – a "buy one, get one free" R rate of 1.5) for a health club by asking new members to commit to consistently attend classes and to promise to refer their friends if (and only if) they achieved the results they were looking for.

For most small businesses, there are two reasons they're not getting a shedload of referrals:

1. They're not asking for them.
2. They don't have enough deliriously happy clients.

If your R rate is lower than you'd like it to be, then I bet you could improve it with a little work on these two areas. Most small businesses don't ask for referrals, they rely on word of mouth, so that's easily resolved. Ask and ye shall receive.

Much harder though is point number two – a lack of deliriously happy clients. You see, the difference between a satisfied customer and a deliriously happy customer is huge. It's the difference between "Yeah, they were OK" and "OMG, they were *amazing*! You simply *have* to try them!"

No one's going to risk looking bad to their friends by recommending you unless they're deliriously happy. Merely satisfied customers are unlikely to refer and those looking at their burger wondering why it doesn't look like the one in the picture definitely won't.

The better your Fulfilment Assets are working, the more deliriously happy clients you'll have. That means all you have to do to get more referrals, increase your R rate, and get the tills ringing is ask.

Tell your customers regularly: "Our customers refer their friends. Our business runs on recommendations and referrals. I've delivered *what you want*. Who do you know who wants ________ too?"

VIRAL ASSETS: CASE STUDIES

Meet Dave.

> *"Hi, I'm Dave Aggiss.*
>
> *I've just signed up for the Hybrid six-week challenge. I've tried a few different things in the past, and nothing's really worked for me.*

I'm not too sure how I'll get on with it, but hopefully this is the one that makes the difference."

Dave is an out-of-shape mortgage broker, who's just signed up for a fitness challenge at his gym. He doesn't like going to the gym but does like Netflix, takeaways, and sedentary desk work.

Dave's also a business partner of mine, running Three Sixty Mortgages, a specialist mortgage brokerage for property investors. I'd been nagging Dave for several years to look after his health but, as Dave admits, nothing has worked.

Until now.

"I've just finished the Hybrid six-week challenge, had great results and lost 20lbs, which is great. I've really enjoyed it. It's been great to do it.

I've struggled a lot in the past to stick to a plan, to lose weight, to eat healthily.

There's a lot of support when you're doing the challenge with other people. The team here is great. I'd definitely recommend doing it if you're looking to lose weight."

It's only been six weeks, but already several of Dave's chins have disappeared and he looks full of energy. The big question though is, will he stick at it?

Well, let's fast forward a year and ask the man himself. You'll have to take my word for it that it is the man himself, because he looks like a completely different person – the extra chins and clothes from Jacamo have been replaced with chiselled cheekbones and a tight-fitting T-shirt to show off Dave's guns.

"Signing up for the Hybrid six-week challenge was the best decision I ever made. This challenge has massively increased my fitness, improved my confidence and given me the physique I've always wanted".

Here's the clever bit: Dave's gym recorded the whole process – capturing his transformation, both with photos and on video. They perfectly captured Dave's fear of the unknown at the start, his scepticism and self-doubt that he would stick at it after six weeks, and his unbridled joy and immense pride 12 months later as he effortlessly swings kettlebells, flings battle ropes, and talks honestly about how it's changed his life.

Remember Jonah Berger's sixth reason things get shared? Stories. Dave's gym gave him what he wanted. But they've wrapped it up in a three-minute human interest story that's easy to remember and easy to share. I'll include a link to the full video in the resources so you can see Dave's story for yourself.

If you walk into Dave's gym, you'll see him immortalised on their wall of fame (complete with before and after photos, measurements, and Dave's story in his own words), along with dozens of other success stories from previous clients.

Somewhere on that wall of fame, there's someone just like you, who got the result you're looking for. The message is clear: This stuff works. Successful clients are Dave's gym's greatest weapon and sharing client success stories is their greatest Viral Asset.

Dave now does the same for his clients – showcasing the life-changing transformations his investors have achieved and making stars of them. Again, Dave's just the guide. His clients are the real stars. Just like the famous restaurant scene in When Harry Met Sally, prospective clients cast envious glances towards success stories and then say: "I'll have what she's having!"

Don't ask, don't get

Most businesses would receive more testimonials and case studies if only they asked for them.

Ask and ye shall receive. A simple: "Could you give me a testimonial please?" will get you results, which is better than nothing. However, those results are likely to be vague, cliched, and not very impactful.

> *"Great to work with."*
>
> *"Did a wonderful job."*
>
> *"Would recommend."*

Do you know who else people say those things about? Everybody. Every other business on the planet, including all your competitors. Bland, beige, boring vanilla testimonials like these are typical of satisfied customers. They're easy to ignore and won't move the needle on your R rate. We don't want vanilla testimonials from satisfied customers. We want raspberry ripple testimonials from deliriously-happy customers.

Book a call with a deliriously-happy client or arrange to meet face to face over a coffee (and a slice of cake). Explain you're looking to showcase some of your favourite, most successful clients (flattery will get you everywhere), and ask if they would be happy to have a quick chat about their experience.

Once you're with them, settle in and make them feel relaxed. Treat the first few minutes as a pure "digging the well" catch up by asking about the kids, how their new hire is settling in, and whether their football team has managed to turn things around since the new manager came in. Then, start to naturally work some of the following questions into the conversation:

- What originally made you look for the product/service that I sell?
- What problem did you have?
- How did that feel?
- What else had you considered or tried before coming to me?
- How did you first hear about the product?
- What were your first impressions?
- Did anything make you hesitate before buying?
- Did you have any objections, worries or concerns about it?
- What happened once you'd bought the product/service?
- What happened next?
- What's your favourite part of the product/service? Why?
- Who would you recommend this for?
- Is there anything else you'd like to add?

Now, you don't want this to come across as an interrogation, but the order of these questions helps to arrange their testimony into something that every person on the planet above the age of two is familiar with – a story.

> *"Once upon a time, I was suffering from ________. Things had got really bad, and I was starting to feel ________. It was even affecting my ________. I tried ________, ________, and ________, but nothing worked. I started researching ________ and discovered ________.*
>
> *That's when I first came across your product/service. It sounded great, but I was worried that it was ________ or wouldn't ________. After reading some of your other case studies, I decided to give it a go. The results were ________.*

I achieved ________, ________, and ________. I no longer ________ and I feel ________. My ________ has never been so ________.

I love the way you ________ and the fact that your product/service does ________ makes all the difference for me. If anyone reading/watching this is suffering from ________ or experiencing ________, I would recommend they give it a go. If they get half the results I did, they'll be over the moon!"

And they all lived happily ever after.

This story is a world of difference from the bland vanilla "would definitely recommend" most people trot out. Sure, it's a lot harder work in the short term but it's an Evergreen Asset in the long term.

If your clients are happy to, ask them if you can record the conversation (or even better, as Dave's gym did, video it). Reassure them this is so you can accurately repeat what they said rather than what you *thought* you remember them saying.

Once you're back in the office, send the recording off to be transcribed (I use rev.com, which delivers accurate transcriptions with a quick turnaround), and then polish up what was said into a nice concise story. You can edit as you see fit and don't have to quote the client word for word. But there is a balance to be struck. You want the copy to flow nicely and be as short and snappy as possible. But you also want it to be an accurate representation of the client's experience and, in my experience, using their words is much more powerful than using your words.

The words your clients use are often the same words your prospects and potential new favourite clients would use. When your ideal client reads these case studies, the thought bubble in their head should say:

"Wow, this person is just like me. That's exactly where *I* am. That's exactly what *I'm* worried about. That's exactly how *I* feel. If this worked for someone *like* me, perhaps it could work for *me*?"

Just one more thing

That final question: "Is there anything else you'd like to add?"

Now, you might be tempted to drop this line of questioning. After all, it doesn't ask anything specific and it just seems like a filler question as we begin to wrap things up and get back to the real job of running our business.

Well, it's that exact disarming nature of the question, left to the end when the tongue is loosened and the brain is warmed up, that produces the true testimonial golden nuggets (which taste delicious when added to raspberry ripple).

How did fictional TV detective Lieutenant Frank Columbo solve 68 murders in 24 years? First, he'd bumble his way through an interview and then exit the room, leaving the suspect under the false sense of security that he or she had literally got away with murder. At which point, the scruffy detective would casually stroll back in with his finger in the air and announce "just one more thing…" before asking the one crucial question that unravelled the entire web of lies.

Asking the Columbo question: "Is there anything else you'd like to add?" almost as an afterthought, when we've wrapped up our main line of questioning, is when the truth is revealed: "Oh no, I think I've covered everything. Oh, apart from this major revelation that's worth its weight in gold."

Just one more thing – but what a thing.

TL/DR:

Case studies tap into the human desire for storytelling.

They capture the entire customer journey from past failures to frightened newbie, early scepticism, through "Hmm, this might just be working", all the way to "this has changed my life". You're not the star of the show though – your clients are. You're just the guide. They're Luke Skywalker. You're Yoda.

Oh, and just one more thing – I'll have what she's having.

VIRAL ASSETS: TESTIMONIALS

Testimonials are the little brother of the case study, condensing the success story to two or three sentences.

We could reduce Dave's Aggiss's three-minute video case study to a few lines:

> *"I've tried a few different things in the past and nothing's worked for me. I struggled to stick to a plan, to lose weight, to eat healthily.*
>
> *Signing up for the Hybrid six-week challenge was the best decision I ever made. This challenge has massively increased my fitness, improved my confidence and given me the physique I've always wanted."*

Even though I've condensed Dave's story from three minutes into four sentences, I've still taken you on the full hero's journey from "nothing's worked" and "I've struggled a lot" up to "the best decision I ever made" and "given me the physique I've always wanted." An important note – don't skip the struggle. Don't scrimp on the heartaches, the fears, and the frustrations. Prospects need to know where Dave was at the start of his journey – especially if that's where they are right now.

Four sentences is a bit of a whistle-stop tour of Dave's story and it's always going to be more impactful for prospects to watch his full case study. But sometimes you need a tiny sprinkling of raspberry ripple, and testimonials deliver great bang for their buck in terms of word count and space, as long as you tell a transformational story with your client as the hero, not you.

Use the case study interview questions above or at the very least ask:

1. What were things like before you discovered us?
2. What's changed?

You should always be on the lookout for testimonials and case studies. Dig the case study well before you're thirsty. Whenever I'm putting together a new piece of marketing, I dive into my testimonials and case studies back catalogue. When I'm promoting the latest Cheltenham Festival magazine, I dig out the case studies of the punters who backed the 80/1 winner in the previous year's magazine.

Each month on the Ambitious Lifestyle Business podcast, Jason and I chat to a One Percenter for 30 to 40 minutes, discovering how they've transformed their business and lifestyle. While we do ask one single question that reminds listeners who their guide was ("how has the One Percent Club helped you?"), 95 per cent of the episode is spent talking about their story and what *they* did. After all, they're the hero and we're just the guide.

Each episode serves as a long-form case study, which I can also edit into shorter success stories and testimonials, sprinkling them throughout my Evergreen Assets ecosystem, using them on order forms, brochures, and leaflets. I'll include one-liners on checkouts, login pages, and Google Ads. I'll pop them on almost every page of my website, in every email I send, and on every piece of Direct Mail that goes out.

I'll also try to deploy them where they'll have the greatest impact.

Product-related testimonials go on the product page.

"So glad I bought it"? That's going on the checkout.

"Signing up was the best thing I ever did?" That's going on my squeeze page.

Every testimonial tells a story and counters an objection – knowing the right story for the right objection is key.

VIRAL ASSETS: REVIEWS

How many deliriously happy customers have you got? Dozens? Hundreds? Thousands? So why, when I google you, do I see "3 reviews" next to your name?

You may have thousands of happy customers, but if they haven't left you a review, I'm going to assume you have none. And so will most of the review snobs like me who also employ this simple shortcut to making better decisions. I watch fewer bad movies because I check IMDb ratings. I don't have many bad meals because I pick restaurants based on their TripAdvisor reviews.

And if I'm shopping on Amazon, it doesn't matter whether I'm buying a £2,000 TV or a £2.50 jar of dark roasted peanut butter, I check the reviews and so do an awful lot of people.

Your customers already have an opinion of you (hopefully a positive one). To massively increase your R rate, simply ask them to share their opinion publicly by leaving you a review.

I love to hear from readers of my books (do email me btw – john@bigidea.co.uk), knowing that my hours spent sitting in a darkened room, furiously bashing my keyboard, actually make a difference in the real world – on the front lines of actual, real small businesses. I'm always happy to chat and help readers take the big ideas in my books and apply them to their own circumstances.

During that chat, I'll ever-so-subtly drop in the following line: "Btw, have you left me a nice Amazon/Audible review? ☺"

Reviews are the lifeblood of any author, so if I want to put food on my kids' plates, I owe it to them to ask for some reviews. I don't usually resort to emotional blackmail to get more five-star reviews, but I'll try anything once.

As well as guilt-tripping readers individually, I also have an email that's part of my Never-Ending-Nurture Sequence. It reads:

> *"I'd like to make one simple request from everyone who's read the book. If you liked it, and found it sparked some ideas that you can use in your business, please leave me a review."*

If you liked the book, please leave a review. Simple as that.

When was the last time you asked a customer to leave a review on Google, Amazon, TripAdvisor, Trust Pilot, ReeVoo, or indeed anywhere that your prospects are looking? Dig the reviews well before you're thirsty. Systematically ask and never stop asking. In my mind, there's no such thing as having "enough" reviews. Which of the following two companies would *you* choose?:

> *3 reviews (5.0 stars out of 5)*
>
> *148 reviews (4.8 stars out of 5)*

The more positive reviews you've got, the higher your business's R rate, and the more exponential growth (and therefore free customers) you can expect.

VIRAL ASSETS: WHO'S GOT MY CUSTOMER?

If I marketed my books to individual readers, I might sell a book or two. Sure, someone might pick up a copy for a friend, buy both paperback and audiobook versions or become a true fan and buy every book I've ever written.

But if I market to the people who already have my customers' trust, I open up a much higher leveraged channel. If I can turn a book club, accountant or business coach into a true fan, a recommendation from them carries far more weight than an advert from yours truly and I could sell dozens or even hundreds of books in one fell swoop.

Never mind two birds with one stone, try 50 birds with one stone.

In between flexing his newly-found biceps and doing squat jumps, my now-ripped mortgage broker friend Dave Aggiss nurtures relationships with – and actively markets to – limited company conveyancing solicitors, property sourcers, property investment trainers, and accountants who specialise in working with property investors.

In short, Dave's asking one question: "Who's got my customer?" Dave's ideal customer is a professional property investor looking to expand their portfolio – those with at least a couple of properties, a few years' experience, and an ambition to scale up.

So who's got Dave's customer? Solicitors and accountants who specialise in working with property investors, property sourcers (people who research and sell attractive property investment deals to portfolio investors), and those training in property investment (although Dave does need to be careful here that he doesn't attract complete newbies who have big plans but end up with a single buy-to-let. He needs to identify those who are training more advanced portfolio-building strategies).

If you're a dog trainer, then dog groomers, kennels, veterinarians, dog walkers, pet shops and breeders all have your customer.

If you're a nutritionist, then allergy clinics, doctors, personal trainers, health coaches and wellness groups have your customer.

If you're a financial advisor, then lawyers, accountants, mortgage brokers, business coaches and investment trainers have your customer.

Once you've identified who's got your customer, you're going to start marketing to *them* in the same way you've marketed to your prospects throughout your Evergreen Assets ecosystem – by giving them what they want, by using The Right Bait, and making them an Offer They Can't Refuse.

Your prospect is no longer the end customer – it's the person who's got your customer.

The product/service you want to sell to the end customer is not, repeat not, what you market to these guys. They don't care how brilliant your product or service is. They only care about two things:

1. What's in it for me?
2. What's in it for my clients?

Remember, people share things that make *them* look good. If you want to woo super-referrers, you need to find ways to make *them* look good to their clients. It's not about you, it's about what you can do for *them*. Will teaming up with you give *their* customers a better experience? Can you look after *their* clients better than anyone else? Will partnering with you make things faster and more efficient or open up a new revenue stream for *them*? Can you share *your* customers with them as well?

Many personal trainers already recommend a high protein diet to their clients, so if your range of high protein shakes, snacks and bars would genuinely help their clients *get what they want*, they'd happily recommend it.

Dave Aggiss happily refers to lawyers he trusts, because it stops his clients' deals from falling through due to legal red tape and overlooked legislation. Dave's clients get what they want, which makes him look good.

You can even team up with your competitors (shock horror, I know). While you may be rivals in the loose term, I bet there are areas where you don't compete and could work together to be the rising tide that lifts both ships. Dave specialises in working with portfolio landlords, but he receives leads and inquiries almost daily from single buy-to-let owners and residential mortgages. These aren't the clients he wants.

Meanwhile, other mortgage brokers who *do* want residential homeowners and single buy-to-let clients also receive occasional inquiries from portfolio landlords. It's a lot more complex and not their area of expertise, so they don't want these clients.

The win-win solution is blindingly obvious in this case, isn't it? Yet, I'll wager that a similar win-win scenario could be found somewhere in your business if you look hard enough.

In my sports betting business, I actively encourage my unconverted prospects to go and sign up with my competitors, who do the same for me. For whatever reason, those leads haven't converted for me, so I'm not losing anything by letting my rivals have a crack at them. And I get to do the same with the leads *they* couldn't close.

We're also working with influencers, such as retired footballers with large social media audiences. These guys have got our customers (sports fans who like to have fun) and we can present a great "what's in it for me?" case to the ex-pro – they'll look good by referring their audience to a reliable service, we'll look after their referrals and treat them well, and the player gets a new revenue stream now that his playing days are behind him.

Those who would self-identify as an “influencer” are already likely to be open to this kind of “50 birds with one stone” (or 50 sales with one tweet) deal. There are a plethora of influencers out there, so the most important thing is to be laser-focused with your targeting. The influencer’s audience should primarily consist of your target market. Simply hoping that there’s a handful of your clients somewhere in the 30,000 random followers they have because they were once on Love Island or Towie will not deliver a healthy ROI.

TL/DR:

You can kill 50 birds with one stone and one question: “Who’s got my customer?”

It requires a slight tweak to your marketing. Your prospects become Super Referrers and the product a joint venture proposal. Your marketing message is: What’s in it for them (and their clients)? You can even work with your competitors, having a crack at each other’s unconverted leads. Some influencers have the power to generate 50 sales with one tweet but only if they have your customer!

Oh, and let me know if you’re looking for a book to feature in your next book club.

VIRAL ASSETS: REFERRAL SYSTEMS

I’d like to share some of the referral systems I’ve deployed in my businesses and with my coaching clients.

The simplest one to get started with right now is simply asking for a referral: “If you’ve enjoyed reading this book, would you mind telling a friend about it?”

There, that wasn't so hard now, was it? That's the minimum effective dose – going from zero to one. Ask and ye shall receive.

Place some variation of that referral question into your Signature Move for all clients. Remember, we want to create a culture of referring, so let's offer more triggers to remind deliriously-happy clients to bring their friends along for the ride.

When I deliver digital copies of our 32-page Cheltenham Festival magazine to our sports betting clients, I include the line: "If you think your mates would enjoy reading this too, please forward this to them." Every time I include that line, hundreds of people send it to a friend.

Social network sharing buttons on your website can also help to spread the word when the trigger is shown at the right time. I own a website that fools visitors into believing they've been caught speeding, resulting in an invitation to view an image taken by the speed camera. When users click the image, they see a "gotcha!" message, a picture of a monkey pulling a funny face – and an invitation to fool a friend, together with social sharing buttons.

One day, my website was featured by LADbible on its social networking channels – and my traffic skyrocketed from the usual 250 visitors a day, to more than 30,000 in the first 24 hours.

But that wasn't the end of the story. My Viral Assets encouraged the newly-fooled to trick their mates with social sharing triggers displayed at the point of the "reveal". As such, I received a further 25,000 hits on the second day. Day three saw 18,000 and, although the traffic slowed, I had an R rate of 1.3 (every ten people sent it to three more), so traffic was still coming in six weeks later. One post turned 30,000 people into 250,000-plus.

A quarter of a million hits, with one stone (and some Viral Assets).

Probably the most complex referral system I've used was our seven-step Direct Mail system for our premium sports betting package. Members were initially asked for details (including home addresses) of their friends who might be suitable for the service. We then sent them a copy of our members-only magazine not from ourselves, but from their friend.

We asked members why they thought their mate would benefit from becoming a member and used their exact words in the letter. We then followed up with a more "salesy" letter from ourselves, making an Offer They Can't Refuse. A further follow-up letter was sent to the referrer asking them to check in with their friend. Two more pieces of Direct Mail were sent, introducing a deadline for the offer (together with a chocolate bar to sweeten the deal) and a final reminder that the offer was going away.

Finally, we called both the referrer and the referee on deadline day to close the deal.

Phew! I'm exhausted just describing that process, which is why we don't use it anymore. It did work and certainly brought in sales. But it was far too much work for my liking. There were too many moving parts, too many things that could go wrong and everything was time sensitive. Creating a culture of referring was far easier than getting this process followed consistently.

For a much simpler Direct Mail system, how about popping a prepaid postcard in with your product (or sending it out as a standalone with a choccy bar for service businesses) asking the question: "Who else do you know who would love ________?" and leaving space for them to give you the details. Then just call/email these people, saying: "So and so asked me to call, because she thinks you'd benefit from what we do."

Keep it simple, stupid!

Bribery always works well, too. Introduce a friend to Sky today and you'll both get a £75 prepaid Mastercard. Refer a new customer to Dropbox and earn free extra storage. Tell ten people about my books and I'll buy you coffee and cake.

Win-win offers tend to work well, because they remove the icky part of "I'm getting paid for this" when making a referral, instead turning it into social currency and practical value ("If I refer you, we *both* get a better deal than the standard offer. I'd recommend this even if I wasn't getting paid, but because you're lucky enough to know me, we're *both* better off").

Affiliates can also deliver a steady stream of referrals. Seventy per cent of the turnover from my sports betting company is from affiliate marketing and I'm building an army of affiliates to promote my brands, paying them a commission for every customer they send me.

Effectively, these are still natural recommendations, but affiliates get paid for kickbacks. It's very similar to the "who's got my customer?" strategy, but on a results-only commission structure. You can encourage your customers to join your affiliate program, letting them earn commission/discounts/bonuses for every person they refer to you. But, again, make sure they're doing it for the right reasons (a natural recommendation) rather than for pure financial gain.

Keep an eye on the quality of these referrals too. You more than likely don't want all of your customers bringing in more customers like themselves. You just want your best customers bringing in more people like them.

TL/DR:

Referral systems can be as simple or as complex as you like.

The simplest way is to just ask. Forward this email. Who do you know? Add social sharing triggers at the right time. Make referring easy. Add complexity if you want even better results (but don't make it too hard). You could create a seven-step direct mail campaign, send a chocolate bar or some other form of bribery – including cold, hard cash. But make sure you're getting high-quality referrals with your best customers replicating themselves, not your worst.

Oh, and if a website tells you that you've been caught speeding, don't believe them!

VIRAL ASSETS: SOCIAL NETWORKS

This isn't about getting a social media post to go viral. No matter how viral that post goes, it's still not an Evergreen Asset. I've had posts that more than a million people have seen, attracted more than a thousand likes and hundreds of comments. And almost every one of those views, likes, comments and other vanity metrics were outside of my target market.

They weren't the right people for me. I can't help them. I don't know what they want. They don't know who I am and certainly aren't likely to be one of my 1,000 true fans.

Evergreen Assets is not a numbers game. It's a relationships game. If you want to take your social networking game viral, then you need to create a culture of referring in your network, continuing to dig the well and nurturing those relationships so when someone in your network spots an opportunity to recommend or refer someone to you, they will do so automatically.

Always remember: What's in it for *them*? Ensure that by referring their customers/friends/colleagues/neighbours to you, *they'll* look good. *They'll* appear knowledgeable. Connected. Sending out the message to their network: "I know amazing people. I can help you solve your greatest problems even outside of my usual area of expertise. Aren't you glad you know me?"

To maximise your R rate, make it as easy as possible for your network to refer. Does your network know what you do? Do they know how you help people and the problems you solve? Are they aware of your dream (or nightmare) clients? Have you shared your case studies and testimonials with them? If so, the easier it is for your network to retell those stories.

Dave Aggiss's gym leveraged his network, sharing his case study video to generate referrals for its next six-week challenge.

Again, make sure you're getting natural referrals. I've been part of networking groups where referrals are anything but optional. If you want to stay in the group, you have to use the group's accountant, the group's printer, the group's web designer. That's not a network, that's a cartel.

The One Percent Club is a network and it always gives me immense pride when One Percenters work together to achieve great things. That's the power of a true network.

But we don't insist on it. In fact, Jason and I go the other way, reminding members we don't officially endorse anyone. Just because they've joined our network, it does not mean they're good at what they do.

One thing that gets my goat is when people confuse "who can you recommend?" with "who do you know?". I see people recommending businesses they've never worked with just because they're in the same networking group or they're friends on Facebook or their kids went to school together.

Prospective clients end up choosing the wrong product or service, just because lots of people know them. Knowing someone is not the same as knowing, liking, and trusting them. Even I've been recommended as a business coach by people I've never spoken with, let alone coached. How can they risk their reputation and vouch for me when they've never worked with me?

I always add the caveat: "I've not actually worked with them, but I've heard good things about Company A" or "You could try Company B. I've not used them myself though, so can't vouch for them". When you recommend, you risk your reputation. When someone recommends you, they've risked their reputation and you hold that reputation in your hands, so treat it well.

You might be tempted to incentivise your network with a kickback, but be careful not to end up with poor quality leads for the wrong reasons. I'd rather make my network look good by treating their referrals well and thanking them personally for making that referral. I may allocate some budget towards rewarding them with a bottle of wine or a box of chocolates, but I want that to be a genuine token of my appreciation rather than a financially incentivised kickback.

I'm sure the referred client would rather the referral was made due to a genuine recommendation than for financial gain too.

If you need to "shake the tree" for a few sales, try asking your network for a referral to the right type of client for you. "Who do you know who ________________?"

The more specific you can be about the type of clients you want (and don't want) to work with, the better referrals you will get.

> *"Who do you know who runs an established small business (any sector), is coachable, and working harder than they need to right now?*

If I ask my network that question, it's clear who I'd like to work with:

- Established small businesses (in any sector).
- Coachable.
- Working too hard.

While I may still get referrals outside of this criteria, I've made it clear who my dream clients are (ambitious, lifestyle business owners). These are the people I can give the best value to and who I enjoy working with the most. My network can be my eyes and ears and spot my ideal clients from a mile away (and hopefully refer them to me before they're two miles away, continuing to work hard in the wrong direction).

VIRAL ASSETS SUMMARY

Can you turn one customer into 1.2? What's the R rate of your business?

People do what they see others doing so create a culture of referring: "Our customers bring their friends."

There are two reasons most small businesses don't get more referrals: They're not asking for them and they don't have enough deliriously happy clients. Merely satisfied customers don't refer.

Make heroes of your best clients, sharing their stories as case studies and testimonials. There is no such thing as "too many" reviews so keep asking for them. Ask and ye shall receive. (If you liked this book, please leave a review. See, that wasn't so hard now, was it?).

Who's got your customer? You can kill 50 birds with this one stone.

Referral systems can be as simple or as complex as you like. You could create a seven-step direct mail campaign, but the simplest way is to just ask. Again, ask and ye shall receive. Your network can be a great source of referrals if you've been digging the well and making it easy for them to refer – making them look good by doing so.

Do you get two free customers with every ten that your Lead, Nurture and Sales Assets generate? Viral Assets help you turn one customer into more than one and compounds as those "free" leads also travel through your entire Evergreen Assets ecosystem.

9. ASSEMBLING THE MACHINE

It's time to put the theory into practice – time to start curating your ecosystem and building your machine. As you've been reading this book, your gut instinct has probably been screaming to let you know which asset class needs your attention first.

Remember the simple, one-sheet Evergreen Assets ecosystem template:

> We help _______ (target market) to _______ (what they want), by _______ (Proven Framework).
>
> We generate leads by _______ .
>
> We build trust by _______ .
>
> We convert to sales by _______ .
>
> We fulfil clients by _______ .
>
> We get paid by _______ .
>
> We turn 1 customer into 1.2 by _______.

Which asset class in your ecosystem has missing cogs, rusty screws and years-old duct tape holding it all together?

If your phone isn't ringing, start with Lead Assets. If they won't take your call, add Nurture Assets. If no one's buying, focus on Sales Assets. If your burgers don't look like the picture, work on Fulfilment Assets. If things aren't working like clockwork, create Admin Assets. And if you want to turn one customer into more than one, let's add some exponential growth with Viral Assets.

Once you know which asset class to focus on, go back and re-read that section and start planning, building, and designing the Evergreen Assets you're going to add to your ecosystem.

As a reminder, here are some of the Evergreen Assets we've covered:

Lead Assets

- One Lead Asset To Rule Them All: The Right Bait.
- Email: Build a list using The Right Bait.
- Websites: Squeeze and Hug pages. Sharing the "big idea".
- Search Engine Optimisation: Give Google what it wants.
- Google Ads: A shortcut to SEO.
- Facebook Ads: The interrupting cow.
- Social Networks: Build 1,000 true relationships.

Nurture Assets

- One Nurture Asset To Rule Them All: Weekly Emails.
- Email: Find out *what they want* and start two-way conversations.
- Websites: Your website is not about you. It's about "people like us".
- Awards: Winning awards is a shortcut to trust.
- Google My Business: People already google you. Control what they see.
- Social Networks: Dig the well before you're thirsty.
- Podcasts: Be Basil Fawlty or Sir Terry Wogan (or just be a guest).
- Books: The best business card you ever had.
- Printed Newsletters: Like an email newsletter, except it'll get read.
- Remarketing: OMG! They're everywhere.

- PR: Become BFFs with the people who have your future customers' eyes and ears.
- Video: Convey tone, emotion, and sincerity ten times quicker.

Sales Assets

- One Sales Asset To Rule Them All: An Offer They Can't Refuse.
- A Proven Framework: The step-by-step process all successful clients follow.
- A Guarantee: Put your money where your mouth is.
- A Small Taste: Try before you buy is tried and tested.
- Make It Easy: If you want to sell more, make it easier for people to buy more.
- A Deadline: "'Too late! too late!' will be the cry, when the man with the bargains has passed you by."
- Email: Create your Signature Move. SPEAR your best prospects and milk the GOAT.
- Websites: Make it easy for busy, lazy, drunk, amnesiac idiots to buy from you.
- Funnels: A deselection process. Don't be Mrs Doyle.
- Direct Mail: Cuts through the noise. Its barrier to entry (cost) is also its greatest asset.
- Google Ads: Target the buyers, not the tyre-kickers and "just looking" brigade.
- Video: Your best sales rep, delivering a perfect pitch every time.
- Remarketing: Shoot fish in a barrel by only advertising to qualified prospects.
- Your Network: Can anyone recommend a ____________?

Fulfilment Assets

- One Asset To Rule Them All: The Quick Win.
- The Kick-off Call: Make sure their burger matches the picture before you drive away.
- The Handover: Not "Terry will be looking after you from now on".
- First 100 Days Checklist: Don't lose 20 to 70 per cent of your customers in the first 100 days.
- Proven Framework: The guardrail that keeps customers on track to getting what they want.
- Video: Don't tell me how it works. Show me.
- Email: Keep the same pre-sale level of razzmatazz going.
- Websites: Make sure your customers do have everything they need.
- Evergreen Products: Be the Netflix in your niche.
- Membership model: Predictable, steady income without too many peaks and troughs.
- Feedback loop: Find out why customers' burgers don't match the one in the picture.
- Direct Mail: We're all in the renewals business. Keeping customers could be a piece of cake.
- Remarketing: Who else follows people around the internet just to make sure they're happy?
- Your Network: Keep digging the well. Your network just got bigger.

Admin Assets

- One Admin Asset To Rule Them All: Company Culture.

- Proven Processes: This is how we do it.
- The Company Handbook: Your bible. The law, according to *you*.
- The Humble Checklist: Your ten (or preferably fewer) commandments.
- Task Management Software: Get people to actually follow the proven processes.
- Email: Use (un)canned responses to add some raspberry ripple to the boring vanilla.
- Self-serve: Only when it's easier for the customer.
- Video: Personal video doesn't scale and that's what makes it so damn effective.
- Finance: Stop driving with the rear-view mirror and become a numbers person.
- The Purge: Keep it simple, stupid. Remove anything that doesn't serve you.
- Slopey Shoulders: Stop trying to do it all yourself –embrace specialisation and exchange.

Viral Assets

- One Asset To Rule Them All: Bring Your Friends.
- Case Studies: Make heroes of your successful clients and tell their stories.
- Testimonials: The little brother of the case study. Use them *everywhere*!
- Reviews: There's no such thing as "too many", so start collecting them now and never stop.
- Who's Got My Customer?: Kill 50 birds with one stone. Just remember what's in it for *them*.

- Referral Systems: Start with a simple, "Who do you know who ________?"
- Your Network: Make it easy for them to refer and make *them* look good when they do.

An important note at this point is that not even I have *all* of these assets in play in my ecosystem and many of the ones I do are not firing on all cylinders. But that's fine because our businesses are a work in progress. They always will be. Just like any strong ecosystem, they're always evolving, doubling down on what works and losing what doesn't.

Constant, never-ending improvement of the ecosystem is the name of the game. If you committed to improving your ecosystem by a mere one per cent each week, after a year you'd see a 68 per cent uplift to your machine. After two years, compounding really kicks in and your ecosystem will be working 181 per cent more effectively.

These massive, game-changing improvements are only possible in the long term by making small incremental improvements every week in the short term – by getting one per cent better at selling, increasing your profit margins by one per cent, and being one per cent more focused. It's about doing one per cent more marketing, reducing wastage by one per cent and training your staff to be one per cent more effective.

Each week, tick off simple one per cent improvements in your finances, mindset, learning, networking, communications, copywriting, negotiation, and people management. Get one per cent more people seeing your ads, persuade one per cent more of them to click on the ad, get one per cent more sign-ups for your lead magnet, and increase your email open rates by one per cent.

Get one per cent more people buying, spending one per cent more money on one per cent more items. Reduce your refunds or cancellations by one per cent. Get customers taking upsells one per cent more often, returning one per cent more often, and referring one per cent more of their friends.

Collect one per cent more testimonials and one per cent more reviews. Interact one per cent more often with your social network, and create an Offer They Can't Refuse that is one per cent better than what you're doing right now.

Do just one of those things every week (or even every month), with a tiny one per cent improvement, and watch the Evergreen Assets ecosystem exponentially compound those gains:

Number of 1% Improvements	Uplift to the Evergreen Assets ecosystem
1	1%
10	10%
25	28%
52	68%
70	101%
100	170%

HOW EVERGREEN ASSETS COMPOUND

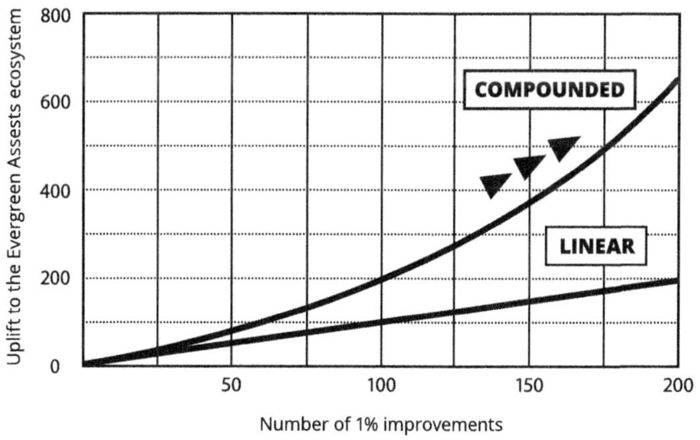

Unless you're already running a perfectly oiled machine with every moving part working at 100 per cent capacity, improving one single element by just one per cent each week should be easily achievable for just about every one of us. And who wouldn't want a 68 per cent increase on their bottom line for a year of stacking up easy one per cent wins?

By now, you certainly shouldn't be stuck for ideas on how to improve your machine. It's much more likely that you're overwhelmed by the sheer volume of tasks you could perform.

There's another Evergreen Asset that will help you figure out what's worth doing and in what order. I call it the "Could Do List". It's the opposite of the traditional to-do list because you're not going to commit to doing anything on this list at all. It's simply a brain dump of everything you *could* do to improve your Evergreen Assets ecosystem.

Grab a piece of paper and start writing down your Evergreen Assets Could Do List. Don't think about anything you're writing or pre-judge whether your ideas are good or bad, how long they'll take or how much they'll cost. We're simply looking to capture *all* your thoughts and ideas now, even if they're ridiculous moon shots or far too much hard work for far too little reward.

Write everything down. Every little thing. Your sole aim is an empty head and a full sheet of paper.

Once everything has been captured, you're then going to triage the lot. You're going to rank everything you've written in descending order of "bang for your buck". The "low effort, high gains" at the top and the "high effort, low gains" at the bottom. From highest ROI to lowest. This will involve some guesswork, but it's better to have a rough idea of your expected ROI and, believe me, the lowest hanging fruit will be blindingly obvious to you.

Once you've triaged your list, simply work your way through it from highest ROI to lowest.

If you're anything like me, that one sheet of A4 will soon become a folder with about a hundred sheets of A4 in it because I'm always capturing ideas to optimise my machine. Every time I read a book, I write a one-page debrief and the action points from this end up in my Could Do List folder. If I listen to a podcast and hear a great tactic, I'll write it down and put it in my CDL folder.

My folder is full to the brim with screenshots, photocopies of books, Kindle highlights, Post-it notes, action points from team meetings, journal entries, and crudely-drawn diagrams and funnel designs. There are a couple of hundred things in that folder that I *could* do to improve my machine.

Most of them, I'll never get around to doing.

But the ones at the very front of the folder *will* get done. I can guaran-damn-tee you that. Because I regularly triage my Could Do List, putting all those highly-leveraged, highest ROI, lowest hanging fruit opportunities at the front.

Spot an idea > document it > triage it > do it. It's a simple system, but it works.

HOW TO BE A CONTENT MARKETING GENIUS

"Better or worse?"

The key question asked by opticians performing eye tests and by marketing geniuses looking to constantly improve every aspect of their Evergreen Assets ecosystem.

The optician plays around with various strength lenses, trying out variants on each eye and asking you which is better. She might start with the prescription she thinks will work best for you. She'll use her knowledge, training, and years of expertise. She'll listen to her gut and go with what she thinks will work best for you.

And she'll probably be wrong.

She usually is the first time. And often the second, third, and fourth time. And that's fine because the optician has built a machine that doesn't rely on her god-like genius to be right. It's called an eye *test* for a reason. The optician tests her hypotheses (I think lens B *could* work better than lens A) and gets real-time user feedback by asking that key question: "Is that better or worse?"

B wins. Let's see if C can beat B. "Better or worse?" B wins again. Let's see how lens D performs. "Better or worse?" Lens D is better. Cool. D is now the control. Is D better than E…and so on.

The optician is playing by the same rules as the pub pool table – winner stays on.

If you employ that same mindset when optimising your Evergreen Assets machine, you too can appear to be a marketing genius simply by playing Winner Stays On. Take any existing asset and consider how you might get it performing better.

The existing asset is the control – version A. You're going to create a B version and pit it against the control, asking enough of your prospects and customers: "Is that better or worse?"

Would you rather do what most people do and rely on gut feeling, opinions, and instinct when engineering your machine? Or would you rather be guided by cold hard facts, results, and money-in-the-bank?

That's highly illogical, Captain

Playing Winner Stays On is how I discovered that adding a grammatical error to a headline increased leads by 48 per cent. It's how I learned that deleting adverts *increased* sales by 16 per cent, and it's how I was able to increase average customer spend by 31 per cent by dropping my prices!

Believe it or not, busy, lazy, drunk, amnesiac idiots behave in illogical ways. So there's no point using logic to try to figure out how they'll behave. I attended a seminar years ago where conversion rate experts asked the audience to guess the winners of several split tests. The room was full of very successful, switched-on marketers – the best in the business. By a show of hands, we voted for what our knowledge, expertise, and instinct – logic – told us.

And we were wrong. Every time. About everything. The horrible looking page outsold the beautiful one. The massive, rambling copy outperformed the short, snappy one. The £297 product had a higher conversion rate than the same product with a £197 tag.

Everything we knew was wrong. All logic went out the window.

This, of course, was the point the experts wanted to make – that you never know the answers for sure until you test. All those marketing experts in the room were probably right, in general. But for that product, that audience, that part of the machine, they were wrong. And, worse, they don't know they were wrong.

Because they're not playing Winner Stays On and finding out if they're wrong.

I've always got at least five A/B tests running at any one time (an A/B test is where you show 50 per cent of people version A of an asset, while 50 per cent see version B. You track the results and the winner stays on). I'm always testing. I want to know if any of the cogs in my machine can be improved. I want to test for myself the ideas and hypotheses I read in books and hear on podcasts. I actively seek out user feedback to discover why people don't buy, why they cancel, and what roadblocks they're reporting.

I love being wrong. I'll put up a B version that I *know* will lose. And then cheer like a loon when it kicks the arse of the control, and when I spot trends, patterns, and user behaviour that I never even considered, let alone expected. As scientist Isaac Asimov said: "The most exciting phrase to hear in science, the one that heralds new discoveries, is not "Eureka" but 'That's funny...'"

There are several ways you can play Winner Stays On. Most advertising and email platforms have a "split test" or "A/B test" option. This allows you to specify a B version, so you can try out a different headline, a different call to action or change some of the body copy.

There's software that will allow you to do the same on your website (I use Google Optimize). Better or worse? You'll know for sure. And when you know for sure, you simply continue to play Winner Stays On. If version B wins, version B stays on, becomes the new control, and we attempt to beat that with a new variant.

As you continue to optimise the machine, your conversion rate will naturally increase, as you'll always have the best performing version of each cog in play so you'll capture more leads, nurture those leads more effectively, convert more of them to a sale, do a better job of "giving them what they want", have your Admin Assets working like the well-oiled machine they're capable of being, and maximise the virality of each customer.

That means each customer is worth more to you. They'll pay you more money, more often. And they'll bring in more of their friends who will do the same. Every lead you capture will also be worth more and this unlocks some pretty amazing doors.

Suddenly, those advertising platforms that were financially out of reach are within your grasp. You can outbid your competition, knowing full well that you're monetising each and every lead better than them because they're still using gut feeling and instinct, and you're using cold, hard facts and data. They're still wrong about just about everything, while you know for sure.

As legendary direct response marketer Dan Kennedy says: "Ultimately, the business that can spend the most to acquire a customer wins." And by playing Winner Stays On and constantly improving your ecosystem of Evergreen Assets, *you* can be that business and a marketing genius to boot.

Two is one, and one is none

Even the best racehorses go lame. The most talented footballer in the world will have to retire eventually. The biggest companies on the planet 50 years ago? Ninety per cent of them don't even exist anymore. Expect everything to fail at some point. If you have two widgets, one of them will fail at some point and then you'll have one. If you only have one widget, that one will fail at some point and you'll have none.

If you've got one asset – one cog that your entire machine relies on and that cog fails (or irreparably breaks) – you're screwed. The more cogs you've got, and the easier you can swap them out for another, the easier it is to keep your machine ticking over with the least amount of downtime.

I own two businesses in two very different sectors: a sports betting company and a small business coaching company. Each business has multiple revenue streams. Each has multiple Lead Assets bringing prospects into the ecosystem, where multiple Nurture Assets warm those prospects up, before introducing them to one of many different Sales Assets. Anyone who becomes a customer then receives dozens of Fulfilment Assets, a plethora of Admin Assets, and a variety of Viral Assets.

In a moment, I'll walk you through all the assets from both businesses to demonstrate the diversity of my Evergreen Assets ecosystem. I'm still adding new assets and always playing Winner Stays On because I know the more cogs I add to my machine, and the more effective I make those cogs, the stronger my foundations will be, the more diverse my ecosystem, reducing the likelihood of my machine grinding to a halt.

Screw you guys, I'm going home

As a kid, I used to play football in our local park with a bunch of lads from school.

Gary always picked the teams. Gary chose the captains (he was always the captain). Gary chose who went in goal (usually me), and who was the star striker (always him). Gary was the referee as well, and usually awarded himself a penalty or two if someone had the cheek to take the ball off him.

Why did we let Gary dictate everything? Because Gary owned the football. A Mitre Delta 1000. A thing of beauty.

They say the golden rule is he who has the gold decides the rules. Well, when it comes to playing football in the park, he who has the football decides the rules. It was Gary's football. Therefore, we played by Gary's rules.

Was it over the line? It depends which team Gary's on. What's the score again? Better ask Gary. How long's left to play? That's up to Gary. If he's on a hat-trick, we'll play until he scores. If he's about to lose, then he'll suddenly remember his mum wanted him home ten minutes ago.

And if you did anything to upset him, you'd hear Gary shout those immortal words: "Screw you guys, I'm going home." Of course, he would take his Mitre Delta 1000 with him. Game over.

If you don't own the football, you've got no control.

Evergreen Assets are long term assets that *you* own and *you* control. They're *your* football. Your football = Your rules.

I built my entire business empire on SEO only to discover it was Google's football when it moved the goalposts.

I built a Facebook page up to 127,000 fans, spending £10,000 a month on Facebook Ads, only to have my ad account closed and my page shut down. Its football. Its rules.

I've had suppliers give me 30 days' notice that they're removing six figures from my bottom line. I've had a PayPal account shut down with no notice after 18 years of trading because they deemed us to be "high risk". Their football. Their rules.

I sell my books through Amazon's Evergreen Assets ecosystem – leveraging *its* sales pages, *its* emails, *its* reviews, *its* network (people who bought *this* also bought *that*), *its* remarketing, and of course *its* patented 1-Click buy button. There's a huge benefit to me in leveraging the behemoth that is Amazon. But I still need to remember that it's Amazon's football and Amazon's rules.

That's why I'm building my own Evergreen Assets ecosystem alongside that of Amazon.

When you build your empire on someone else's land, it's like playing football with Gary. It's great fun for a while, but if at any point they want to move the goalposts, change the team or play "next goal wins", they're fully entitled to do so because it's *their* football.

How about you get your own football?

Once you control an ecosystem of Evergreen Assets, you can still play with other people's balls (oo-er missus!), but it won't be "game over" if and when they take their football home with them.

10. I'LL SHOW YOU MINE...

Throughout this book, you've read examples, stories and anecdotes to demonstrate how these ideas and concepts work on the front lines in the real world. Now, I will take you behind the curtain to show you what happens backstage in my businesses and how I've created my Evergreen Assets ecosystem.

For each business, you'll see how all the moving parts fit together and how each asset compounds on the others.

HERE'S THE ECOSYSTEM FOR MY SPORTS BETTING BUSINESS:

Lead Assets

We've created The Right Bait (such as a 32-page Cheltenham Festival magazine, a 75/1 acca for this weekend's matches or free tips for the Grand National). We share our "big idea" (having access to professional tipsters will help you make better betting decisions) on our website, using both squeeze and hug pages.

We've written detailed blog posts about the most popular horse races, betting strategies and explained some of the more complex terms in our industry. This gives Google what it wants and we get lots of free SEO traffic as a result.

We have Google Ads and Facebook Ads running to generate leads, as well as key partners from our network ("who's got my customer?"), and a thriving social network where we're digging the well every day.

Nurture Assets

We've written a comprehensive book, *47 Horse Racing Betting Systems*. We send weekly emails that don't sell anything but simply find out what they want and start two-way conversations. Our website isn't about us – it's about our members. It's full of case studies, testimonials and "people like us".

We've appeared as expert guests on podcasts and written guest horse racing tips for several major newspapers.

Sales Assets

We make an Offer They Can't Refuse (a free 30-day trial, a half-price first month or bonus tips when you join before the deadline). We have a Proven Framework (The Simple Six), and give people a small taste to try before they buy.

We've made it as easy as possible for busy, lazy, drunk amnesiac idiots to buy and constantly play Winner Stays On to keep the improvements stacking up. We leverage sales campaigns – including emails, funnels and webinars (such as a free training video or a Cheltenham Festival preview evening).

We have a Signature Move so that people can tell us to "shut up and take my money", and we SPEAR our best prospects. When we want to shake the tree, we send an eight-word email.

Fulfilment Assets

We deliver quick wins (the quickest was an 80/1 winner on day one of the Cheltenham Festival). We have a first 100 days checklist to keep new members on track within our Proven Framework, so we don't lose 20 to 70 per cent of them.

We keep the razzmatazz going after they've bought and have a feedback loop (without a noreply@ email address in sight) to make sure that their burger looks like the one in the picture. We send them cake on their anniversary and we never forget that it's a relationships game.

Admin Assets

Everyone in our team knows our "why" – to help everyday punters make better betting decisions. We have our proven processes collated in a digital company handbook, which is managed by task management software.

We've got a handful of simple checklists for the stuff that matters and red flag alerts to mystery shop and quality check. We've embraced self-serve only where it makes things easier for the members (an automated daily tipping competition and a SaaS model).

We've also automated invoicing, billing, and bookkeeping. Cart abandonment processes and (un)canned responses are in place, and my shoulders are as slopey as they've ever been – fully embracing specialisation and exchange. Every month, we purge thousands of emails from our list, keeping deliverability and open rates high.

Viral Assets

We've got an army of affiliates and joint venture partners working with us ("who's got my customer?"). We tweak our Signature Move for clients, asking for referrals instead of a sale. We're always looking to make heroes of our most successful clients – interviewing them to create case studies and testimonials.

We never stop collecting reviews and never stop asking: "Who do you know who…?"

We turn one customer into 1.2.

AND HERE'S MY COACHING BUSINESS ECOSYSTEM:

Lead Assets

I use The Right Bait (free sample chapters of my books) to build an email list. I share my "big idea" (improving your business by one per cent each week leads to huge improvements over the long term) on my website, again using both squeeze and hug pages.

I've written dozens of SEO blog posts, giving Google what it wants. I dig the well with my social network. I've also run Facebook Ads and Google Ads to generate leads.

Nurture Assets

I've been writing weekly emails for the past four years (head to www.bigidea.co.uk if you'd like to get them).

I've also written three books (including this one), appeared as a guest on more than 200 podcasts, and hosted more than 80 episodes of my podcast. I've done countless public speaking gigs. I leverage video to have maximum impact.

Sales Assets

I make prospects an Offer They Can't Refuse (my team's help to improve your business by one per cent every week). I've created a Proven Framework (The One Percent Way), a step-by-step process that all successful clients have already followed. I back this up with a "money-where-my-mouth-is" guarantee but have a strict deadline (I only have two sales windows per year: in March and September).

Again, I SPEAR my best prospects and shake the tree with an eight-word email. I remember that funnels are a deselection process and don't force anyone to buy.

Fulfilment Assets

I want to deliver a quick win, so aim to deliver their first one per cent gain on the very first day. New One Percenters immediately get a kick-off call with Jason (who they've already been introduced to as he's part of the A-team), and a razzmatazz video welcome from yours truly.

Using our first 100 days checklist, we'll then aim to keep newbies on the One Percent Way Proven Framework, as well as sending them an onboarding survey (to find out what they want). There's also plenty of surprise and delight baked in (which wouldn't be a surprise if I wrote about it here), and the ever-crucial feedback loop to make damn sure they're getting what they want.

Admin Assets

Again, everyone in the team is crystal-clear on the company's "why" – to help ambitious, lifestyle business owners improve their business *and* lifestyle by one per cent each week.

We have proven processes and a digital company handbook with everything collated and managed by our task management software. We know why we do it, we know how to do it, and the TMS makes sure it gets done correctly and on time.

We leverage automated billing and invoicing, cloud accounting and bookkeeping, and enable members to self-serve (to update payment methods, access our Netflix-style back catalogue of videos and masterclasses, or change their membership) *if* that's the easier option for them. If they prefer to speak to a human, they can do that too.

We've designed red flag "slipping away" processes to alert us when members are becoming less engaged, enabling us to reach out and remind them: "I'm here for you and I care. I'm going to help you to get what you want. And I'm not going to stop until I'm damn sure you've got what you want. Your success matters to me."

Viral Assets

By creating an environment that our members truly love, they naturally want to bring their friends along, too. When they do so, we need to work even harder in those first 100 days because it's no longer just *our* reputation on the line. We need to make our referrer look good to their friend. People share what makes *them* look good.

Every month, when Jason and I record the Ambitious Lifestyle Business podcast, we're creating another case study and making another hero out of one of our most successful clients by telling their story. They're the hero – we're just the guides.

I'll never stop asking for reviews of my books (as we're approaching the end of this book, have you left me a nice review yet? If you don't ask, you don't get!) because I know there's no such thing as "enough" reviews.

We turn one One Percenter into 1.2.

I DIDN'T START AT THE FINISHING LINE

After going on that whistle-stop tour of both businesses' ecosystems, you may well be thinking: "This all sounds like a lot of hard work!" And you wouldn't be wrong. But that's the result of years of constant, never-ending improvement of the machine.

My sports betting business began as a simple one-page website (acting as a Lead, Nurture and Sales Asset). It got traffic from SEO and nowhere else. I didn't sell any of my own products, instead referring clients to affiliate partners to look after fulfilment. Because the business was simple, my admin was simple. Viral Assets? Zero. None. Nada. Oops!

That was where I started. Over many, many years, I then added an email capture form, then our own services, then an Offer They Can't Refuse, then squeeze pages (and hug pages), then invested heavily into SEO, then Google Ads, then Facebook Ads, then The Right Bait, then a support team, then printed newsletters, then working with JV partners, then more and more marketing pillars, and more and more assets.

My coaching business started with six people sitting around my kitchen table. I reached out to my network (an existing Nurture Asset) and offered six people a free, six-month trial (an Offer They Can't Refuse). I found out what they wanted and made damn sure they got it.

Everything else – all those other assets – were added and evolved over time. I started a podcast. Then I wrote a book, launched a website, and started sending weekly emails. I simply kept adding new assets into my ecosystem one at a time and built it up over several years. Another book. More blog posts. New relationships.

That's how ecosystems work, you see. They evolve. They get better over time, as compounding kicks in, and you build upon what works and lose what doesn't.

Start simple. Then evolve. Play Winner Stays On and improve what you've already got before adding more. Revolutionary results are achieved through an evolutionary process.

11. YOU'RE PROBABLY THINKING...

Whenever I present the Evergreen Assets framework to audiences, the Q&A section at the end is always my favourite part because it's where the rubber meets the road. It's where theoretical ideas get turned into actionable, concrete plans. It's where you get to connect the dots in your head and answer one of two burning questions:

1. "Yeah, but what about ____________?" (Where ____________ is the one thing that's stopping you from taking action).
2. "Yeah, that sounds great in theory. But what should I do?"

While I've received hundreds of different questions on the topic of Evergreen Assets, they all fall into these two categories. There's either one big stumbling block that's stopping you from "getting it" and taking action, or you're struggling to connect the dots to translate the theory into the real world and know what *you* should do. Where should *you* start? How will *your* ecosystem look? What asset should *you* tackle next?

I've answered the most frequently asked questions over these next few pages. If your specific question isn't answered, don't panic. You can email me (john@bigidea.co.uk) and I'll happily help you connect those dots.

How do I calculate the ROI?

It's incredibly easy to create content for content's sake, call it an asset, and not actually improve your business in the slightest. In other words, to be a busy fool. For some assets, working out the ROI will be a piece of cake. Pop some tracking code on your website and you'll know whether that new sales page is doing better or worse than the old one. Google Ads will report which headline works best and you can simply glance at your email open rates and clickthrough rates to calculate improvements.

But how do you work out the ROI on a book, checklist, or a review? That's much harder.

Where it's more difficult to calculate ROI, I like to justify my investment in the asset (whether I'm investing cold hard cash or my more finite resources of time, energy, and focus) by answering the following question:

> *Will this asset help me get or keep more customers?*

If the answer's a "hell yeah!", then it's a good investment. But the minute I feel the need to try to justify it to myself – "Well, it *could* in the long term. Someone *might* read this piece of content, and that *could* be the thing that triggers them to buy" – I know I'm unlikely to see a return *of* my investment, let alone a return *on* it!

Ask yourself: "Will this asset help me get or keep more customers?" If your answer contains any (or all) of the words *could*, *might* or *maybe*, then save yourself the hassle and focus on a different, more highly-leveraged asset.

My business is different/boring/complicated. Will Evergreen Assets still work for me?

I hear this from many new clients who think their business is special. I'm sorry to burst your bubble guys, but while your products and services may differ considerably, and your target market can vary wildly, your business shares 95 per cent of its DNA with every other business out there.

All businesses need to:

- Generate leads.
- Warm up potential buyers.
- Make sales.
- Fulfil client needs.
- Do admin.
- Generate future business.

Most small businesses have the same problems and run in very similar ways, regardless of their size, industry, or sector.

I run one business that is entirely creative and another that is highly regulated. Evergreen Assets works for both. Sure, I need to change the marketing message for each and I can't simply copy and paste an asset from one business to another, but I can swipe and deploy. I can adapt and adopt.

Rather than shutting down your brain by saying, "That won't work for my business", try asking your brain to solve the problem: "How can I make that work in my business?"

Jay Abraham insists that "breakthroughs increase in direct proportion to the amount of networking, brainstorming, and masterminding you do with like-minded, success-driven people outside your industry."

I used to think that because I owned an internet marketing business, I could only learn from other internet marketers. But my truly game-changing breakthroughs have come not from internet marketers, but by connecting the dots from influences as wide-ranging as hedge fund managers, musicians, scientists, gardeners, builders, lawyers, farmers, accountants, and property investors.

I can't copy and paste anything from these industries, but I can swipe and deploy the overarching Proven Frameworks – the guiding principles – then connect the dots to my own business and make them my own.

How much should I give away for free?

Enough. And no more. That's going to require a little trial and error to find out where the ideal "free line" (where free ends and paid starts) should be. People worry about getting this wrong, either refusing to give anything away (banks chaining their pens to the desk) or giving it all away (the coach who just wants to help, but never asks for the sale).

Don't spend all your time creating Nurture Assets and delivering a tremendous amount of value for free, only to find that there's nothing left to pay for.

Another useful rule of thumb is to give away "what" to do (a high-protein, low-carb diet with HIIT workouts three times a week), but not "how" to do it (Your Proven Framework meal and exercise plan, plus personal coaching, and accountability).

It depends on how knowledgeable your prospects are. They might already know what to do, but need more actionable advice on how to do it. Or they may be completely clueless and not know what to do, let alone how to do it. This is where the free/cheap line could blur:

- Free: *What* to do, zero *how*. You could use this as The Right Bait.
- Cheap: *What* to do, plus a basic overview of the *how*. This could be a tripwire or a low-priced evergreen product.
- Paying clients: *What* to do and exactly *how* to do it in granular, personalised detail. This could involve giving them all the tools to successfully DIY or it could be DWY (Done With You) or DFY (Done For You). Either way, this is on the paying client side of the free line.

Ultimately, it's your football, so you get to choose where to place the free line. Put it wherever you feel comfortable and remember that you can always move it (although it's always easier to move it in the direction of giving more stuff away than less).

One thing I'll say is that I've never felt I've lost out by giving tons of free content away, as long as it serves the purpose of greasing the wheels of my machine. Will this free content help you get or keep customers?

I'm swamped with live client work – how can I find the time to create Evergreen Assets?

You'll never *find* the time. You need to *make* the time. So block out some time in your calendar.

I'm a big fan of regular routines, so whether that's one day a month or an hour a week, just make an appointment with yourself for that time and do not allow anything else to be booked into that time slot.

In his 2011 letter to shareholders, Warren Buffett said: "Investing is often described as the process of laying out money now in the expectation of receiving more money in the future."

Well, investing in Evergreen Assets is often described (by me) as the process of laying out time, money, and energy now in the expectation of receiving more time, money, and energy in the future.

Creating Evergreen Assets is an investment in your future. The reason you don't have time now is that you didn't invest in your Evergreen Assets ecosystem five years ago. Will future-you be grateful for this investment five years from now or will you still be making excuses about not having time?

By sacrificing some time (and quite possibly some revenue if you have to turn away paying clients to create space in your calendar) now to generate evergreen, compounded future revenue streams that could be far, far larger in the long term, you become an investor in the true sense of the word.

As your assets start to bear fruit, you can begin to pivot further away from "live" work, leaning into more Evergreen Assets, further compounding and accelerating your results.

When will I start to see results?

Evergreen Assets are a long-term strategy and you shouldn't expect to build Rome in a day. I always worry when people ask this question, because it's a great indicator of short-term thinking, which is not helpful for long-term business success.

Charlie Munger (97 years old at the time of writing and with a net worth of more than $2billion) summed this up perfectly when he was asked a similar question: "We get these questions a lot from the enterprising young. You look at some old guy who's rich and you ask, 'How can I become like you... except *faster*?'"

My answer, I'm afraid, is one that no one likes to hear: "It depends." I simply can't calculate the return on investment without knowing your business model and current ecosystem inside-out. Even if I did, it would still be a "best guess".

What I will say, though, is that you can affect the rate of return by focusing your resources (time, energy, headspace, and money) on those asset classes and individual assets that will have a disproportionate effect on your entire ecosystem.

That's why I started my coaching business by simply connecting two large cogs (a well-nurtured network and an Offer They Can't Refuse). Hey presto! I was up and running and able to see an almost instant ROI.

If you've already got an ecosystem, any improvements you make to the machine will compound, thanks to all the other cogs. Your individual model, your margins, and the rate you turn prospects into cash in the bank will dictate how soon you will see a positive ROI from your improved ecosystem.

The larger cogs make more of an impact, so you should see results pretty quickly if you're working on these. But if you're tinkering with a tiny cog or you've got very few leads coming into your machine, you can't expect to see the needle move very much until you create the right conditions for it to do so.

When deciding where to invest your resources, always ask yourself: Will adding or improving this asset get (or keep) more customers?

Finally, there's the real beauty of Evergreen Assets – their "do it once, reap the rewards again and again (and again)" nature. So, rather than ask, "When will I start to see results?" let's ask, "What can I do to see permanent, everlasting, never-ending results?"

When will my ecosystem be finished?

Another popular question with an unpopular answer. When will your ecosystem be finished? Ideally, never. I still work on my businesses' ecosystems every day. I've got a folder crammed full of ideas to make them better. Every book I read, every podcast I listen to, every coach I hire, every mentor I seek out, every seminar I attend, and every TED talk I watch all spark new ideas, innovations, and improvements that I *could* make to my ecosystems.

Every day, I'm playing Winner Stays On with one simple goal – constant, never-ending improvement. Better? Or worse? Better? Or worse?

Walt Disney was an animator and the best in the world at creating animated movies. Fifteen years after producing Snow White and the Seven Dwarfs – the world's first feature-length animated movie – and collecting a host of Oscars (one "big" Oscar and seven "dwarf" ones), Walt walked away from the movie business to focus his attention on theme parks.

Walt explained his reasoning thus: "Disneyland will never be finished. It's something we can keep developing and adding to. A motion picture is different. Once it's wrapped up and sent out for processing, we're through with it. If there are things that could be improved, we can't do anything about them anymore. I've always wanted to work on something alive, something that keeps growing. We've got that in Disneyland."

Something alive. Something that keeps growing. That sounds like an ecosystem to me!

Walt Disney played Winner Stays On for the rest of his life, creating the happiest place on Earth. It's a process that continues to this day. When I visited the Magic Kingdom a few years ago, several attractions were being demolished and replaced with new ones. Others were being upgraded and modernised. New technology was being integrated wherever possible. We were surveyed (feedback loop) several times during our visits.

Seven decades after Disneyland first opened its doors (and almost as long since Walt's death in 1966), it's still not finished. And if Walt has his way, it never will be.

Disneyland will *never* be finished and neither will your Evergreen Assets ecosystem.

12. CONCLUSION

The lazy way

> *"I used to work hard. The 18-hour days. The seven-day weeks. But I didn't start making big money until I did less – a lot less."*

Believe it or not, that's *not* a quote from me.

While it could so easily have been lifted directly from the pages of my first book *Big Ideas... for Small Businesses*, the passage above was written 44 years earlier by a gentleman called Joe Karbo in a sales letter to promote his book, *The Lazy Man's Way To Riches*, which sold more than three million copies despite never being available in bookstores.

How did Joe sell three million copies of a book without being in bookstores? He used a simple direct mail sales letter. In it, Karbo writes: "This ad took about two hours to write. With a little luck, it should earn me 50, maybe a hundred thousand dollars."

It didn't. It actually earned Joe a whopping $10million, which was a lot of money in 1973. $10million for two hours' work? That certainly sounds like The Lazy Man's Way To Riches to me.

Of course, Joe put in a lot more work behind the scenes than simply writing a sales letter and hitting the beach. He had to write the book. The book had to deliver value from his decades of business success. He had to set up fulfilment centres, upsell readers onto courses and seminars and eventually start doing infomercials.

Joe had to:

- Generate leads from prospects interested in learning more.
- Get those prospects to know, like and trust him.
- Sell books (as well as courses and seminars).
- Fulfil orders.
- Handle admin for more than three million customers.
- Turn one customer into 1.2.

Joe worked smart, not hard. He understood the leverage a great sales letter can bring. Investing two hours into writing that sales letter created an Evergreen Asset that served him for decades (and is still studied by marketing students and copywriters all over the world as a shining example of great sales copy). Joe did the work once and reaped the rewards three million times – and to the tune of $10million.

What will *you* do with your next two hours? Watch the footie or binge-watch on Netflix or create an Evergreen Asset that could serve you for decades to come?

13. LET'S GET TO WORK

"The way to get started is to quit talking and begin doing." - Walt Disney

If you've read any of my books before, you'll know what's coming. This is the part where I implore you not to be the frog in the library, chanting, "Reddit! Reddit! Reddit!", finishing one book, and immediately starting the next one. This is where I get on my soapbox and lecture you about not just "reading the book" but also "following the instructions".

Your Evergreen Assets ecosystem isn't going to improve by reading a book about it. Theory alone doesn't cut it. You need to turn theory into action. You need to do something. You need to create, improve, and design. You need to dig the well. You need to give the world's largest merry-go-round a push in the right direction. You need to start making your burgers look like the one in the picture.

The subtitle of this book is "do the work once, reap the rewards again and again (and again)". When I crowd-sourced that subtitle from beta-readers, everyone loved the idea of reaping the rewards. There was a lot of love for reaping those rewards again and again (and again). But very few people mentioned the most important bit. The first three words: "Do the work."

For many years, I've described myself as a "lazy entrepreneur". The opening line of my first book was a Tim Kreider quote: "I hate being busy. I'm the laziest ambitious person I know".

But don't confuse my laziness with idleness or inactivity. I work hard so that I don't *have* to work hard. I work hard creating Evergreen Assets, so those assets work hard for me while I'm slacking off.

I work hard once, and reap the rewards again and again (and again). Then, when I want to (my ideal job description is doing what I want, when I want, how I want, where I want… if I want), I'll work hard once more so I can reap even more rewards again and again (and again).

It's time to start. It's time to find out what they want, give them what they want, and make damn sure they've *got* what they want. Decide which asset class (Leads, Nurture, Sales, Fulfilment, Admin, Viral) you want to invest in first. Then, turn back to that chapter and start planning your first investment.

Remember:

- Lead Assets bring prospects into the machine.
- Nurture Assets warm them up.
- Sales Assets convince prospects to get their wallets out.
- Fulfilment Assets give them what they want.
- Admin Assets make sure that things run like clockwork.
- Viral Assets turn one customer into 1.2.

Evergreen Assets are not about "what's working right now". They're not about "what's your favourite biscuit?" engagement-bait, vanity metrics or throwing enough shit at the wall in the hope some of it sticks.

Evergreen Assets are about doing the work once and reaping the rewards again and again (and again.).

It's time to do the work.

14. WHAT'S NEXT?

Thank you so much for investing your time in reading this book. It has been a pleasure sharing my work with you. I hope it's triggered some inspiration, got the cogs turning in your head, and encouraged you to create your Evergreen Assets ecosystem.

I'd love to hear from you if this book has resonated with you in any way. Send me an email at john@bigidea.co.uk and let me know what asset(s) you're going to create first.

If you're looking for something to read next, allow me to offer a suggestion. If you've enjoyed reading Evergreen Assets, then you may well enjoy my other writing as well. I send out free weekly articles every Wednesday lunchtime to my email subscribers. You can get these at my website: www.bigidea.co.uk.

Subscribers are also the first to hear about new podcast episodes, my latest books and also have access to my recommended reading list – a comprehensive list of my top 100 must-read books that I've hand-picked, covering a wide range of topics, such as sales and marketing, productivity, health, relationships, mindset, customer service, financial, investment and motivation, as well as inspirational biographies and autobiographies.

You can download the full top 100 list from www.bigidea.co.uk, where you will also find links to the Ambitious Lifestyle Business Podcast, as well as details about the One Percent Club and how to join the waiting list for our March and September intakes.

RESOURCES

You can access all the resources mentioned in this book at www.evergreenassets.co.uk, including:

- The Evergreen Assets one-page ecosystem template.
- Tools and resources to improve your conversion rates, SEO and email deliverability.
- A 99-minute Evergreen Asset Masterclass.
- A 74-minute webinars masterclass.
- Dave Aggiss's transformational video case study.
- Example of company handbook.
- Interviews with many of the people and businesses mentioned in this book.
- Bonus video content and podcast interviews about the Evergreen Assets ecosystem.
- Some ideas on other books you might like to read next.

ALSO BY JOHN LAMERTON

Big Ideas… for Small Businesses

The blueprint for running a successful, ambitious, lifestyle business. Centred around John's ideal job description: "To do *what* I want, *when* I want, *how* I want, *where* I want… *if* I want", *Big Ideas…* is full of simple, practical tools and tactics to help your small business grow.

Available in: Paperback, Kindle and Audiobook (narrated by John himself) via Amazon.

Routine Machine

Consistency is a superpower. In *Routine Machine*, John explains how a "normal bloke from Plymouth" achieved more success than he ever dreamed (or deserved) by following a simple, everyday plan to achieve his goals that required neither superhuman effort nor natural-born talent (which is just as well).

Available in: Paperback, Kindle and Audiobook (narrated by John himself) via Amazon.

ABOUT THE AUTHOR

John Lamerton is a serial entrepreneur and investor. He is a former civil servant who started a dotcom company back in 2000 despite having no skills, knowledge, or experience ("But then, neither did most of the other dotcom businesses at that time, so I was in good company").

He's owned a website that told students where to get free sachets of shampoo, one that told people they'd been caught speeding (when they hadn't), and one that told football fans where to get the best pies.

Before he knew it, he was running a dating website, selling office space, working with florists to sell online, and selling package holidays to the Algarve. He's also owned a bingo website, a finance blog, sold mobile phone insurance, and streamed live sports events.

Trust me, that's the short version. John has owned and operated more than 100 different websites since that first one in 2000. Most have been either sold or closed down and he now works primarily in two sectors:

- Sports betting: John owns a number of online sports betting brands and specialises in building large, loyal communities of sports betting fans.
- Coaching: John's main passion these days is coaching ambitious lifestyle business owners. Together with his business partner

> Jason Brockman, John runs a paid group coaching programme (the One Percent Club), and hosts a free podcast. You can find details of both at: www.bigidea.co.uk.

John is also a perennial optimist, firmly believing that the mighty Plymouth Argyle will one day play in the top-tier of English football. So far, though, he's witnessed five promotions and six relegations. Still, it only takes a couple of back-to-back promotions.

He lives in Plymouth with his wife Sarah and two children, Jack and Harrie.

He's also a bit of a fanboy of Warren Buffett.

And he can always, *always,* be bribed with cake.

Mmm, cake...

BIBLIOGRAPHY

Abraham, J. (2001). *Getting Everything You Can Out Of All You've Got.* Little, Brown Book Group.

Berger, J. (2013). *Contagious: Why Things Catch On.* Simon & Schuster.

Brunson, R. (2017). *Expert Secrets: The Underground Playbook for Creating a Mass Movement of People Who Will Pay for Your Advice.* Morgan James Publishing.

Carnegie, D. (1936). *How to Win Friends and Influence People.* Simon & Schuster.

Catalano, F., & Smith, B. E. (2000). *Internet Marketing for Dummies.* John Wiley & Sons.

Clear, J. (2018). *Atomic Habits: An Easy & Proven Way to Build Good Habits & Break Bad Ones.* Avery.

Coleman, J. (2018). *Never Lose A Customer Again: Turn Any Sale Into Lifelong Loyalty in 100 Days.* Portfolio.

Dalio, R. (2017). *Principles: Life and Work.* Simon & Schuster.

Gawande, A. (2009). *The Checklist Manifesto: How to Get Things Right.* Metropolitan Books.

Jarvis, P. (2019). *Company of One: Why Staying Small is the Next Big Thing for Business.* Portfolio Penguin.

Jervis, N. (2017). *Law Firm Growth Formula: How smart solicitors attract more of the right clients at the right price to grow their law firm quickly.* Rethink Press.

Karbo, J. (1973). *The Lazy Man's Way to Riches: How to Have Everything In The World You Really Want!* F P Publishing Co. Inc.

Keller, G., & Papasan, J. (2014). *The One Thing: The Surprisingly Simple Truth Behind Extraordinary Results.* John Murray Learning.

Kiyosaki, R. T. (2000). *Rich Dad Poor Dad: What the Rich Teach Their Kids About Money That the Poor and Middle Class Do Not!* Warner Books.

Kroc, R. (1977). *Grinding It Out: The Making Of McDonald's.* St. Martin's Press.

Krug, S. (2000). *Don't Make Me Think: A Common Sense Approach to Web Usability.* New Riders Press.

Kurtz, B. (2019). *Overdeliver: Build a Business for a Lifetime Playing the Long Game in Direct Response Marketing.* Hay House Inc.

Lamerton, J. (2017). *Big Ideas... For Small Businesses: Simple, Practical Tools and Tactics to Help Your Small Business.* Let's Tell Your Story Publishing.

Lamerton, J. (2019). *Routine Machine: How successful people improve their morning routine, daily habits and guarantee themselves results.* Let's Tell Your Story Publishing.

Matthews, L. (2017). *A Marvellous Reputation: 10 Lessons From My Life As A PR Insider For Entrepreneurs Who Want To Be Talked About.* Rethink Press.

Miller, D. (2017). *Building a StoryBrand: Clarify Your Message So Customers Will Listen.* HarperCollins Leadership.

Mullins, C. (2015). *Bog-Standard Business: How I Took the Plunge and Became the Millionaire Plumber.* John Blake Publishing Ltd.

Norris, D. (2020). *Compound Marketing: How Smart Entrepreneurs Use Asset-Building Marketing Strategies for an Unfair Growth Advantage.* JETLAUNCH.

Olson, J. (2005). *The Slight Edge: Turning Simple Disciplines Into Massive Success and Happiness.* Momentum Media.

Priestley, D. (2017). *24 Assets: Create a digital, scalable, valuable and fun business that will thrive in a fast changing world.* Rethink Press.

Ridley, M. (2010). *Rational Optimist: How Prosperity Evolves.* Harper.

Samed, D. (2000). *Earn With Your Art: The Creative Freelancer's Guide to Business & Marketing.* Independently published.

Schramko, J. (2017). *Work Less, Make More: The counter-intuitive approach to building a profitable business, and a life you actually love.* SuperFastBusiness.

Sivers, D. (2020). *Hell Yeah or No: what's worth doing.* Hit Media.

Smith, T. (1885). *Successful Advertising.* Thomas Smith Agency.

Veness, S., & Veness, S. (2016). *The Brit Guide to Orlando 2017.* W Foulsham & Co Ltd.

Printed in Great Britain
by Amazon

71780739R00203